T0175900

FISMA
Principles and
Best Practices

Beyond Compliance

OTHER INFORMATION SECURITY BOOKS FROM AUERBACH

Building an Enterprise-Wide Business Continuity Program
Kelley Okolita
ISBN 978-1-4200-8864-9

Critical Infrastructure: Homeland Security and Emergency Preparedness, Second Edition
Robert Radvanovsky and Allan McDougall
ISBN 978-1-4200-9527-2

Data Protection: Governance, Risk Management, and Compliance
David G. Hill
ISBN 978-1-4398-0692-0

Encyclopedia of Information Assurance
Edited by Rebecca Herold and Marcus K. Rogers
ISBN 978-1-4200-6620-3

The Executive MBA in Information Security
John J. Trinckes, Jr.
ISBN 978-1-4398-1007-1

FISMA Principles and Best Practices: Beyond Compliance
Patrick D. Howard
ISBN 978-1-4200-7829-9

HOWTO Secure and Audit Oracle 10g and 11g
Ron Ben-Natan
ISBN 978-1-4200-8412-2

Information Security Management: Concepts and Practice
Bel G. Raggad
ISBN 978-1-4200-7854-1

Information Security Policies and Procedures: A Practitioner's Reference, Second Edition
Thomas R. Peltier
ISBN 978-0-8493-1958-7

Information Security Risk Analysis, Third Edition
Thomas R. Peltier
ISBN 978-1-4398-3956-0

Information Technology Control and Audit, Third Edition
Sandra Senft and Frederick Gallegos
ISBN 978-1-4200-6550-3

Intelligent Video Surveillance: Systems and Technology
Edited by Yunqian Ma and Gang Qian
ISBN 978-1-4398-1328-7

Managing an Information Security and Privacy Awareness and Training Program, Second Edition
Rebecca Herold
ISBN 978-1-4398-1545-8

Mobile Device Security: A Comprehensive Guide to Securing Your Information in a Moving World
Stephen Fried
ISBN 978-1-4398-2016-2

Secure and Resilient Software Development
Mark S. Merkow and Lakshmikanth Raghavan
ISBN 978-1-4398-2696-6

Security for Service Oriented Architectures
Bhavani Thuraisingham
ISBN 978-1-4200-7331-7

Security of Mobile Communications
Noureddine Boudriga
ISBN 978-0-8493-7941-3

Security of Self-Organizing Networks: MANET, WSN, WMN, VANET
Edited by Al-Sakib Khan Pathan
ISBN 978-1-4398-1919-7

Security Patch Management
Felicia M. Nicastro
ISBN 978-1-4398-2499-3

Security Risk Assessment Handbook: A Complete Guide for Performing Security Risk Assessments, Second Edition
Douglas Landoll
ISBN 978-1-4398-2148-0

Security Strategy: From Requirements to Reality
Bill Stackpole and Eric Oksendahl
ISBN 978-1-4398-2733-8

Vulnerability Management
Park Foreman
ISBN 978-1-4398-0150-5

AUERBACH PUBLICATIONS
www.auerbach-publications.com
To Order Call: 1-800-272-7737 • Fax: 1-800-374-3401
E-mail: orders@crcpress.com

FISMA
Principles and
Best Practices

Beyond Compliance

Patrick D. Howard

CRC Press
Taylor & Francis Group
Boca Raton London New York

CRC Press is an imprint of the
Taylor & Francis Group, an **informa** business

AN AUERBACH BOOK

CRC Press
Taylor & Francis Group
6000 Broken Sound Parkway NW, Suite 300
Boca Raton, FL 33487-2742

First issued in paperback 2019

© 2011 by Taylor & Francis Group, LLC
CRC Press is an imprint of Taylor & Francis Group, an Informa business

No claim to original U.S. Government works

ISBN-13: 978-1-4200-7829-9 (hbk)
ISBN-13: 978-0-367-38290-2 (pbk)

This book contains information obtained from authentic and highly regarded sources. Reasonable efforts have been made to publish reliable data and information, but the author and publisher cannot assume responsibility for the validity of all materials or the consequences of their use. The authors and publishers have attempted to trace the copyright holders of all material reproduced in this publication and apologize to copyright holders if permission to publish in this form has not been obtained. If any copyright material has not been acknowledged please write and let us know so we may rectify in any future reprint.

Except as permitted under U.S. Copyright Law, no part of this book may be reprinted, reproduced, transmitted, or utilized in any form by any electronic, mechanical, or other means, now known or hereafter invented, including photocopying, microfilming, and recording, or in any information storage or retrieval system, without written permission from the publishers.

For permission to photocopy or use material electronically from this work, please access www.copyright.com (http://www.copyright.com/) or contact the Copyright Clearance Center, Inc. (CCC), 222 Rosewood Drive, Danvers, MA 01923, 978-750-8400. CCC is a not-for-profit organization that provides licenses and registration for a variety of users. For organizations that have been granted a photocopy license by the CCC, a separate system of payment has been arranged.

Trademark Notice: Product or corporate names may be trademarks or registered trademarks, and are used only for identification and explanation without intent to infringe.

Visit the Taylor & Francis Web site at
http://www.taylorandfrancis.com

and the Auerbach Web site at
http://www.auerbach-publications.com

Dedication

To Daniela and Peter:
Thank you for all the joy you have brought me.

Dedication

Contents

Preface

Over the last seven years, federal agencies have come to understand the requirements of the Federal Information Security Management Act (FISMA), have learned the routine for periodic reporting of FISMA compliance, and also generally comply with the requirements of the act, particularly with respect to system authorization, weakness remediation, and awareness training. However, most agencies continue to struggle with finding resources to maintain compliance and with balancing FISMA compliance with other ongoing needs for the continuous protection of agency data. Most agencies find that resources to support information technology security are limited and are growing more constrained. Hence, agencies are being forced to be more efficient in how they implement security controls and manage information technology (IT) security programs. Threats are intensifying; and an agile defense posture must be employed.

The purpose of this book is to help the reader understand how efficiencies can be gained in the implementation of a FISMA-based, agency-level information technology security program, and to share ideas about how compliance requirements can be balanced against overall organization needs for security. It is my contention that FISMA legislation is sufficiently comprehensive and flexible to permit an agency-level Chief Information Security Officer (CISO) to balance compliance requirements against overall needs for security, and that FISMA provides a sound framework for the implementation of essential system security controls, providing a solid foundation for the establishment of an effective IT security program. Further, an IT security program established and implemented to comply with FISMA can result in an effective program that meets an agency's broader needs for information security. I am equally convinced that implementing security that aims to merely satisfy FISMA reporting requirements has little hope of success in providing effective security of agency information systems and information. Unfortunately, this has been demonstrated all too often since FISMA was enacted in December 2002.

This book presents real-world examples to describe an approach to establishing and implementing a coherent enterprise information security program that fuses compliance review, technical monitoring, and remediation efforts. It is based on my experiences as an agency-level Chief Information Security Officer charged with developing, implementing, and maintaining enterprise FISMA-based information technology security programs at three major Federal agencies. My hope is that readers will discover insights, ideas, and practices they can employ to not only improve the level of FISMA compliance in their organizations, but also to successfully balance those efforts against agency mission requirements through the employment of risk management principles and practices.

Havre de Grace, Maryland

Acknowledgments

This book is a result of my experiences in three U.S. Government agencies since 2003 as both a government employee and contractor. What I observed in each of these agencies taught me valuable lessons about information security in general and best practices for managing compliance with the Federal Information Security Management Act (FISMA), specifically. During this time, I was supported, taught, and led by information security and information technology professionals of the very highest caliber.

At the Department of Transportation, Vicki Lord and Kelvin Taylor were instrumental in the department's successful implementation of a FISMA-compliant and cost-effective certification and accreditation methodology for which I was given responsibility. Lisa Schlosser, the Chief Information Officer at the Department of Housing and Urban Development (HUD), provided unending support to me as Chief Information Security Officer, which permitted the department to make notable improvements in its enterprise information security program. Providing further support in my efforts at HUD were John W. Smith, Mike Milazzo, and Homa Zarrinnahad, each of whom I trusted fully and turned to daily for advice and assistance. I relied on their unswerving support in implementing and managing the department's information technology security program. Finally, at the Nuclear Regulatory Commission, my service as

Chief Information Security Officer was given the full and unqualified support of Darren Ash, the Chief Information Officer and Deputy Executive Director for Corporate Management, as well as the entire Computer Security Office staff, and particularly the FISMA Compliance and Oversight Team. Paul Ricketts, Alan Sage, Shalom Nevet, and Keisha Marston demonstrated on a daily basis the principles I describe in this book, and continually proved that security and compliance are not mutually exclusive.

PART I

INTRODUCTION

Today, most organizations have at least indirectly felt the impact of government regulation in the area of information systems security. With the advent of international standards for information security, and in the United States the Government Information Security Reform Act (GISRA) and its replacement, the Federal Information Security Management Act (FISMA), there is an increased emphasis on, and measurement of, the ability of government organizations and companies subject to these mandates to protect information and systems in ways specified by external entities. Outside scrutiny of information security programs has been increasing for the better part of ten years, and there is no indication that this level of legislative oversight and public interest will ebb. Consequently, both public and private organizations must seek ways to ensure they comply with these new and ever-more stringent requirements, while simultaneously maintaining an overarching information security program.

Roughly, over the past five years there has been something of a backlash against the concept of information security compliance within the U.S. Government. Primarily, this has taken the form of reaction to the certification and accreditation process, considered by many to be the embodiment of FISMA, as a wasteful, ineffective use of government resources that does little to provide "real security." Consequently, meeting compliance requirements has come to be defined as a paperwork exercise providing little or no value to the overall security of agency data. In response to this reaction, a variety of recommendations for legislation to update FISMA have been introduced to correct the perceived weaknesses in the original legislation.

This book provides a practical prescription for addressing information security requirements mandated by FISMA for government

agencies and private concerns that process government information. The book addresses FISMA compliance as an outcome of an organization's overall information security program anchored on FISMA.
It offers workable solutions and approaches for establishing and managing an agency-level information security program that ensures
the security of sensitive information while complying with FISMA
requirements. The book addresses what I think are the ten most essential considerations in successfully implementing a government information security program, including gaining management support
for the program, designing and staffing a compliance organization,
program planning, development of policies and procedures, training
and awareness, establishing an effective relationship with the audit
function, compliance monitoring tools and techniques, addressing
FISMA throughout the system development life cycle, and building
organizational relationships.

INFORMATION SECURITY PROGRAM IMPLEMENTATION CHECKLIST

1. Does senior management support the program?	Yes/No
2. Is there an independent information security organization in place to manage the program?	Yes/No
3. Is the information security organization appropriately staffed to perform its assigned functions?	Yes/No
4. Have strategic and tactical plans for implementing and maintaining the information security program been developed?	Yes/No
5. Is the information security program based on documented policies and procedures?	Yes/No
6. Does the program provide for training and awareness of users and those assigned to significant security roles?	Yes/No
7. Is there an effective working relationship between the information security function and the inspector general?	Yes/No
8. Have monitoring mechanisms been implemented to permit continuous assessment of security control effectiveness and risks to agency information?	Yes/No
9. Have information security program requirements been fully integrated into the system development life cycle?	Yes/No
10. Does the information security function prioritize customer service in its provision of support to agency organizational elements and personnel?	Yes/No

The book describes security processes, practices, and procedures
that comply with FISMA, but go well beyond compliance and mere
generation of security documentation, with the aim of showing how
FISMA can be leveraged to develop and implement a risk-based
information security program.

In this volume, I address many implementation considerations and provide thoughts and recommendations based on my experiences in building and implementing information technology security programs at the U.S. Nuclear Regulatory Commission (NRC), the Department of Housing and Urban Development (HUD), and the Department of Transportation (DOT) for more than seven years, and other experiences in the security field over the past thirty-five years. This practical approach to mastering the challenge of balancing security and compliance provides readers with a prescription that can be applied to respond to requirements for compliance not only with FISMA and agency-level directives based on FISMA, but also with ISO 27002, and other security mandates and frameworks.

The purpose of the book is to describe how an organization can meet its requirements for complying with FISMA through the establishment of a FISMA-based agencywide information security program. It is written from the perspective of an agency Chief Information Security Officer, but will prove useful to anyone involved in the implementation of FISMA irrespective of their duty position. It is designed to describe an approach for organizations to achieve risk-based information security management through FISMA compliance. The book is a resource for both public and private organizations in implementing effective processes that will help them exercise due diligence in complying with primary federal law related to information security management. Further, the book can help the reader understand the general nature of security compliance management, allowing it to be useful in this broader context.

The goal of the book is to provide a practical guide for complying with the requirements of FISMA. To achieve this goal, the book is made up of two parts: Part I addresses the background of FISMA and government compliance requirements for information security management, an analysis of the FISMA legislation itself, and current FISMA reporting requirements promulgated by the Office of Management and Budget (OMB). Then in Part II, I offer ten keys for establishing and maintaining an effective FISMA-based information security management program. This approach provides a description of requirements for FISMA compliance as well as a prescription for managing FISMA compliance in an efficient manner. This book seeks to address not only the historical basis for FISMA reporting, but also the very latest reporting requirements from OMB. Additionally, in the conclusion, the book addresses a number of proposed changes to the FISMA legislation and their potential impact on how the government's current approach to information security management may be affected. However, it should be noted that at the time of this writing there are at least eight pieces of proposed legislation in varying stages of review that could affect FISMA.

This book assists in understanding the primary considerations in the establishment of an effective FISMA-based information security program. It is my intention for the reader to benefit from my experiences in implementing requirements of the FISMA at three of the twenty-four U.S. Government Chief Information Officer (CIO) Act organizations. The book addresses how an agency-level information security program can be designed or improved to better meet an organization's security and compliance goals. The book provides insights into how management support for such a program can be attained and maintained through the process of maturing the program. The book describes processes, practices, and principles involved in managing the complexities of FISMA-based security that can be applied to requirements of multiple mandates, and varying audit standards and organizations.

The value of this book to the reader is to present practical and proven, real-world FISMA-related security solutions and approaches that are based on my experiences in developing and managing FISMA-based information security programs for two cabinet-level U.S. federal departments, and an independent federal government agency to help them in the performance of their compliance management or support roles. Most of what I know relative to FISMA has been learned "the hard way," through trial and error. Many of the solutions and approaches I used were previously identified as best practices at other government organizations, and were tailored to meet specific agency requirements as I adopted them for local implementation. The book also addresses recent developments related to FISMA and government information security management, and as such can also aid in preparing for addressing key aspects of proposed FISMA legislation and to prepare for the Office of Management and Budget's new requirements for FISMA reporting.

It is my hope that this book will be a reliable resource for those information security managers and practitioners working in government agencies or for firms under contract to the federal government that seek to improve the security of government information with which they have been entrusted. It is those dedicated professionals working in this challenging endeavor for whom this book is written.

1

ANALYSIS OF THE FEDERAL INFORMATION SECURITY MANAGEMENT ACT (FISMA)

Public Law 107–347 was passed by the 107th U.S. Congress and signed into law by President George W. Bush on December 17, 2002. Known as the "E-Government Act of 2002," its stated purpose is the enhancement of "the management and promotion of electronic Government services and processes by establishing a Federal Chief Information Officer within the Office of Management and Budget, and by establishing a broad framework of measures that require using Internet-based information technology to enhance citizen access to Government information and services, and for other purposes." Although the security of information is not specified in this preamble, Title III (Information Security) of the statute requires federal agencies to establish agency-level information security programs that protect the information and information systems supporting agency operations and assets.

Title III, also known as the Federal Information Security Management Act or FISMA, was passed by Congress to permanently authorize, streamline, and strengthen information security programs, evaluation, and annual reporting requirements for U.S. Government agencies. These requirements had been previously introduced in the Government Information Security Reform Act or GISRA, which was enacted in 2000. GISRA required each department or agency head to ensure that information security was provided throughout the life cycle for all agency information systems, and to ensure that agency officials assessed the effectiveness of the information security program, including the testing of information security controls. Other GISRA requirements for agencies are shown in the following table:

Other GISRA Requirements

Employment of a risk-based, entitywide management approach

Development and implementation of cost-effective, risk-based policies and procedures to protect information used by the agency, another agency, or a contractor

Periodic risk assessments for information systems

Development and maintenance of minimum security controls

Oversight through annual independent evaluations of agency information security practices

Development of a remediation process to address significant deficiencies

Provision of training for employees and contractors on security awareness and for information security personnel on their security responsibilities

This table presents some of the key aspects of GISRA: a focus on risk management, acceptance of the value of an enterprisewide program that addresses the protection of information wherever it may reside, definition of minimum security controls, regular evaluation of security compliance, and emphasis on remediation of weaknesses, as well as on requirements for awareness and role-based training. All of these GISRA themes were carried forward in the new FISMA provisions. However, the new legislation went further to strengthen two of these areas, which had been considered weaknesses in GISRA. These were additional requirements for annual assessments of information system security controls effectiveness, and for mandatory minimum information security standards.

Agency-Level FISMA Requirements

The purpose of this chapter is to review the requirements of FISMA that relate to government agencies, their information security programs, information, and information systems. These requirements are recorded in Title III of the E-Government Act, which is provided in Appendix A in its entirety. There are four subsections in Title III that establish the primary information security requirements levied by FISMA on government agencies. These subsections address the purposes of the information security portion of the legislation, responsibilities of federal agencies for information security, federal agency information security programs, and agency information security reporting requirements. The following sections provide an analysis of these four subsections to highlight their significance for agency-level information security programs.

Purposes

Subsection 3541 documents six specific purposes for the information security subchapter of FISMA. The six purposes specified are to:

1. "Provide a comprehensive framework for ensuring the effectiveness of information security controls over information resources that support Federal operations and assets;"
2. "Recognize the highly networked nature of the current Federal computing environment and provide effective governmentwide management and oversight of the related information security risks, including coordination of information security efforts throughout the civilian, national security, and law enforcement communities;"
3. "Provide for development and maintenance of minimum controls required to protect Federal information and information systems;"
4. "Provide a mechanism for improved oversight of Federal agency information security programs;"
5. "Acknowledge that commercially developed information security products offer advanced, dynamic, robust, and effective information security solutions, reflecting market solutions for the protection of critical information infrastructures important to the national defense and economic security of the nation that are designed, built, and operated by the private sector; and"
6. "Recognize that the selection of specific technical hardware and software information security solutions should be left to individual agencies from among commercially developed products."

In general, two of these were particularly germane to federal agencies in that they reflect the importance the statute places on developing and maintaining minimum security controls necessary to protect government information and systems. Because of the focus on controls and systems, much of the work to implement FISMA has concentrated on the security of individual information systems. The track record for agency-level FISMA implementation is that this system focus has been undertaken at the expense of developing information security programs that holistically apply to the entire enterprise. Additionally, paragraph four placed emphasis on the need for improvement of oversight of agency-level information security programs, setting the stage for enhancement of the role of independent audits and creating tension between the need for implementing risk-based security as introduced in GISRA and found elsewhere in FISMA and achievement of regulatory compliance.

Federal Agency Responsibilities

Subsection 3544 identifies requirements for federal agencies, with particular emphasis on responsibilities of key agency officials, aspects of agency information security programs, and agency reporting requirements.

- *Agency Head Responsibilities*: The subsection includes among the responsibilities of the agency head the need to provide risk-based information security for information systems that are used by or on behalf of the agency or those operated by another agency, a contractor, or another organization on the agency's behalf. Agency heads are to comply with FISMA requirements as well as with related policies, procedures, standards, and guidelines for all information systems, including those containing national security information. Also, they are required to integrate information security management processes with agency strategic and operational planning processes (such as the agency's mission-based strategic plan, information resources/information management strategic planning, and the system development methodology). The agency head is also required to ensure senior agency officials secure the information and information systems under their control, and this subsection stipulates that these officials must do this through assessment of risks to their systems and information; by determining levels of security appropriate for their protection (information/system categorization); by implementing cost-effective, risk-based policies and procedures; and through periodic testing and evaluation of security controls to ensure that they are effectively implemented.

  Agency heads are also required to ensure that the agency has sufficient trained personnel to assist with agency compliance with FISMA as well as related policies, procedures, standards, and guidelines. Finally, the agency head must ensure that the agency Chief Information Officer (CIO) coordinates with appropriate senior agency officials to prepare an annual report for the agency head on the effectiveness of the information security program and the status of remediation activities.

- *Chief Information Officer (CIO) Responsibilities*: The subsection further requires the agency head to delegate to the agency CIO the authority necessary to ensure compliance with FISMA requirements imposed on the agency. Specifically, the CIO is charged with development and maintenance of an agency-level information security program and information security policies, procedures, and control techniques (i.e., mechanisms and processes) needed to meet the requirements of the agency information security program; training and oversight of personnel assigned significant information security responsibilities (e.g., project managers, system administrators, developers); providing assistance to senior agency officials (e.g., authorizing officials, system owners, information system security officers, etc.) in fulfilling their information security responsibilities.

- *Chief Information Security Officer (CISO) Responsibilities*: Under the CIO responsibilities paragraph of Subsection 3544, the CIO is assigned responsibility for designating a "senior agency information security officer." This has been accepted by most government agencies as the CISO function. Requirements for this position are to carry out the CIO's responsibilities for information security; have the necessary training and experience to perform effectively (i.e., the CISO must be qualified to perform the requirements of the position); have information security assigned as his primary duty (that is, information security management will not be performed as a collateral responsibility); and be in charge of an organization given the necessary resources to carry out its mission of ensuring that the agency complies with the provisions of FISMA.

Agency-Level Information Security Programs

Section 3544 requires each federal agency to "develop, document, and implement an agencywide information security program" that has been approved by the Director of the Office of Management and Budget. The objective of this program is to secure agency information and information systems that support agency operations and assets. This requirement is not limited merely to those systems and information under the direct control of the agency, but also to those systems and information managed by a contractor, another federal agency, or by some other provider. This subsection specifies that agencywide programs are to include the following elements:

- *Periodic Risk Assessment:* Agency information security programs are to go beyond compliance and perform periodic assessments of potential risks resulting from "unauthorized access, use, disclosure, disruption, modification, or destruction of information and information systems" the agency uses to support its operations and assets. This requirement focuses on the need to dynamically understand the nature of relevant threats and vulnerabilities and their securty impacts and probability of occurrence as a basis for establishing program needs.

- *Policies and Procedures*: The requirement for agency programs to have risk-based, cost-effective policies and procedures reinforces the previously stated requirement for periodic risk assessments ensuring their results will be taken into consideration in policy and procedure development and maintenance. The notion of cost-effectiveness is reinforced in the stated requirement for information security to be addressed in all stages of an information system's life cycle. This subsection also mandates that agency-level policies and procedures comprehensively address requirements from both external and internal sources to include FISMA, Office of Management and Budget (OMB), NIST, authorities responsible for standards for national security systems, as well as agency-specific system configuration requirements.

- *Security Plans:* In this subsection, FISMA requires that the agency information security program include requirements to develop and maintain "subordinate plans" that ensure adequate security is provided for all agency information technology assets, and specifically, "networks, facilities, and systems or groups of information systems." Reference to these plans as "subordinate" implies a requirement for consistency with, and integration into, the overall agency program.

- *Security Awareness Training:* Agency information security programs are required by FISMA to include the provision of security awareness training of employees, contractors, and other system users who support agency operations and assets. This training is required to address the information security risks associated with their use of agency systems, and their responsibilities for protecting these systems and reducing these risks through compliance with agency information security policies and procedures. The key elements here are the requirements for training of all users irrespective of their employment status, the focus on making them aware of risks to the systems they use, and the need for user awareness of their responsibility for reducing these risks through compliance with policies and procedures. Although this particular subsection is limited to user awareness training requirements, additional requirements for role-specific training is addressed elsewhere in the statute (e.g., responsibilities assigned to the CIO).

- *Periodic Testing:* FISMA requires that the effectiveness of policies, procedures, and security practices be evaluated periodically. The frequency of effectiveness testing is to be established according to risk (e.g., greater frequency for higher-sensitivity systems), but must be performed at least annually. Other testing requirements in this subsection specify that testing will be performed on all types of security controls (i.e., management, operational, and technical controls) and that the scope of testing will include every information system that is identified in the agency's systems inventory. Further, this testing may be used in support of the annual independent audit specified in Section 3545 that is described later in the statute. Note that the requirement for testing according to risk implies that there is not a need to test every control annually, and that the rigor and type of testing is also not specified, but only that the effectiveness of controls is ascertained. Although this permitted agencies to determine controls testing procedures according to their own discretion, most followed available

NIST guidance such as Special Publication 800-26 initially, and later SP 800-53A as the need for mature controls testing increased across government.

- *Deficiency Remediation:* If there are requirements for identification of weaknesses that limit the effectiveness of policies, procedures, and practices, then there must also be requirements related to remediation of these weaknesses. Hence, agency information security programs are required by FISMA to develop and implement a process to address remediation of deficiencies. This process—and note there is to be a single agency process for this—is required to provide provisions for remediation planning, implementation of corrective action, evaluation of the effectiveness of corrective action, and documenting remedial action in response to identified deficiencies. Following guidance from the Office of Management and Budget and from NIST, agencies have taken the approach of developing plans of action and milestones (POA&M) processes in response to this requirement.

- *Security Incident Procedures:* FISMA requires in this subsection that agency programs include procedures that allow detection, reporting, and response to security incidents. Other security incident requirements call for containment procedures to mitigate incident-related risks before substantial damage results; notification and coordination with the federal information security incident center (that is, today's U.S. Computer Emergency Readiness Center) established in Section 3546 of Title III on security incidents; and notification and consultation appropriate to the security incident with law enforcement agencies and Offices of Inspector General in situations where investigation of security incidents is warranted; authorities responsible for incidents involving national security systems; and any other agency or office, according to law or as directed by the president. These provisions emphasize the importance of timely notification by agencies to allow higher-level response and support when security incidents occur.

- *Systems Continuity of Operations Planning:* The agency information security program is also required to include establishment of plans and procedures that ensure the continuity of operations of critical agency information systems. The system-specific plans called for by this FISMA requirement are generally referred to as contingency plans and are developed by agencies following NIST Special Publication 800-34 guidance. To ensure continuity of operations as specified, there must be a plan for how agency officials are to respond to emergencies and the potential for extended outages to protect system availability, and procedures for testing the effectiveness of these plans on a periodic basis, and updating them appropriately.

Agency Reporting

Section 3544 also establishes requirements for government agencies to provide an annual report on the adequacy and effectiveness of information security policies, procedures, and practices, and compliance with the requirements of this subchapter, including compliance with each requirement related to the agency information security program specified earlier. This report is required to be submitted to the authorities listed in the following table.

Recipients of Annual FISMA Reports

Director, Office of Management and Budget

Committees on Government Reform (currently Oversight and Government Reform) of the House of Representatives

Committee on Science (currently Science and Technology) of the House of Representatives

Committee on Governmental Affairs of the Senate

Committees on Commerce, Science, and Transportation of the Senate

Committee on Appropriations of the House of Representatives

Appropriations Committee of the Senate

Comptroller General

This report is generally known today at the agency level as the Annual FISMA Report. FISMA reporting requirements are detailed further in Chapter 2.

Additionally, to reinforce the expectation that information security will be integrated into agency-level strategic and operational processes, agencies are required to document in various agency plans and reports the adequacy and effectiveness of agency information security policies, procedures, and practices. Specifically, Section 3544 requires agencies to reflect this information in the following plans and reports:

- Annual agency budgets
- Information resources management
- Information technology management
- Program performance
- Financial management
- Financial management systems under the Federal Financial Management Improvement Act
- Internal accounting and administrative controls under the Federal Managers Financial Integrity Act (FMFIA)

Finally, Section 3544 requires agencies to report any significant deficiency in an information security policy, procedure, or practice that has been identified as part of the agency reporting requirements as a material weakness, and if it relates to financial management systems, as an instance of a lack of substantial compliance under the Federal Managers Financial Integrity Act of 1982 (FMFIA). This FISMA provision, which links the specification of information security program deficiencies to designation of material weaknesses, proved to be a powerful means of enforcing FISMA. Over the years, there have been many agencies that have had to deal with material weaknesses related to their information security programs and intensified scrutiny and oversight such deficiencies require.

Annual Independent Evaluation

Subsection 3545 establishes the requirement for an annual independent evaluation of the agency information security program and practices in order to determine their effectiveness. It specifies that this will be achieved by means of testing of information security policies, procedures, and practices for a representative sample of the agency's information systems. Also, based on the results of this testing, the independent evaluation is also to include an assessment of compliance with FISMA requirements, and with related information security policies, procedures, standards, and guidelines.

The subsection stipulates that the independent evaluation would address the effectiveness of information security for national security systems by means of separate presentations as appropriate. Agency inspectors general, at their discretion, may perform the annual evaluation using assigned personnel or an independent external auditor. Heads of agencies not authorized as inspectors general are required under this subsection to engage an independent external auditor to perform the evaluation. Agency heads must also ensure that the portion of the evaluation pertaining to vulnerabilities in controls of national security systems is protected according to risk and applicable laws to prevent disclosure of information that coud be used to exploit government systems.

According to this subsection, evaluation may be based on existing audits, evaluations, or reports that have been previously conducted on agency programs or practices related to the subject of the evaluation. Both agencies and evaluators are directed in this subsection to apply risk-based protection to information that could adversely affect its security if disclosed. The subsection states a requirement for agency heads to submit to OMB the results of the annual evaluation no later than the date established by OMB. Finally, Subsection 3545 calls for the OMB director to summarize the results of agency evaluations in its report to Congress. The director's report to Congress under this subsection si required to summarize information relating to the security posture of national security systems in such a manner as to ensure appropriate protection for information associated with any information security vulnerability in such systems that is commensurate with the risk and in accordance with all applicable laws.

National Security Systems

Subsection 3547 makes each agency head who either operates or exercises control over a national security system responsible for ensuring that the agency provides risk-based information security protection for the information contained in national security systems, and for implementation of information security policies and practices in accordance with standards and guidelines for national security systems.

FISMA Requirements Case Study

In analyzing FISMA and breaking down its requirements from an agency perspective, a useful approach for the CISO to take is to clarify its requirements in four categories: general requirements,

requirements for senior agency officials, requirements for CIOs, and requirements for agency information security programs. These categories are addressed in the following four sections, in which agency perspectives are reflected according to what I have observed in my experiences with implementing FISMA-based information security programs at the federal agency level.

General FISMA Requirements

There are four requirements in this category. These include establishment of the agency information security program, integration of information security management into agency processes, annual reporting, and availability of trained personnel.

- *Information Security Program:* Agencies normally meet this requirement by developing and maintaining an agencywide information security policy document. This policy may be written in varying degrees of detail, but at a minimum establishes the authority for the program and its related roles and responsibilities. The scope of the policy document may also vary by agency in that it may cover all aspects of information security, or may be limited to specific subsets such as information technology security, security of classified information, security of nonautomated information, etc.

- *Process Integration:* Agencies integrate information security management processes with agency strategic and operational planning processes in response to FISMA requirements by linking them to processes for managing the agency strategic plan, the information resource/information management strategic plan, the enterprise architecture, capital planning and investment control, enterprise IT architecture, system development life cycle, and IT project management. Requirements documented in the information security policy are linked to these processes to ensure that critical security activities are performed and are completed in a timely and cost-effective fashion.

- *Annual Reporting:* The general requirement for the CIO to report to the agency head annually on the effectiveness of information security program and status of remedial actions is normally accomplished through submission of the annual FISMA Report. This may be accompanied by expanded documentation on the health and posture of the program as specified by agency executive management, and a formal presentation to the head of the department or agency on this topic. Additional reporting may result from quarterly FISMA reporting being channeled to the agency head for information or approval, as well as other, more frequent reporting resulting from the agency continuous monitoring process.

- *Training:* The requirement for the agency to ensure that there are sufficient trained personnel available for the information security program falls under the purview of the CISO who manages the program, and supporting functions. This extends to the CISO's management of the staffing of dedicated security personnel for his office, as well as overseeing the designation and training and performance of personnel assigned to other established information security roles, including authorizing officials, system owners, and information system security officers. The CISO fulfills this requirement through the use of staffing plans in concert with human resources personnel, and by means of agency-level performance measurement plans and processes.

Requirements for Senior Agency Officials

This second category encompasses requirements applicable to senior agency-level officials given responsibility for the security of information and information systems, and includes four process-specific requirements for these official to address: risk assessment, categorization, policies and procedures, and systems certification.

- *Risk Assessment:* Designated senior agency officials, normally system owners and authorizing officials, are required to ensure that risk to the information and information systems under their control are assessed for the probability and impact of its "unauthorized access, use, disclosure, disruption, modification, or destruction." To satisfy this requirement, owners of agency systems must ensure that NIST SP 800-30-compliant risk assessments are performed as part of the system authorization process and are included in the system authorization package for use by the authorizing officials to accredit the system. System owners are also charged with performing risk assessments when systems undergo significant change.

- *Categorization:* To comply with FISMA requirements in this area, system owners evaluate the information processed, stored, or transmitted by their information systems using NIST SP 800-60 and Federal Information Processing Standard (FIPS) 199 to categorize the system to serve as a basis for determining the appropriate levels of protection required. The result of this process is identification of system information types and categorization of the system as high, moderate, or low, based on the system's security requirements for confidentiality, integrity, and availability.

- *Policies and Procedures:* The responsibilities of the senior agency officials referenced in this requirement are normally fulfilled by system owners, who must implement the requirements of the information security policy and procedures in the form of security controls to cost-effectively reduce risks to information and information systems under their responsibility. In response to this requirement, system owners document security controls in system security plans and note weaknesses in plans of action and milestones following the guidance of NIST SP 800-18, 800-37, and 800-53.

- *Systems Certification:* This requirement calls for the periodic testing and evaluation of information security controls and techniques to ensure they have been effectively implemented. Security certification or security testing and evaluation processes have been employed by government agencies to meet requirements of this type as part of the system authorization process, which requires reaccreditation every three years, or when significant changes to information systems are proposed. Guidance for performing testing and evaluation activities is provided in NIST SP 800-37, 800-53, and 800-53A.

Requirements for CIOs

This third category comprises requirements applicable to agency CIOs, who are given authority by the agency head to ensure compliance with agency-applicable FISMA requirements. The CIO category includes four requirements relating to designation of an agency CISO: provision of security assistance, development of policies and procedures, system configuration, and specialized security training.

- *Senior Agency Information Security Officer:* The CIO is charged under FISMA to designate a senior agency information security officer (SAISO) whose primary duty is information security and who leads an office in the performance of his or her functions. Agencies typically meet this requirement by appointing a full-time CISO under the direction of the CIO, although other position titles are often used. The CISO carries out the CIO's information security responsibilities, most often heads an office assigned the information security or information technology security function, and competes with other agency elements for resources necessary to fulfill the information security mission.

- *Security Assistance*: The CISO acting on the behalf of the CIO provides assistance to senior agency officials concerning their information security responsibilities, including risk assessment, categorization, policies and procedures, weakness remediation, and systems certification. Many agency CISOs perform this assistance function through the use of security service and support contracts to provide support to system owners in meeting these requirements. Additional assistance in performing information security responsibilities is provided through information sharing (e.g., ISSO councils), periodic outreach, and publication of guidelines and instructions.

- *Policies and Procedures:* Under FISMA, the CIO must develop and maintain information security policies, procedures, and control techniques to address all applicable FISMA requirements, including those issued by OMB. This function is carried out for the CIO by the CISO and includes documentation of the information security policy, standards, procedures, guidelines, instructions, processes, and templates.

- *Specialized Security Training:* The CIO is charged with training and overseeing personnel assigned significant information security responsibilities as part of their duties, and normally relies on the CISO to develop and deliver role-based training according to NIST SP 800-16. This training is targeted at individuals performing duties as authorizing officials, system owners, ISSOs, system administrators, project managers, developers, as well as IT managers, operators, and executives.

Information Security Program Requirements

The fourth category addresses the requirements found in Section 3544(b), which pertain to agency information security programs. Such programs must be applicable agencywide and must be approved by OMB. In this category, we find eight requirements relating to periodic assessment of risk, development of policies and procedures, security planning, awareness training, periodic controls testing, remediation of deficiencies, security incident response procedures, and continuity of operations for information systems.

- *Risk Assessment:* In addition to the requirements levied on senior agency officials as noted earlier, the agency information security program must provide for periodic assessments of risk to information and information systems. This should include provisions for annual updates of existing risk assessments, and completion of a risk assessment as part of periodic information system reauthorization.
- *Policies and Procedures:* In addition to related requirements for the CIO and for senior agency officials, FISMA requires the agency program to include development and maintenance of cost-effective information security policies and procedures that reduce risks to an acceptable degree, ensure that security is addressed throughout the life cycle of agency information systems, and ensure compliance with FISMA, OMB, NIST, agency-specific, and national security systems directives and guidance. In response to this requirement, agencies find it necessary to develop policies and procedures that address specific provisions of NIST guidance such as the controls

requirements of NIST SP 800-53, and also publish security configuration baselines to document agency-specific, minimally acceptable configurations standards.

- *Security Planning:* The agency information security program must include provisions for subordinate plans for protecting agency networks, facilities, systems, or groups of systems. To do this, agencies document requirements for security plans for its information systems in accordance with NIST Special Publication 800-18, and require security plans to be included in system authorization documentation.

- *Security Awareness Training:* The agency program must address requirements for training of all users on risks associated with their activities and on their responsibilities for complying with agency information security policies and procedures. In response to this requirement, agencies provide user-level security awareness information (often computer based) to employees and contractors at least annually, and on an occasional, as-needed basis, through e-mail messages, announcements, newsletters, etc.

- *Controls Testing:* Periodic testing and evaluation of the effectiveness of information security policies, procedures, and practices must also be a part of the agency information security program. This must include testing of management, operational, and technical controls for every system listed in the agency inventory based on the level of risk to the system, but no less frequently than annually. Agencies devised plans for conducting annual controls testing that first aimed at testing all controls of all systems, and the NIST SP 800-26 self-assessment approach was normally used to meet the requirement. NIST refined guidance to encourage the testing of a subset of controls for each system according to risk, to which agencies responded by identifying core controls for annual testing and a combination of biennial or triennial testing for the remaining controls. To lessen the burden of this requirement, certification testing of systems undergoing reaccreditation was accepted for this requirement. More recently, agencies have used the incremental testing associated with their continuous monitoring efforts to meet this requirement.

- *Remediation of Weaknesses:* The agency information security program must provide for a process to plan, implement, evaluate, and document remediation of deficiencies in agency policies, procedures, and practices. For this, agency CISOs rely on the plan of action and milestones (POA&M) process, and use the process to consolidate information on security weaknesses, support it with automated mechanisms to create a primary repository of vulnerabilities, and use it to track remediation activities in coordination with system owners.

- *Incident Response:* Procedures for incident detection, reporting, and response to security-related incidents must be addressed in the agency information security program. The program must also include mitigation of risks resulting from the incident and appropriate notification to internal and external officials having a need to know. To achieve this, agency CISOs establish incident response capabilities that provide a means of receiving, responding to, analyzing, reporting, and documenting security incidents during and beyond normal agency operating hours. This capability is supported by documented operating procedures that also provide guidance on performing these tasks as well as identification and detection of incidents, and coordination and investigation roles and responsibilities.

- *Continuity of Operations:* Finally, the agency program must also include plans and procedures for ensuring the continuity of operations for agency information systems. To meet this requirement, CISOs develop policies and procedures for development, testing, and update of system-level contingency plans, and assign system owners responsibility for compliance. Inclusion of these plans in system authorization packages is often a requirement, as is annual testing and update of these plans in accordance with the testing guidance of NIST SP 800-34.

Potential Changes

In the years since FISMA was enacted, its critics have recommended a multitude of changes to address particular concerns that have arisen. For example, there has been concern that FISMA does not provide enforcement authority for the agency CISO, which would give that official a greater ability to ensure compliance with the requirements of the agency information security program and policy. Another often-seen recommendation is to eliminate the requirement that the CISO be subordinate to the agency CIO. The thinking behind this proposal is that the CISO could be more effective and the program could be more visible if the CISO were positioned elsewhere, perhaps higher in the agency organizational hierarchy. Consolidation of operational security tasks with information security oversight tasks under the authority of the CISO has also been an often-heard proposal. This would give the CISO not only the authority, but also the operational capability to enforce security policy and would permit more immediate response to violations. And, calls for updating FISMA to include provisions for a governmentwide CISO council are longstanding and aim to give agency-level CISOs a means for information sharing among their peers similar to the CIO Council.

There has also been a substantial amount of activity in Congress to reform FISMA. As an example of this, an effort in mid-2010 by the Senate Homeland Security and Governmental Affairs Committee was nearing success in coordinating legislation that would result in reform of FISMA which would, among several significant new requirements, require agencies to implement real-time monitoring of threats to their networked information systems. Generally, the proposed legislation would also reform the way the government recruits, hires, and trains cybersecurity personnel; would require developing a strategy to deal with supply chain risks of information technology products; and would establish the National Center for Cybersecurity and Communications (NCCC) within the Department of Homeland Security with responsibility for developing, overseeing, and enforcing information security throughout the federal government, and for coordinating protection of the nation's computer networks, power grid, and critical infrastructure. However, most significant for agencies and for CISOs in particular are its provisions in the following areas:

- The annual performance evaluations of all managers, senior managers, senior executive service personnel, and political appointees would be required to include information security performance measures.

- The CISO would have the authority to name senior agency officials as accountable for the impairment of the agency information infrastructure, resulting in the withholding of any bonus and cash awards.
- The CISO would be granted the authority and budget necessary to ensure and *enforce* (rather than merely ensure) compliance with FISMA.
- The CISO would be charged with overseeing a security operations center that is technically capable through automated and continuous monitoring to handle incidents, address vulnerabilities, evaluate risks, to collaborate, and to report. This provides a more active role for the CISO in operational security.
- Agencies would be required to permit and facilitate access of the NCCC to the agency networks, systems, storage, and security architecture. This would provide a far greater level of scrutiny of agency information resources than currently.
- The CISO (rather than the CIO) would report to the agency head on the effectiveness of the agency information security program at least annually.
- The agency information security program would have to be approved by the NCCC rather than by OMB.
- The agency information security program would be required to include risk assessments at least twice each month, and provisions for recommending to the agency head removal or migration of information systems when warranted.
- The program would also have to include testing and evaluation of security controls at least twice a year of every information system identified in the agency inventory.
- And the program would be required to include "… the effectiveness of ongoing monitoring, including automated and continuous monitoring, vulnerability scanning, and intrusion detection and prevention of incidents posed to the risk-based security of information and information systems."

The net result of these changes promise increased coordination of government information security at the national level, enhanced authority for agency-level CISOs, and improved capabilities for holding agency officials accountable for the security of their information and systems.

Conclusions

FISMA as currently written provides a sound framework for the implementation of necessary system security controls and the establishment of an effective information security program. An information security program established and implemented to comply with FISMA can result in an effective program that meets an agency's risk-based needs for security. However, implementing security that aims to satisfy FISMA reporting requirements will not necessarily lead to an effective information security program. FISMA requirements are sufficiently comprehensive and flexible to permit a CISO to balance compliance requirements against overall needs for security. However, such flexibility also allows agencies—should they so desire—to focus their efforts on satisfying reporting metrics, thereby achieving a minimum acceptable level of security. While such an approach is permissible under current government policy, it is inconsistent with the risk management principles of FISMA. That is why the manner in which agencies are required to implement FISMA's provisions should be addressed in more stringent reform legislation.

2
PRINCIPLES OF FISMA REPORTING

Probably the most significant aspect of FISMA since its enactment has been its requirement for periodic reporting. The requirements for reporting and the manner in which FISMA reporting has been implemented have elevated the visibility of government information security management activities, heightened the awareness of senior agency officials, and stirred significant controversy.

At the highest level, FISMA requires the director of OMB to report to Congress annually (in March) on agency compliance with FISMA, including the following: a summary of the results of annual independent evaluations of agency information security programs, an assessment of compliance with standards developed by the National Institute of Standards and Technology, significant deficiencies in agency information security practices, and planned remedial action to address such deficiencies. In support of OMB's reporting requirement, agencies are required to report to the director of OMB annually on the adequacy and effectiveness of information security policies, procedures, and practices, and their compliance with FISMA. The agency report must also be provided to the Committees on Government Reform and Science of the House of Representatives; the Committees on Governmental Affairs and Commerce, Science, and Transportation of the Senate; the appropriate authorization and appropriations committees of Congress; and to the comptroller general. The agency chief information officer (CIO), in coordination with other senior agency officials such as the chief information security officer (CISO), plays the lead role in agency FISMA reporting by complying with FISMA requirements that mandate an annual report to the agency head on the effectiveness of the agency information security program, and progress in remediating weaknesses in information technology security controls.

A cursory read of the legislation shows that status reporting is a major FISMA focus area. Consequently, upon the law's publication, the timelines established by Congress and by OMB for FISMA reporting requirements forced agency officials to concentrate their initial efforts primarily on reporting the status of its information security posture, and secondarily on complying with the many requirements of the law. This is because the effort required to develop the capability to comply with reporting requirements necessitated significant planning and resources. This alone took most agencies several years to master.

The impact of FISMA reporting requirements was doubly intensified when agency officials recognized first that the agency OIG was now required to conduct an annual evaluation of the agency information security program to fulfill its FISMA mandate; and second, that the annual report required the OIG's input to be integrated into the overall agency report. For agencies that were already adverse to IT audits of all types, this was a significant escalation of OIG involvement in agency IT operations and activities. Annual FISMA reporting requirements mandated a level of cooperation between agency IT officials and OIG, to which many agencies were not fully accustomed. A high level of cooperation was now required between the CIO and OIG staffs by the new FISMA legislation, in order to ensure development of a coordinated annual report that the agency head could approve without having to take sides.

Beyond the OIG–CIO coordination issue, the most controversial aspect of FISMA reporting was the decision by the House Committee on Government Reform to review annual FISMA reports and assign letter grades to each of the twenty-four agencies that were members of the CIO Council. This report allowed easy comparison of the relative effectiveness of the information security programs of these agencies, which quickly triggered a move among agency heads to focus more attention on FISMA compliance and reporting in order to avoid a bad grade in information security. Unfortunately, the growing importance of the FISMA Report Card and the emphasis of OMB on FISMA-related performance metrics led many agencies to adopt a compliance-based "check the box" approach in response to FISMA in order to achieve a good FISMA grade.

Annual Reporting

To meet its responsibilities under FISMA, OMB published instructions annually to guide agencies in reporting on the status of their information security programs, policies, and practices. OMB normally published reporting instructions for use by both the agency CIO and OIG in the third quarter (April through June) of each year. These instructions provided information about which aspects of the agency information security program would have to be reported on by the CIO organization and by OIG in his or her independent evaluation. At the agency level, these reporting metrics would subsequently influence and drive the majority of FISMA-related activities for the last third of each fiscal year.

Knowing what OMB was interested in through its reporting instructions, many agencies responded by focusing their time and effort on improving their programs primarily in response to the metrics, rather than creating holistic programs that ensured critical controls were implemented. Because of the nature of reporting guidance, agency reporting also focused almost exclusively on *information systems*, without much regard for the need to build a sound agency-wide program. Agencies were not given additional funding to meet FISMA requirements, but had to reprogram from existing funding to meet the additional information security requirements. Because dollars for information security were scarce, agencies had to prioritize their response to FISMA accordingly, and resources generally were invested in developing processes necessary to improve their FISMA Report Card grade. Certification and accreditation efforts, security training, and contingency planning and testing activities were the primary beneficiaries of dollars early on following FISMA's enactment. Because OMB did not phase in FISMA by restricting certification and accreditation to systems under development only, agencies strove to certify and accredit all of their information systems to get to or as close to 100% completion as possible. Agencies identified hundreds of weaknesses in security controls protecting legacy systems that they could never hope to correct, because these systems were in advanced stages of their life cycles. OMB reporting only required that operational systems be certified and accredited, and agencies in their short-sightedness only focused on systems in development after most all legacy systems had been taken care of. This caused certification and accreditation to be viewed as a distinct and separate security process to be addressed at the conclusion of the system development effort, rather than as an integrated part of the system development life cycle.

For instance, let us take a look at the reporting instructions for FY 2004. Areas of emphasis were the results of OIG's independent assessment, status of processes completed on agency information systems, incident reporting; security awareness and training, and status of remediation activities. For each of these areas, here are some of the issues that agencies had to consider:

- *System Inventory*: Agencies were required to report the number of information systems recorded in their system inventories. This is indicative of the importance agencies gave to defining their systems as either general-support systems or major applications in accordance with OMB Memo A-130. The agency had to account for every system in the inventory in terms of applying FISMA-related security processes.

- *Effectiveness of Security and Privacy Controls*: Agencies were required to report on the percentage of general-support systems and major applications that had been certified and accredited. Based on this reporting requirement, agencies would have to invest significant effort to develop an acceptable methodology to ensure that certification and accreditation had been completed for each system in its inventory.

- *Security Costs Included in the System Life-Cycle Costs*: For FY 2004, agencies were required to report on the percentage of systems for which security costs had been included in the life-cycle costs for the system. Inclusion of this metric required agencies to link resource requirements for information security into their existing capital planning and investment control processes.

- *Tested Security Controls*: Agencies were required to provide information in the report as to the number of systems in the inventory that had undergone security controls testing within the last year. This report metric required agencies to establish a process for testing controls protecting information systems and data annually. This initially took the form of a self-assessment conducted by system owners using NIST Special Publication 800-26, and later NIST SP 500-53.

- *Tested Contingency Plans*: The annual FISMA report required agencies to report on the number of systems in the inventory that had tested contingency plans. To achieve reporting requirements, first a contingency plan had to be developed for each general-support system and major application in accordance with NIST SP 800-34, and second, it had to be tested annually following NIST guidance.

- *Information Security Awareness and Training*: In this area, agencies had to report to OMB the number of assigned employees, including contractors and the number of users who had received information security awareness training in the reporting period. Agencies were graded highest on the annual FISMA report card if 96% or more had completed information security awareness training during the year. Also, agencies were required to report the number of information security staff, including contractors who were assigned significant information security responsibilities. At this time, it was assumed that only information security staff performed significant security responsibilities, an assumption that changed in the years that followed. Agencies then had to report on the number of these personnel who had undergone specialized security training during the reporting period. Finally, agencies were required to report the cost of training per capita.

- *Weakness Remediation*: In FY 2004, agencies also had to report on their progress in remediating weaknesses identified in POA&M. This required them to establish plans and programs for tracking weaknesses and the actions taken by system owners in closing them. For large agencies with dozens of systems, the ability to achieve with any level of efficiency was extremely difficult without the use of an automated tool designed for this purpose. Over the years, the burden of FISMA reporting led to the development of many reporting tools that minimized the impact of POA&M tracking as well as the status of other security documentation.

Additionally, OIG was required to report on the agency areas that were related to those reported on by the CIO. This included an assessment of the effectiveness of the agency's processes for systems inventory and categorization, oversight of contractor systems, agencywide management of plans of action and milestones, certification and accreditation, contingency plan development and testing, security controls testing, privacy program and privacy impact assessment, configuration management, incident reporting, and security awareness training. OIG's annual evaluation generally consisted of two parts: the OMB-prescribed spreadsheet used to record responses to specific questions about the agency's information security program, and the narrative report that was used to elaborate on these responses as well as to document other aspects of the agency's program such as agency compliance with mandated OMB requirements and compliance with NIST guidance.

Although it was quite difficult in many agencies to reconcile the CIO and OIG sections of the report, most agencies found ways to achieve this through negotiation, knowing that the agency head was required to approve and submit a consolidated report over his or her signature. However, there were occasions in which the CIO would feel compelled to submit an accompanying memorandum with the agency's final annual FISMA report stating his or her disagreement with the findings of the independent evaluation.

Quarterly Reporting

Beyond the annual reporting requirements, OMB also established quarterly reporting requirements for agencies. These were essentially a subset of the annual reporting metrics. For example, in FY 2005, agencies were required to report quarterly according to risk impact level (high, moderate, and low) and by bureau, in a spreadsheet the total number of systems, and the number of systems that have a current certification and accreditation, a contingency plan tested within the past year, and security controls tested within the past year. For the POA&M portion of the report, agencies had to report the total number of weaknesses at the start of the quarter, the number for which corrective action was completed, the number for which corrective action is ongoing and on track for scheduled completion, the number of weaknesses for which corrective action has been delayed with an explanation, and the number of new weaknesses that surfaced during the quarter. The POA&M information was to be presented for each agency bureau as applicable, and weaknesses had to be broken out by program level and system level. An example of the quarterly POA&M submission is shown in Table 2.1.

The basic elements I have described for the annual and quarterly FISMA reports remained the primary areas of focus for OMB through FY 2009 without significant variation. As a result, agencies that were able to report success with respect to these metrics, and were validated by the results of the independent evaluation, were able to achieve high Report Card grades during these years. Consequently, without varying the main reporting metrics, reporting was not used to incentivize agency management.

Report Preparation

As noted earlier, OMB normally publishes reporting instructions for the annual FISMA report in the third quarter of the fiscal year. Because this only allows roughly three to four months to prepare the final report, it is imperative that the CISO immediately coordinate the reporting effort with all staff offices that will have input to the report. This includes coordination with the information technology operations staff on issues such as asset inventory, perimeter controls, and configuration baseline implementation; the privacy staff on the privacy impact assessment status, System of Record Notice submissions, and protection of personally identifiable information; identity and access management function for HSPD-12 implementation status; the incident response function on incident reporting information, policies, and processes; and the oversight and compliance staff. Meeting with key FISMA reporting stakeholders ensures that all those required to provide input to the report are clear on reporting requirements, timelines, and agree on definitions used, and provides an opportunity to bring up questions on the reporting instructions early in planning for the annual submission. In fact, OMB usually calls for feedback from agencies on the reporting instructions, and a

Table 2.1   POA&M Summary Table

BUREAU		TOTAL NUMBER OF WEAKNESSES IDENTIFIED AT THE START OF THE QUARTER	NUMBER OF WEAKNESSES FOR WHICH CORRECTIVE ACTION WAS COMPLETED (INCLUDING TESTING) BY THE END OF THE QUARTER	NUMBER OF WEAKNESSES FOR WHICH CORRECTIVE ACTION IS ONGOING AND IS ON TRACK TO BE COMPLETED AS ORIGINALLY SCHEDULED	NUMBER OF WEAKNESSES FOR WHICH CORRECTIVE ACTION HAS BEEN DELAYED, INCLUDING A BRIEF EXPLANATION FOR THE DELAY	NUMBER OF NEW WEAKNESSES DISCOVERED FOLLOWING THE LAST POA&M UPDATE AND A BRIEF DESCRIPTION OF HOW THEY WERE IDENTIFIED (E.G., AGENCY REVIEW, (INSPECTOR GENERAL) IG EVALUATION, ETC.)
Bureau						
	Program-level					
	System-level					
Bureau						
	Program-level					
	System-level					
Total						
	Program-level					
	System-level					

report coordination meeting provides a means for consolidating agency feedback. Additionally, this meeting is an important way to establish reporting responsibilities and deadlines for having feedback available for the CISO staff to consolidate and prepare for the approval by the agency head. Close coordination with the agency administrative staff is necessary to ensure that the report can be approved in time for submission to OMB on schedule, formerly around October 1st, but currently November 15th (for FY 2010).

A meeting of those involved in providing input to the report also affords an opportunity to perform a check on where each office stands with respect to its assigned area of responsibility and allows establishment of priorities to address known shortfalls. For instance, in reviewing the implementation of various configuration baselines, requirements for addressing missing baselines, needs for updating baselines, and for implementing updated baselines can be identified, and a plan of action to achieve compliance before submission of the annual report can result. An assessment of the availability of control mechanisms necessary to generate required report data can also result from early coordination of this nature, so that gaps can be identified and plans can be made to procure and implement needed capabilities.

In coordination meetings such as these, there may be discussions over whether the agency should take such a course of action, for it may be considered to be merely "checking the box." If this is the intent of the recommendation, then I would propose that it not be initiated, because such an effort would be ineffective in the long run. Resources in this case can be better used elsewhere. Agencies that employ a strategy of just doing the minimum necessary to meet compliance requirements are merely playing a game that in time they will surely lose. Such an approach also fails to recognize the value and importance of the FISMA approach to information security management. Agencies must make the effort to understand the nature of all compliance requirements, accept them as bona fide components of the overall information security program, and honestly seek to integrate their implementation into their plans for improving the overall information security posture of the organization. CISOs who continually try to make the choice between "real security" and compliance are at least short-sighted, and fail to understand that one must complement the other.

Another action that the CISO should take once reporting instructions are received is to meet with the agency inspector general staff or other IT auditors who are charged with conducting the FISMA audit and submitting input to the annual report. This meeting allows each to compare notes on reporting instructions and to come to common conclusions about the instructions. This ensures that report input is integrated between the CIO and OIG staffs in terms of report submission deadlines and identification of possible areas of overlap. There are areas in the annual report that need to be closely synchronized between these two organizations, such as system inventory, system categorization, etc. One of the primary goals a CISO should have is to come to full agreement with OIG on their submission. In fact, this requirement was made explicit in the FY 2008 reporting instructions, which mandated that agency heads would resolve any discrepancies between the CIO's and OIG's submissions prior to forwarding their report to OMB. Philosophically, there should always be a desire to come to terms with the agency IG and agree with their input because both should have a shared view of compliance status. There is only a single "truth," and both should see it. Agencies that failed to do this in the past, and submitted memos describing why there were disagreements between the submissions only hardened the positions, thereby weakening the working relationship between the parties involved.

Requirements for quarterly reporting are not as expansive as those for the annual report. Nevertheless, time should be taken to coordinate in advance the report input to ensure that it is consistent from one quarter to the next, comports with the annual report when it is submitted, and matches any internal organizational performance reports. The quarterly report has traditionally placed emphasis on documenting the status of weaknesses in security controls and progress toward their remediation.

Weaknesses in FISMA Reporting

That there were significant problems with the way FISMA was being implemented in government agencies was broadly accepted by FY 2007. There was a general understanding that agencies were committing significant resources to develop processes that would lead to a good Report Card grade without necessarily providing an improved level of security. At the direction of Congress, the Government Accountability Office (GAO) published on March 12, 2008, a report focused on FISMA compliance titled "Information Security: Progress Reported, but Weaknesses at Federal Agencies Persist" (report number GAO-08-571T). To respond to Congress, GAO evaluated the "state of federal information security and compliance with FISMA." In this report, GAO concluded that annual FISMA reporting by the major government agencies had shown continuing progress in their information security activities according to OMB performance measurements. This included "increasing percentage of systems governmentwide had been tested and evaluated, had tested contingency plans, and had been certified and accredited." However, GAO also found that identified key weaknesses in FISMA implementation at the time included the continued existence of significant deficiencies in security controls; failure to implement access controls for computer networks, systems, and information; ineffective management of network device configuration; failure to employ separation of duties principles; and lack of "complete continuity of operations plans for key information systems." GAO concluded that the reason for this situation was the fact that agencies had not yet "fully or effectively implemented agencywide information security programs." This conclusion, according to the GAO, was demonstrated by the increasing number of security incidents government agencies were experiencing. The report also found that the effectiveness of information security within government agencies could be improved if federal agencies would take action to correct significant deficiencies and security program shortfalls identified in prior GAO and IG audits. Additionally, the report recognized the benefit to agencies of employing governmentwide initiatives such as information systems security line of business (ISSLOB) common processes and functions for information systems security management, and adoption of secure configurations developed by the National Institute of Standards and Technology and Departments of Defense and Homeland Security. The report also documented that improvements were also necessary in the areas of security control testing, FISMA reporting, and performance of annual IG evaluations of agency information security programs.

Recent Improvements

In April 2010, OMB published the much-awaited revised FISMA reporting instructions. These instructions are provided in Appendix B. The new instructions were significant in that they documented a substantially new approach to FISMA reporting.

The primary thrust of this change was to shift toward real-time monitoring of information systems and away from evaluation of processes documenting compliance with FISMA. The change was instituted by OMB to require agencies to continuously monitor security-related information across the enterprise through the use of automation as fully as possible. According to OMB, agencies are now required to "develop automated risk models and apply them to the vulnerabilities and threats identified by security management tools." These new instructions were recorded in OMB FISMA Memo 10-15, "FY 2010 Reporting Instructions for the Federal Information Security Management Act and Agency Privacy Management." Beginning in FY 2010, agencies are required to submit annual FISMA reports through the use of a new, online interactive collection tool called CyberScope, and are now due on November 15, 2010, instead of the traditional October 1st submission date. The new reporting requirements levied on chief information officers are based on a three-tiered approach that includes the following:

- *Data feeds directly from security management tools:* In lieu of quarterly reporting, CIOs will now be required to report monthly beginning on January 1, 2011, by means of data feeds directly to CyberScope on inventory, systems and services, hardware, software, external connections, security training, and identity management and access. This new approach shows movement toward implementation of continuous monitoring, but must still be considered as reporting on a "snapshot" basis. OMB encouraged agencies to avoid creating separate systems for reporting because the goal is for reporting to be a "by-product" of continuous monitoring tools. Consequently, OMB identified data elements that promote submission through the use of agency security monitoring systems. The new information was first required for agency submission for the third quarter of FY 2010, and would continue for the fourth quarter of FY 2010 and first quarter of FY 2011. However, beginning on January 1, 2011, agencies were required to report this new information on a monthly rather than quarterly basis. The new information comprised summary information on agency systems inventory, hardware and software assets, external connections, security training, and identity and access management.

- *Governmentwide benchmarking on security posture:* In addition to the data feeds identified earlier, major agencies are also required to report their answers to a set of questions regarding security posture using CyberScope. Separate questionnaires were created for the CIO, OIG, and the Senior Agency Official for Privacy. The questionnaires for FY 2010 are provided in Appendix C.

- *Agency-specific interviews:* As a follow-up to the questions described earlier, a team of government security specialists conducts an individual interview with all agencies to obtain information about their specific security posture and issues. The focus of these interviews is specific threats related to the unique mission of each agency. OMB further clarified that these interviews were designed to "shift our efforts away from a culture of paperwork reports" toward implementation of "... solutions that actually improve security." The information gathered from the agency-specific interview process is also included in the annual report to Congress required by FISMA.

The new requirements for inspectors general expand and improve the metrics previously collected by the IGs during their annual FISMA audits. As part of their annual independent evaluation, OIGs are still required to assess agency management performance in certification and accreditation, configuration management, security incident management, security training, remediation/plans of actions and milestones, contractor oversight, and contingency planning. However, there are now additional requirements to assess performance in the areas of remote access, identity management, and continuous monitoring.

The privacy section of the annual report to be submitted by the Senior Agency Officials for Privacy is largely unchanged and continues to follow the guidance of OMB Memorandum M-07-16, dated May 22, 2007, "Safeguarding Against and Responding to the Breach of Personally Identifiable Information." Agencies are required to submit as part of their annual FISMA report, through the use of CyberScope, their breach notification policy (should it have changed significantly since the previous report), a progress update on reducing the use of Social Security numbers, and an update on agency activities undertaken to review and reduce the amount of personally identifiable information (PII).

Conclusions

The detailed reporting requirements that have resulted from FISMA have actually proved to be a greater driver for FISMA's implementation than has the statute itself. Consequently, the charge that FISMA has been a monumental waste of resources has resulted in the generation of unnecessary paperwork at the expense of "real security" is more a function of the metrics that agencies have had to report on rather than of FISMA proper. Although most would agree there is room for improvement with FISMA, the most significant problems associated with FISMA are related to its implementation resulting from how it was measured primarily in annual FISMA reporting. Recent changes in FISMA reporting requirements aim to move agencies toward implementation of continuous monitoring and real-time risk assessment in hopes of improving their ability to counter realistic attacks with agility and speed. The effectiveness of these changes in FISMA reporting in changing agency behavior and performance remains to be seen, because agencies have been conditioned through past FISMA reporting measures to monitor the effectiveness of security controls. There is a substantial difference between monitoring controls and monitoring risks.

PART II
Managing
FISMA
Compliance

The purpose of Part II is to explore key areas that can make or break the information security program. These are the priority areas on which the CISO must focus his attention to ensure the success of the program. These are the areas he must get right, for if he does not, his work will be considerably more difficult if not impossible.

Before we can delve into each of these areas of emphasis, it is necessary to set the philosophical foundation for achieving FISMA compliance. And that is, compliance is best accomplished through the implementation of good security management principles, rather than through practices and processes designed to achieve mere compliance. This is a crucial distinction. It means that efforts to ensure compliance with FISMA are a subset of the overall information security program.

As demonstrated in our analysis in Chapter 1, FISMA essentially mandates establishment of an agency-level program for managing information security based on risk. This means that a focus on security risk management provides an effective way to achieve compliance with FISMA. Or, as specified in Section 3543, paragraph (a)(2) requires agencies

> To identify and provide information security protections commensurate with the risk and magnitude of the harm resulting from the unauthorized access, use, disclosure, disruption, modification, or destruction of information collected or maintained by or on behalf of an agency; or

information systems used or operated by an agency or by a contractor of an agency or other organization on behalf of an agency.

It is worthwhile for the CISO to broaden his program objectives beyond compliance with the specific aspects of FISMA, and instead establish an information security risk management program that addresses regulatory compliance as one of perhaps several program requirements. Because FISMA targets security management, the CISO should establish effective security management as his goal rather than compliance. The chapters in Part II address the high-level requirements of FISMA that were analyzed in Chapter 1, and show how they can be met or exceeded by a well-grounded approach to management of a risk-based enterprise information security program.

Security Risk Management

With this approach in mind, we must conclude that efforts to establish a security compliance program rather than a risk management program are misdirected and fall short. FISMA does not require agencies to appoint Chief Compliance Officers. Rather, agencies must designate Senior Agency Information Security Officers, generally known as CISOs. It should be noted, however, once again based on the aforementioned analysis, that the provisions of FISMA can effectively serve as the basis for an effective security risk management program. FISMA not only mandates establishment of a security risk management program that provides adequate protection for an agency's information resources, but also provides a practical pathway for achieving this goal. There is no provision in FISMA that prohibits what many refer to as "real security," and actually establishes a risk management framework that promotes implementation of security that addresses real security needs.

An enterprise security risk management program must begin with an enterprise perspective on, and definition of, risk. This is unique to each agency and must take into consideration agency-specific assets, threats, vulnerabilities, and safeguards as well as the agency mission. Such an approach would lead to consideration of compliance as a business risk among many such risks affecting the security of agency information resources. Failure to comply with the provisions of FISMA (or with any other regulatory requirement for that matter) is a risk that senior management must be aware of and accept the consequences of any level of noncompliance.

Unfortunately, since its inception, FISMA has been considered in terms of compliance rather than risk. And the response to it has been consistently considered to be a compliance effort. It is well established that the term *compliance* connotes something negative because it is taken as merely meeting preestablished requirements with little latitude for deviation, or thought to impacts or resource constraints. It is therefore a primary task of the CISO to deemphasize FISMA compliance as the primary security driver and alternatively to emphasize security risk management as the goal of the information security program, which, as described previously, is what FISMA actually calls for. The advantage of this strategy is that security risk management is much more positive than compliance management; compliance is black and white, while risk management is relative and situational; and compliance aims at doing something because somebody said so (OMB) rather than because it addresses a real business need. One must consider also that NIST guidance goes beyond mere compliance with minimum security requirements and actually encourages the application of a risk-based approach through the "scoping guidance" it recommends, as it relates to the process for tailoring established security controls to meet the specific security needs of information systems.

Security Program Management

The chapters in this section of the book support the needs of agency-level security managers and personnel in managing the enterprise information security program. They build on and reinforce key security management concepts. For instance, there is an emphasis on accumulating the information necessary to know the status of the various components of the program and being in a position to share that information in a timely fashion, as well as having a vision of what is coming in the future and a plan for continuously improving and maturing the program, and a means for keeping it on track through good security management techniques and practices. Following the idea that you must define the program for the organization in order to manage it, these chapters highlight the need to define the scope of the program by defining its components (for example, incident response, training, security architecture, and compliance and oversight), as well as defining what the program does not include (i.e., operational security tasks, privacy, etc.), and dispels false notions about the program and its goals, roles and responsibilities, dependencies, and capabilities. Requirements related to complying with specific requirements stipulated in the FISMA legislation will be addressed in these chapters, but will be covered in terms of achievement of the goal of managing the information security program. Compliance must be considered as part of all organizational initiatives that have an information security component, and it is the job of the CISO as information security program manager to include the agency's position on all matters relating to information security management and FISMA compliance along with other compliance requirements such as HIPAA, Sarbanes–Oxley, and Clinger–Cohen.

Critical Tasks for Information Security Program Management

The structure of this section of the book centers on the ten most critical tasks to be performed in information security program management at the government agency level. Each of these critical elements is explored in its own chapter, which provides tips, pitfalls, and best practices I have come to know (most often through trial and error), and have found to be critical in establishing and maintaining an effective agency information security program that not only complies with FISMA requirements, but is capable of effectively securing agency information resources.

Critical Information Security Program Management Tasks

Obtain and maintain the support of senior management.
Design the information security organization.
Staff the information security organization.
Develop a strategic plan for implementing the program.
Establish information security policies and guidance.
Provide information security awareness and training.
Support audit requirements.
Monitor security controls and risk, and ensure compliance with
  information security policies and procedures.
Integrate information security into the system development methodology.
Share program information and provide customer support.

The following paragraphs provide a short summary of each of the chapters in Part II:

- *Obtain and maintain management support for the program*: This critical element is far and away the most important. An agency whose management is not committed to the need for an effective information security program will never have one. If that management is satisfied by merely complying with FISMA requirements and checking the box, that agency will never have a program mature enough to consistently provide adequate security for the information it needs to support its mission and objectives. Management support is addressed first, indicating its importance to program success.

- *Design the information security organization*: Each government agency must have an information security organization that is right-sized to the needs of the agency. Careful consideration is necessary to determine what that size is, where it will be located in the organization, the roles and responsibilities for program components, and what functions it will provide in support of the agency information security program. An out-of-the-box approach or adoption of a structure that works somewhere else normally misses the mark by over- or underestimating program requirements, and the CISO must be able to take the lead in designing the information security organization and ensuring that it is capable of managing program requirements.

- *Staff the information security organization*: Having the right people staffing the security organization ensures that it delivers on its promises. The right people are not just those who are smart, experienced, and credentialed, but are also able to function as a team, who have knowledge of the mission of the agency, and who understand risk and how security can enable mission accomplishment.

- *Develop a strategic plan for implementing the program*: Planning for the implementation of the information security program is vital to its success, not only in the early weeks and months when an agency is perhaps dealing with the aftereffects of a major security incident or coping with a failing audit, but also for the long haul, where real program effectiveness is only realized. The nature of security program planning relies on knowledge of the "as-is" state of the program today and identification of the "to-be" state of the future. Each of these is of great importance and presents great challenges for the information security program manager. But his knowledge of each permits him to employ strategic planning to address the gap between these two states.

- *Establish information security policies and guidance*: Documenting requirements of the information security program through policies, standards, procedures, and guidance is the critical foundation for the program in that this documentation establishes the authority for the program and permits consistent implementation of program requirements according to management directive. The challenge of developing and maintaining useful and coherent information security policy and guidance is exacerbated by the dynamics of modern information technology and the proclivities of the federal workforce and user population.

- *Provide information security awareness and training*: It has often been said that the biggest bang for your security dollar is security awareness. This is because of the importance of system users to the success of the program. Each individual user has powers to do both good and evil that may be beyond their understanding. Giving them this understanding is the goal of security awareness and training. They must have a continuing awareness of their role in the protection of agency information and an understanding of the consequences of their mistakes and omissions. Dollar for dollar, training users is the most cost-effective use of information security program resources.

- *Support audit requirements*: Evaluating the effectiveness of the information security program is an important part of the agency's audit strategy. FISMA and the number and nature of security breaches and vulnerabilities in today's government computing environment has intensified the frequency, scope, and intensity of external audits, which aim to measure the effectiveness of agency information security efforts and to recommend corrective actions where necessary. The information security function plays a critical role in not only managing the agency's information security program, but also in preparing the agency for external audits of the program and its various components. The effectiveness of the information security team in understanding the nature and value of external audits and how they support program effectiveness is a critical component that can make or break the program and its ability to maintain management support.

- *Monitor security controls and risk, and ensure compliance with information security policies and procedures*: The information security function in most government agencies performs oversight of the agency's information security program in order to ensure that sensitive information is secure at all times. This means the IT security function must employ monitoring capabilities to identify vulnerabilities when they occur. This requires a combination of technologies and processes to provide the CISO visibility of the agency's security posture and awareness of the level of compliance with agency policies and procedures.
- *Integrate information security into the system development methodology*: The integration of security requirements, activities, and processes into the development and acquisition of information systems is the most effective path to building in security rather than bolting it on. A continual problem in government agencies is that the information security function is not engaged in new projects until late, leading to the situation where system requirements do not adequately address security, causing costly retrofitting of security controls. Therefore, timely engagement should always be a crucial objective of the information security program.
- *Share program information and provide customer support*: The information security function is a customer service organization, in that it must continually elicit support for the security program and must reach out to entities that play a critical role in the success of the program. FISMA apportions responsibility for information security across government agencies through assignment of a number of mutually supporting roles, and the information security function plays an integrative

role rather than an operational one. Therefore, an effective outreach program can lead to a well-coordinated approach to implementing security where all the moving parts have full knowledge of the information security program and its purpose and its goals, understand their individual roles and responsibilities for program requirements, and work together rather than at cross purposes.

By properly addressing these ten areas, the chief information security officer can make significant strides toward building a mature information security program that provides assurance that agency information assets are protected while concurrently ensuring compliance with external mandates such as FISMA.

3
MANAGEMENT SUPPORT

How does a new chief information security officer (CISO) go about gaining management support for the information security program? One often hears that it takes take a digital "Pearl Harbor" in order to get support from executive management. That is, something has to go terribly wrong before an organization's leadership will finally pay attention to its security compliance program. There are numerous recent examples of data loss incidents that help support that contention. Of course, this is not an ideal situation for a new CISO to step into. First of all, there is the pressure to make rapid and highly visible progress in addressing vulnerabilities. Then, there is the obvious situation of knowing that your predecessor was just fired, and the same thing could happen to you.

In government, FISMA has provided another driver for getting management to focus on security. For some agencies, a couple of cycles of poor FISMA scores has been enough to convince their executive leadership that something has to be done to show that they are serious about their information security posture. To agency executives, a poor FISMA grade is an embarrassment, and their contemporaries have a ready means of measuring performance. This has often led to heroic efforts to improve their rates of compliance to demonstrate that they are not substandard. Programs established on this basis, however, often fall apart once better scores are achieved, and management begins to turn its attention to other priorities. Additionally, FISMA has caused many agencies to shift emphasis to compliance almost exclusively at the expense of establishing a good all-around security program. Limited budgets have forced many agencies to concentrate on compliance rather than security because there are not enough resources to achieve both, and compliance is cheaper than implementing risk-based security. Additionally, Congress has held agencies strictly accountable for poor FISMA compliance levels. By crashing to ensure their agencies achieve FISMA requirements, agency management can avoid being called to testify before Congress. Short-term strategies such as these can also help CIOs avoid material weaknesses in audits and preclude intensive inspector general and GAO audits.

Management support is the most valuable single indicator of the success or failure of an information security program. Without the backing of upper management, the ability of the CISO to implement an effective program is more a matter of luck than skill. Executive management must take active ownership of the program and must visibly demonstrate its support in word and deed, by how it addresses resource requirements and by how involved they are in the oversight of the program. Experienced executives in most cases have come to know the importance of securing information by trial and error, based on cases where security has fallen short or based on having learned the ropes from mentors who already know its importance.

With the advent of FISMA, executives now have another reason for implementing programs designed to secure their organization's information. By means of the FISMA compliance report card, major agencies are given a letter grade annually, making it very easy to compare the relative status and progress of their security programs. Whether or not this is a fair or accurate means of grading security program effectiveness, this approach at least focuses the attention of management on the need for information security or at least FISMA compliance. It creates a spirit of competition between agencies and is regarded as another means of demonstrating excellence. The annual FISMA audit can be used to draw attention to areas where support is needed, but it should not be wielded as a hammer. Instead, audit findings should be should be considered on the basis of their relationship to an actual risk-related need rather than the sole justification for corrective action. For instance, measure support maturity vertically by evaluating the effectiveness of various information security program roles such as approving officials, system owners, project managers, etc., or measure support horizontally across the organization by assessing the level of support by each element within the scope of the program.

One approach to measuring the level of management support that the information security program enjoys is to assess it against a management support maturity model. Such a model focuses on the need to build management support incrementally, one part at a time. Through such an approach, support is gained incrementally by prioritizing program requirements.

CISOs must set priorities for support. It is wishful thinking for CISOs to believe that they will be able to obtain their optimum level of resources. They, therefore, will need to set priorities for using the resources that they do have or that they hope to have provided. This applies to hiring actions, services that must be performed, and to tools and products that must be purchased. Needs such as these should be viewed as part of a longer-term resource strategy, which allows CISOs to incrementally build toward a well-defined future state.

Once success is achieved, the CISO will find that maintaining management support becomes increasingly challenging. When success is demonstrated and compliance goals are met, organizational leadership may divert attention from the program, and its support can gradually shift elsewhere. The principle that the squeaky wheel gets the grease applies as there are numerous competing priorities for management to be concerned with, and the CISO must work hard to maintain the level of support required to maintain progress beyond short-term and intermediate goals. An effective strategy for maintaining support is to intensify efforts to keep senior leadership informed of the current status of the program, the need for continued improvements, and the presence of new risks when they are identified. This builds awareness of and support for initiatives leading to continued program improvements.

Support for compliance efforts is best gained in the first, early days of the CISO's assignment. This can prove to be fleeting, however, and early successes must be built upon to ensure that an adequate level of support is provided. Although support from upper management can often be expected early on, one should not expect full support from the entire management team, nor from across the organization on day one. The effectiveness and credibility of the CISO have great bearing on the speed with which nonsupporters can be won over, and the level of resources provided for the program. Lack of trust, unresolved issues, failure to achieve goals, and negative feedback all erode the CISO's position and lead to diminished management support.

Executives can usually tolerate an isolated negative incident as long as there is no evidence of malfeasance and the response is on target. But multiple negative incidents are indicative of a CISO who is not in control and who has no effective plan for responding. Certainly, there are cases where the CISO can and should be fired for a single incident. However, executives understand the nature of the position and are willing to overlook individual incidents that arise from time to time. Management support of the CISO in such situations depends on the value of the CISO to the organization as demonstrated by his or her accomplishments and credibility.

CISO Characteristics

In order to earn and maintain management support for information security, the CISO must prove his competence, credibility, and trustworthiness. The basis for expectation of such qualities should be revealed during the hiring process. The CISO must ensure that the requirements he articulates are filtered for practicality, reasonability, and realism. One should not underestimate the importance of character and leadership in determining the effectiveness the CISO may have. Honesty and integrity are essential qualities for the CISO to be effective, and the CISO can never afford to fall short in these two areas. The CISO can never afford to fall short in these two essential areas. In performing the role of the CISO, there is no room for half-truths, differing standards and stories, and worst of all, ethics violations. Naturally, consistency in the performance of the CISO's duties is critical, particularly in terms of policy interpretation, prioritization of work, and in response to incidents and violations. The people with whom the CISO deals have a right to expect consistency in these matters. The CISO must be careful to place great importance on customer service, and must always give priority to customer satisfaction. Finally, and perhaps most importantly, professionalism is an essential quality for the CISO. The CISO must be professional in all of his dealings with others. He cannot afford to be sloppy in his work. He must be sensitive to the needs of his peers and customers, fully understanding their expectations and their perspectives on the information security program.

CIO Support

As a priority, any CISO should focus his efforts on achieving management support from the chief information officer (CIO). Under FISMA, the CISO is a subordinate of the CIO, and a CISO who cannot win over his boss on security is in for a tough time. The CIO must be made to understand the impact of security incidents, the importance of security, as well as recognize that continuous monitoring is essential to the success of the program. To achieve this, the CISO must speak to the CIO in terms that he understands and that are important to him. This includes expressing the value of security in business terms rather than simply as compliance mandates. He must be reasonable in the requests that he makes to the CIO. There should be no gold plating of requirements; seek only the resources necessary to meet an actual business requirement, not nice-to-haves. The CISO must also ensure that he knows the organizational culture and the agency's strategy prior to making requests for support. This will permit him to make a better case for the impact of his fulfilled request on the organization and the priority it may have on an enterprise level. Support from the CIO must be based on sound planning done well in advance and avoidance of panic requests. The latter will rapidly become tiresome. The CISO must be realistic about his prospects for support; the CIO has competing interests, and it is not likely that security will be able to win every battle. When asking for his support, the CISO must strictly avoid putting the CIO in a difficult position. The CISO will be well served to have a plan B in the event that his initial request cannot be filled. He should be prepared to negotiate in such cases to make the best of the situation. The CISO must be careful to try to win the war if not the battle. In dealing with the CIO, the CISO should use incidents and situations that arise to promote support. He can do this by keeping an eye on situations as they arise and by developing the capability of evaluating them as to how they can be leveraged to achieve willing support. This must be done quickly, and the CISO must communicate his requirements while the impacts of the event are fresh in the minds of senior leaders including the CIO. The CISO should strive to ensure that security is part and parcel of the CIO's worldview.

The CISO should seek the CIO's support im promoting participation by authorizing officials. The CIO's help in achieving active engagement by authorizing officials will broaden senior level support for the program, and the CISO will find his efforts to achieve this will pay long-term dividends. Whatever happens, the CISO must keep the CIO informed. The CIO must be aware of program resource needs, and it is the CISO's responsibility to keep him regularly informed.

Senior Executive Support

Obtaining support for the information security program from the highest levels of the organization should be a clear goal for the CISO. To do this, he must find out who the power brokers in the organization are. This could include the secretary, deputy secretary, chairman, assistant secretaries, chief financial officer, etc. There will be at least one player at this highest echelon of the organization that will prove critical to the success of the program. Support from the executive suite can serve the CISO well in setting the tone for broader support across the organization.

Although it may be tempting to start at the top of the organization to get executive support right away, executive management should not be the CISO's first target. Rather, the CISO must understand the agency culture and must become expert in the processes, particularly budget formulation and contracting, in order to obtain long-term support across the organization. Nobody likes cheaters, and those who invoke the name of the agency head too often stand to suffer repercussions, growing hostility, and lack of cooperation. It is better to learn the ropes, know the rules, and work within the system, only using get-out-of-jail-free cards from upper management when absolutely necessary.

Support of Business Unit Leaders

The support of senior executives will normally facilitate support of senior leaders in organizational business units. To achieve this high-level support, the CISO must speak in business terms that help them understand how security enables the accomplishment of organizational goals. He must also help them understand the risks associated with the use of sensitive information and information systems in layman's terms. It is not helpful to bury business unit leaders in terminology they do not understand and process. The CISO must clearly tell them what you need. Get to the point, and be clear about what you are asking for. Also, make it clear to them how you can help them meet their goals and how security supports their business needs. Take the time to learn what their critical business drivers are, and what their immediate business and information technology needs are. The CISO must find ways to integrate these business unit leaders into the system approval process. Make sure that they know what their security responsibilities are with respect to the operation and maintenance of information technology systems under their control.

Support of Security and IT Specialists

The CISO's approach to gaining the support of information system security officers (ISSOs) and system administrators (SAs) should be to help them support the information security program. Individuals in these positions are already assigned security responsibilities. The job of the CISO with respect to personnel in these positions is to help them perform their duties more effectively, thereby promoting the effectiveness of the information security program. This can be done by making ISSOs and SAs aware of information security policies, the information security program, and the current strategy for attaining information security program goals. The CISO should establish a framework to support ISSOs and SAs that promotes information sharing, elevates their authority and credibility, and gives them a voice in the area of policy and program implementation. They should be given ample training opportunities, not just role-based training but technical training provided from external sources. Professional certification of ISSOs and SAs should also be a consideration.

Support of System Owners

As noted earlier, system owners play a vital role under FISMA in the protection of information technology systems. System owners must be educated on their FISMA responsibilities. They must understand system categorization, certification and accreditation, continuous monitoring, risk assessment, and weakness remediation. They must understand that they own security for the systems under their control. The CISO must not only train them in what they are responsible for, but must also help them perform their security tasks. This is done by providing timely guidance and tools that will help them prepare security documentation and perform security tasks that ensure the protection of sensitive data processed by their systems.

Support of Project Managers and Supervisors

To gain the support of personnel in these positions, the CISO must make the case for security with them by stressing its importance to their projects or to their operations. The CISO must offer them value and must articulate the needs of the program from their perspective. With regard to policies, standards, procedures, and tools, the CISO must be consistent in what is provided and how it is interpreted. The decisions that the CISO makes with respect to employing security controls with given IT project must be sound, enforceable, and consistent, and must warrant continued, unswerving adherence. To obtain the willing support of the project managers, the CISO will find it valuable to bring gifts. In other words, to add value. This is done by helping them solve a problem, assisting them in keeping their project on schedule, or offering an easier or more cost-effective means of meeting a security requirement. Partner with them to identify areas where the information security function can make their life easier. It is also helpful for the CISO and his staff to make themselves available to project managers and supervisors whenever needed. Thinking in terms of customer services permits the level of responsiveness necessary to achieve the continuing support of individuals performing these critical roles. The CISO must ensure project managers know who he is, what he can do for them, and who on his staff can serve as a point of contact for them. At the same time, the CISO must make sure they know what his needs are and how they can help support the information security program. This should be reinforced continually, particularly in role-based training and in frequent contacts with them.

Support from Other Managers

The CISO will always be well served to seek out managers across the organization who are in a position to support the information security program. He should tell his story to the CFO, political appointees, the staff of the agency head, information technology operations management, inspectors general, and directors of business units with regard to how they can and should use their funds for security. The CISO's story must be told in a way that these individuals can readily understand, through the use of terminology and examples related to their business needs. The CISO must ensure that they are aware of the impacts of not being able to obtain the resources necessary for the program and how that translates to them and their organizations and operations.

When seeking support for funding and resources, the CISO should present clear, understandable scenarios that make known the consequences and risks of failing to support these requirements, and he must articulate what the current level of resources means with respect to achieving the agency's goals as well as information security goals. Such "what-if" scenarios help managers understand the impact of their decisions on pending actions; and when seeking additional funding or when trying merely to hold on to existing program resources, it may be useful to help them visualize the impacts of various scenarios. For instance, a winning argument may be that the agency will only have 75% of its systems certified and accredited, leaving it behind the governmentwide average of 88%. Then the CISO must ensure that management knows how to support you, and what the impact of their support means to mission achievement.

Naturally, management support is easier to obtain when the CISO is in a position of strength, or has a record of accomplishment. A CISO who is perceived as being ineffective, unreasonable, or incompetent should not expect business units to willingly offer their support and surrender scarce resources that will then be wasted by a spendthrift.

To build credibility and to demonstrate effectiveness, the CISO should look for low-hanging fruit and quick wins. These opportunities should be assessed carefully and chosen wisely to ensure that they actually benefit the organization and are not simply a mirage. Once competence, achievement, and progress have been made, the CISO should trumpet these successes and leverage them to gain support. This approach can be effective in winning supporters and champions in business units to broaden support across the organization. The CISO can then work to nurture these business unit champions to build their confidence in his program and initiatives. Asking trusted counterparts to pilot new processes before they are fully implemented helps to identify shortcomings and areas needing improvement, and provides an excellent means of assuring success once it is rolled-out on a broader scale.

The CISO must take advantage of all formal opportunities to articulate program needs for support. Periodic meetings of agency leadership, various governance council meetings, program reviews, all-hands meetings, senior leadership conferences, etc. are all examples of forums where the CISO can provide updates on the status of the program, and to describe shortfalls and needs for additional support.

Another effective use of informal relationships is for the CISO to use them to test ideas before broadcasting them more broadly. The CISO should look for critical voices among his supporters in order to get an honest perspective about how program initiatives may be received by a larger audience, and this may very well help him avoid political landmines.

Through such informal, trusted relationships, the CISO can come to know the agency's hot buttons, key initiatives, and what its critical projects are. This will help him negotiate more effectively and may help him either avoid becoming engulfed in some quagmire or, on the other hand, may allow him to become involved and contribute in resolving a long-standing problem.

The CISO must be able to identify the individuals (chief financial officer, deputy) and groups (enterprise architects, authorizing officials) that have the authority to influence resource decisions either positively or negatively. Relationships with these individuals should be fostered and nurtured. However the CISO chooses to do this, he must ensure that program needs are made known so these officials can either actively support your program needs, or at least do not stand in the way of your achieving your goals. The CISO must always be reasonable with his requests, and he can only do this by knowing what is unreasonable. For instance, the CISO should know what is in the budget and the amount that can be requested without appearing to be foolish.

Nature of Support

How will the CISO know when he is getting good support from upper management? What does proper management support look like? There are several ways to tell this. First of all, management support must be continuous. It must be evident over an extended period of time rather than an intense one-time burst of energy in order to come into compliance with some external requirement. In other words, management support will have to express itself by focusing on the implementation and maintenance of a comprehensive program rather than merely a project to meet a compliance requirement. Support for the information security program must be more than superficial. It must translate into necessary funding for the program, modifications in organizational priorities to support the program, and staff and contracting support to ensure that sufficient human capital resources are available to implement and maintain the program. One of the key outcomes of good management support is the full-time dedication of personnel to oversee and implement security. While it may be easy for upper management to talk about the importance of the program on the basis of governmentwide emphasis on security these days, their support must amount to much more than that. It must deliver tangible results. This should include support in remediation of weaknesses in security controls that have been identified in security controls. This will take dollars, emphasis, and attention to progress being made. Effective support is that which is provided on a timely basis when it is needed, not when it is convenient. Often, with security, incidents occur and require immediate attention. In such cases, time that is lost in dithering about the impacts of decisions to be made can result in missed opportunities, and can also expose the organization to significant vulnerabilities. Finally, the CISO should strive to ensure that management support is not based on fear of noncompliance, but is based on a logical business case that he is able to make.

Support in System Operation

Another good measure of the level of management support that a CISO has is by determining how much authority he has to refuse to let unsecure systems go into production. At the most basic level, the CISO must be able to keep risky systems from going into or remaining in operation. This means that the CISO must be able to win battles when going head to head with business leaders when it comes to security vis-à-vis achievement of other business requirements. The fact that showdowns over this decision occur is a fair indicator that security at least is a consideration for management, and actual victory in such battles is an even better measure of how much credence management gives to security considerations.

Support in Acquisitions

A measure of management support is how much authority the CISO has in authorizing the acquisition of information technology products and services. In order to ensure that risks are considered and that compliance requirements have been addressed, security always needs to be considered in acquisition decisions, and proper management support for the information security program should ensure that the security function is consulted as part of the approval process. Support is evidenced through opportunities to review statements of work and other procurement actions, by acceptance of standard security language in contract terms and conditions, and by computer security team involvement in configuration control boards, business meetings, and project teams.

Support in System Authorization

Finally, one more means of gaining management support is for the CISO to consider the system authorization process functions in the organization and measure the effectiveness of the role of the FISMA-required authorizing official within the organization. The authorizing official plays a very important risk management role under FISMA in that he is the senior management official who must decide whether or not an information technology system should be allowed to operate on the basis of the risk it poses to agency operations. Because of the nature of this responsibility, the individuals performing the role must have a fundamental understanding of information technology risks, knowledge of what those risks are to the organization in business terms, and they must have a basic knowledge of important security processes such as systems certification and accreditation, and integration of security into the system development life cycle. Because of his responsibility for accepting risks that operation of the system causes, the CISO should recognize that the authorizing official is in a position to serve as a champion for the information security program. Every opportunity should be taken to educate the authorizing official on FISMA requirements and his role, and then to involve the authorizing official in maintaining the security of the system. This can be accomplished by providing the authorizing official an initial briefing on the information security program, FISMA requirements, security risk management, and the certification and accreditation process. Conducting a brief thirty- to sixty-minute desk-side briefing gives the new authorizing official an opportunity for direct information exchange on an important function. This should be accompanied by briefing slides and job aids as long as they are not overly voluminous or detailed. Following this, the CISO should make a concerted effort to keep the authorizing official engaged in the security of the system. Prepare to brief him whenever there is a change in risks to the system, when security controls need to be changed, or when the system operating environment changes. These occasions should be viewed as opportunities for heightening the security sensitivity and security awareness of the authorizing official. The authorizing official is required to make decisions relative to significant changes in the system, and repetition of tasks related to making such decisions increases understanding of the importance of security.

Summary

In order to maintain management support, managers at all levels of the organization must be aware of the role they play in supporting the information security program. The CISO must work to ensure that each player knows what the other players are doing and what they are responsible for. This will help them understand that their support of the program is not isolated and that they are part of a much larger picture.

4

THE INFORMATION
SECURITY ORGANIZATION

This chapter focuses on organizing to comply with FISMA information security objectives that are required of government agencies. To properly organize an information security function, the chief information security officer (CISO) must answer questions about its mission, its size, its placement within the organizational structure, its responsibilities, the functions it must be able to perform, its lines of coordination, and its authority and responsibility vis-à-vis other elements of the organization. The surest path to success with FISMA compliance is through the establishment of a highly functional and well-thought-out information security function. A cross-organizational team that can effectively manage the information security program can also ensure that the agency's FISMA compliance goals can be readily achieved.

FISMA Requirements for the Information Security Function

FISMA requires the establishment of an organization-wide information security function. To establish an enterprisewide security program such as one required by FISMA, centralization makes it far easier to implement such a program. Centralized program management facilitates the program's penetration enterprisewide, into all business units, across all geographical locations, and applicable to all users of the organization's information technology resources. Centralization permits dissemination and enforcement of a single information security policy that applies to the entire enterprise, and is more advantageous than the management of multiple security policies, which will almost always prove difficult to integrate.

Defining Requirements

One of the first steps in designing an information security function to ensure compliance is to conduct a needs assessment. This foundational step is designed to lead to the identification of all security-related activities and resources in the agency in order to determine who is currently performing a security-related role. The CISO should determine where information security is performed in the organization and who is performing security functions, as a basis for the formulation of a coherent strategy and for the creation of a functional information security organization. This can be quite revealing. This exercise should be followed by identification of what the information security function needs to look like, based on known requirements affecting the information security program. Identification of this future state will establish the target information security organization. With the current state and the future state organizations determined, a gap analysis between the two can be conducted to identify unmet needs and a path forward for meeting them. An example of this approach is the development of an information security strategic plan in which all of an agency's information-security-related functions are first comprehensively identified, requirements for the information security program are defined and documented, and gaps are identified, and recommendations for improvements in the agency's enterprise information security program are made.

Organizational Placement

FISMA mandates that the CISO and information security function be under the authority of the CIO. As related in Chapter 1, FISMA has come under some criticism on this score since its enactment, with critics recommending a more prominent place for the CISO. Apparently, in some agencies, visibility of the information security function requires improvement under the current arrangement, and reforming FISMA to break the linkage between the chief information officer (CIO) and the CISO is considered by some to be an appropriate solution.

Visibility of the program is indeed a major factor in determining where the information security function should be placed in the organization.

Organizations should designate a CISO to emphasize the importance of the function, as well as to demonstrate due diligence. The CISO should be given requisite authority to manage the organization's information security program. Inherent in this is his ability to gain access to upper management. The information security function cannot be buried deep in the organization and expect success, and the CISO should not have to constantly compete for upper management's attention.

The information security function fits best closely alongside the information technology operations function. Whether or not the information security function is also given responsibility for operational security as envisioned by FISMA 2.0, or is chartered to focus on oversight and compliance without operational security responsibilities, in either case it is important to clearly establish the division of labor with the information technology operations functions. The information security function must find the line of demarcation that best satisfies the needs of the organization. In any case, those engaged in compliance should avoid the temptation to perform information technology operations tasks. A strict separation of these functions provides checks and balances that are necessary for each to thrive. The security compliance function should not be burdened with implementation tasks such as system security administration, patch management, intrusion detection system monitoring, and access management, all of which jeopardize their independence in performing their compliance and oversight functions.

Wherever the information security function is placed in the organization, it must be integrated with the rest of the staff, that is, with the entire CIO team. It is important that the members of the information security team are seen as, and consider themselves to be, team players who can be counted as part of the larger CIO organization. In particular, they must cooperate closely with the enterprise architecture staff, the information technology investment management team, the privacy office, eGovernment personnel, the system development function, and with the information technology operations staff.

Functional Capabilities

To determine what functions must be performed by an information security organization, it is useful to begin with FISMA and with

Office of Management and Budget and NIST guidance relative to FISMA implementation. According to these, the primary tasks identified for performance by the information security function include compliance monitoring and oversight, development and maintenance of security policy, security training and awareness, incident response and situational awareness, and security architecture development. The information security organization should be designed to support the requirements of each of these functional areas, and distinct teams should be established for each. (See Figure 4.1.)

The compliance and oversight team should be assigned the primary tasks of managing certification and accreditation activities, FISMA reporting, system definition and inventory, security categorization/classification, plan of action and milestones (POA&M), and remediation tracking, interagency agreement development and tracking, oversight of contractor-operated systems, periodic review, and common controls definition among other tasks. The policy and training team should be assigned responsibility for developing policies, procedures, guidelines, and standards; managing exceptions and waivers; interpreting policies; publication of policy notices; training and awareness for general users; provision of role-based and specialized security training; and publication of periodic refresher messages and dissemination of policy updates on current topics. The security architecture team should be structured to support the security compliance effort by managing tasks related to system engineering activities, requirements definition, security architecture integration, and consultation on system design.

The situational awareness function supports security compliance through the conduct of threat analyses, vulnerability identification and tracking, trend analysis, assessment of new technology, interfacing with security operations, conducting penetration testing, vulnerability scanning, and performing forensic analysis. Incident response is related to situational awareness, and seeks to contain, report, investigate, and coordinate response to incidents. This naturally includes protection of evidence, as well as testing and evaluation of remediation, and dissemination of user alerts. Other related tasks include contingency planning (plan development, training, testing, and coordination) and annual controls assessment monitoring.

Additionally, the information security organization must be organized to perform information security program management

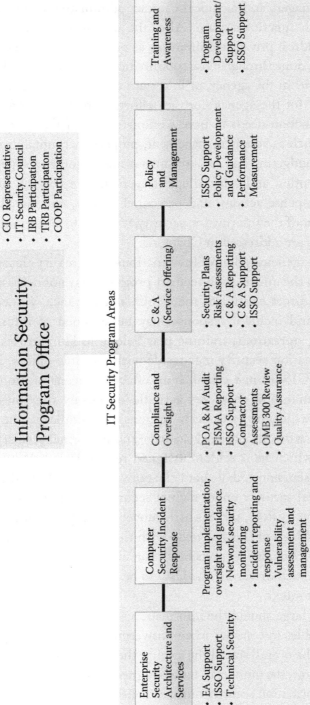

Information Security Program Office

- CIO Representative
- IT Security Council
- IRB Participation
- TRB Participation
- COOP Participation

IT Security Program Areas

Enterprise Security Architecture and Services
- EA Support
- ISSO Support
- Technical Security

Computer Security Incident Response
- Program implementation, oversight and guidance.
- Network security monitoring
- Incident reporting and response
- Vulnerability assessment and management

Compliance and Oversight
- POA & M Audit
- FISMA Reporting
- ISSO Support
- Contractor Assessments
- OMB 300 Review
- Quality Assurance

C & A (Service Offering)
- Security Plans
- Risk Assessments
- C & A Reporting
- C & A Support
- ISSO Support

Policy and Management
- ISSO Support
- Policy Development and Guidance
- Performance Measurement

Training and Awareness
- Program Development/ Support
- ISSO Support

Figure 4.1

functions, a requirement that is best met by ensuring that trained project managers and technical contract administrators are assigned within each functional team. Also, the organization must be prepared to address privacy requirements as part of its compliance activities. This is done through close coordination with the external privacy function within the agency, or in certain cases by making the CISO responsible for the agency's privacy efforts. Finally, the information security function needs to have administrative capability to address activities such as supply management, property accountability, space planning, budgeting and resource management, contract supervision, visitor reception and scheduling, correspondence control, management of suspense actions, and personnel actions, etc. The skill sets needed to staff the information security function to perform the foregoing tasks are addressed in Chapter 5.

In some agencies, some of the functions that are very closely associated with the information security program may not necessarily be under the direct control of the CISO. For instance, vulnerability scanning and incident response may be assigned to information technology operations, training may belong to Human Resources, and information security may reside with multiple offices. In such cases, the CISO must establish an effective means of monitoring the performance of these key activities to ensure they mesh with those for which he is directly responsible. Similarly, the CISO must work with the physical security and personnel security functions, for which he is seldom assigned responsibility. While there is much discussion today about the convergence of logical security and physical security under a chief security officer throughout the greater security field, there is little movement in government in this direction. Much of this has to do with the FISMA requirement for the CIO to exercise responsibility for information security, while there is no such driver for the CIO to be responsible for security in a broader context.

So, how large should the information security office be? There are many variables to consider when answering this important question, including the overall size of the agency, the number of operating units and, of course, the number of tasks assigned to the office. However, an agency information security office established in response to FISMA normally consists of at least ten full-time employees, and can exceed fifty in certain cases.

Formalization of the Organization

There are several documents that must be developed consequent to the establishment of the information security function. A mission statement is important to document what the office is chartered to accomplish. A vision statement usually accompanies the mission statement to define how the CISO envisions accomplishment of the mission. Also, a statement of values provides members of the information security team as well as those outside the organization a statement of those characteristics, beliefs, attitudes, and behaviors that are considered by the CISO to be important to the accomplishment of the mission.

A documented value proposition offers customers of the information security office an idea of what benefit the office expects to provide to them, and provides them a benchmark against which to evaluate the services the office renders.

To establish how the office will function, standard operating procedures are required to provide members of the information security organization with the steps necessary to perform routine, recurring tasks. To guide external customers in areas for which the office is responsible, a documented concept of operations is necessary. This will cover activities such as penetration testing, weakness remediation, contingency planning and testing, and annual controls testing.

A strategic plan for the office defines the goals and objectives to be achieved over a relatively long period of time, normally three to five years. It provides milestones to be achieved and establishes priorities and sequences for tasks that the organization must perform. Development of the strategic plan must be consistent with the overall agency strategic plan and information technology strategic plan. How this is to be achieved is further detailed in Chapter 6.

Roles and responsibilities of each team and each member should be clearly defined and documented, and must be integrated to avoid overlaps, gaps, and confusion. For every task, a lead role and a support role should be specified to explain how various teams are involved in the action. For example, while the compliance team may be assigned lead responsibility for developing templates for security documentation, the policy team has secondary responsibility through its responsibility for the Web site, where all security-related policies, guidance, and tools are posted. Every task should be defined in this way to provide understanding across the team and to ensure depth. For each position, a "smart book" can provide an informal means of documenting precisely how the incumbent of a position routinely goes about performing various aspects of his assigned duties. This is particularly helpful in transitioning newly assigned personnel into new positions. In the process of defining office roles and responsibilities, the CISO should not forget to establish focal points or information access points for various activities that are posted for customers to know. When these are applied consistently, it will reduce confusion within the team and will promote customer confidence. However, care should be taken to permit customers to use personal relationships with team members to communicate their security needs and to surface issues to the team. For example, customers who call an acquaintance on an action should be able to continue to work the issue through them even though they do not own the issue. You cannot afford to be too rigid in communications channels; it jeopardizes the effectiveness of informal relationships.

Based on documented roles and responsibilities, job descriptions are developed for each position and are supported by performance plans that map to the office strategic plan. Finally, a staffing plan is necessary to document a prioritized approach to staffing the organization and filling key vacancies.

The CISO should ensure that he has control over who is hired to be part of the security organization. This includes exercising authority over selection of individual contractors and consultants who provide services to the information security function.

Organizational Compliance Roles

Naturally, the organization required to assure agency FISMA compliance is extends beyond that CISO and his staff. Therefore, the CISO must coordinate his efforts carefully and fully. The internal staff of the information security compliance team must also be on board with the need to work with other elements of the organization to achieve the mission. This includes close coordination with OIG on security matters of mutual interest (i.e., audit findings), with the Office of the General Counsel on legal aspects of security policies and activities, with Contracting on security-related acquisitions and contract language, with the CFO on internal controls, with Human Resources on disciplinary actions, with the eGov office on ensuring that security is addressed in governmentwide initiatives the agency is involved with, and with information technology operations on disaster recovery, infrastructure protection, and systems development activities. To facilitate coordination with and support of other organizational elements that affect the information security program, the CISO organization must be fully integrated into information technology governance processes in the areas of capital improvement and investment, eGov forum, configuration control, enterprise architecture, information technology business planning, and information technology strategic planning.

There are three groups of individuals outside the information security organization proper that play an extremely important role in the effectiveness of the agency information security program. The CISO must properly organize these groups to assure their support and to ensure their contributions to the program are as effective as possible. As detailed in the following sections, the roles of system owner, information system security officer, and authorizing official are critical to the success of the information security program.

The System Owner Role

Owners of information technology systems play a crucial role in the information security program, and should be considered a key component of the information security compliance organization. According to NIST SP 800-37, an information system owner is defined as an "official responsible for the overall procurement, development, integration, modification, or operation and maintenance of an information system." System owners have the responsibility for ensuring the security of their information system. Because of their broader responsibility for the business process that the system supports, it is wise for the system owner to appoint an ISSO to oversee the performance of security tasks for their information technology system. The central information security function must work very closely with system owners in the performance of their security tasks, and even more closely with the ISSOs they appoint to handle system-level security functions on a day-to-day basis. If the agency has an effective ISSO structure, the CISO relationship with system owners will be one that concentrates on information sharing. Without reliable ISSOs, communications between the CISO and the system owner will be much more frequent and intense.

The ISSO Framework

The information security organization needs to be supplemented by the establishment of an ISSO framework of security points of contact throughout the agency. ISSOs should be appointed in writing by senior management for every general-support system and major application as well as for every major organization within the agency. The ISSOs should be given a voice through an ISSO forum that is based on a formal charter, meets periodically with its own leadership, and is given authority to influence decisions regarding implementation of the agency information security program. The ISSO structure will serve as an extension of the information security organization and, as a collective, will provide valuable input on information security program initiatives, policies, and activities. The duties of ISSOs should be standardized across the organization to provide consistency, and the CISO should strive to ensure that performance measures for the ISSO role are integrated into the performance plans and evaluations of each ISSO. Additionally, the CISO should prioritize training of ISSOs to enhance their capabilities and the credibility of the position by developing a standard training curriculum and learning plan for individuals assigned to this function. These should specify the knowledge, skills, and abilities required for successful performance of ISSO duties, and should identify internal and external training opportunities for attaining them. The CISO should recognize strong performance by ISSOs and should provide incentives such as cash and time-off awards accompanied by public announcement of their accomplishments. The CISO should grant individual ISSOs ready access to foster a higher level of communication, to solidify their credibility, and to permit more rapid resolution of policy questions and implementation issues. ISSO credibility is also enhanced by their attainment of professional certifications, and the CISO should set certification goals and encourage participation by application of funding strategies and by stressing the importance of certification at the management level. The security compliance team can also support an effective ISSO framework through the development of documented procedures to guide primary ISSO activities to include preparation of useful templates for creating security documentation.

To be effective as an ISSO, there are certain qualities that required. When making a selection or recommending assignment of individuals for this role, one should consider the problem-solving abilities of the individual. Their ability to quickly grasp the complexities of new issues that arise and their attention to detail are both key traits that should be sought. Other ideal qualities are abilities to work with others, and to effectively communicate requirements, interpersonal skills, and project management.

Authorizing Official Framework

The authorizing official framework is as important as the ISSO structure to the overall ability of the information security organization to accomplish its mission. FISMA requires that a senior management official authorize the operation of each of the agency's information technology systems. How the agency goes about doing this can vary widely, but an organized approach to identifying who the authorizing officials are going to be, preparing them to perform this role, and then managing their activities is a critical success factor for the program.

The number of authorizing officials will depend primarily on the number of information technology systems that an agency has and how the agency is organized. There should be a strict separation of the roles of system owner and authorizing official. According to NIST SP 800-37, the authorizing official should be "a senior (federal) official or executive with the authority to formally assume responsibility for operating an information system at an acceptable level of risk to organizational operations (including mission, functions, image, or reputation), organizational assets, individuals, other organizations, and the Nation." Many agencies find it advantageous to centralize the role of the authorizing officials and thereby limit their number. This reduces the amount of turnover that many organizations experience and lessens the number of senior agency officials who require training in, and familiarization with, the role. Another alternative is to associate the role of authorizing official with a specific level of authority or position. For example, every deputy assistant secretary serves as the authorizing official for all of that office's information technology systems.

As noted earlier, authorizing officials must be familiar with important aspects of their role in order to be effective. They must have a basic understanding of FISMA, must have knowledge of the agency's business processes, and must understand the concept of risk acceptance. That is, they must be aware that there is a certain level of risk that often must be accepted in order for an automated business process to operate, and that striking a balance between security and business is indeed possible. It is incumbent on the CISO to ensure that each authorizing official is aware of these critical aspects of the position, and this is done by documenting requirements for authorizing officials, providing face-to-face training upon their initial selection or assignment to the role, and then keeping them apprised of changes in the threat environment as it evolves.

Organizing to Communicate

It is not possible for the security team to "overcommunicate" with other elements of the organization in order to understand business needs for security and to help business units understand compliance requirements. To maintain a high level of team awareness, the CISO must continually look for and find ways to keep his security staff informed of what he knows about the organization and what is going on elsewhere in the organization from his perspective. At the same time, he must make the entire agency aware of the status of the information security program and his team through various means. He must participate in organizationwide meetings whenever possible, he should hold frequent team meetings, and he must meet regularly with team leaders, holding both scheduled meetings and meetings on demand. Other ways that should be considered for communicating with all or parts of the agency include holding meetings on special interest issues as necessary to lead to their resolution, establishment of SharePoint or other information-sharing sites, active use of an information security function Web site, submission of periodic reports (weekly/monthly) to upper management with direct input by the staff, participation in off-site planning meetings, participation in workshops, and judiciously providing information copies of correspondence to managers who have a need to know.

Traits of an Effective Information Security Organization

First of all, the information security organization must be relevant and appropriate for the organization. An information security organization that is appropriate is one that positions the information security program for success without wasting resources or creating an atmosphere of fear and dread. It allows for effective decision making by agency executive management. The structure of the security compliance team must enable support of peer-to-peer relationships across the organization, and allow it to operate on an equal footing with other offices in the performance of the organizational mission.

The information security organization, of course, must be consistent with regulatory requirements and should comport with National Institutes of Standards and Technology guidance as much as possible. The ideal organizational structure will permit efficient delivery of information security services while at the same time support efforts to ramp up to meet short-term surge requirements. A well-organized security compliance function will allow for the effective management of assigned personnel to ensure they are fully engaged in performance of meaningful tasks, challenged and fulfilled by the work they are assigned, and permitted to grow as professionals and as individuals.

The security compliance team must be large enough to manage the needs of the entire organization on an equal basis. If there are regional or field offices, there must be a capability for addressing the special needs of parts of the organization that may be geographically remote. The team must be structured to provide depth of capability in order to permit recovery from personnel losses. Its ability to continuously deliver quality services must be sustainable, and plans for succession of key positions must be taken seriously. Training needs must be integrated into normal operations, so as to allow training to be performed without adversely affecting the delivery of services to customers. Also, an effective security compliance organization will have a comprehensive set of interlocking, mutually supporting position descriptions that are based on well-documented roles and responsibilities for each position.

Mechanisms for performance measurement must be built into the fabric of the team structure to ensure that all members know what is required of them, with the expectation that their performance is being observed, measured, and rewarded as appropriate. Supervisory responsibility within the organization must be clearly stated, and the number of supervisors should be assigned on the basis of two to five employees per supervisor. This is due to the highly specialized nature of the duties that must be performed by the members of the team.

Another trait of an effective information security team is that team members work well together. This means that every individual on the team must be committed to the goals of the office and how they are to be achieved, speak with one consistent voice when dealing with customers, and discuss differences of opinion in private and not in the presence of customers.

In developing the compliance team, it must be remembered that support of the organization is paramount. The CISO should seek to answer the question, "How can we provide the best possible support?" There is no need for an ivory tower organization, but rather one that is ready to get its hands dirty. One should not expect unquestioning support from business units, at least initially. Therefore, the structure and placement of the information security organization should lend itself to maximum support for business unit needs. You should be prepared to do things for them—to hold their hands, in other words.

Independence

To properly exercise its compliance role, the information security function must be independent of elements required to comply with security mandates. This separation is essential for providing assurance that business units are not capable of hindering compliance-monitoring activities. Consequently, the information security function in its compliance role needs to be known across the organization as an independent organization. To reinforce the necessary degree of independence, the information security office must have control of its own budget, justified in its own business case, and must have its own operating space to permit proper protection of its own sensitive data.

Because the information security function is responsible for overseeing compliance, it has this in common with other organizational elements also engaged in compliance efforts. The Office of the Inspector General and the chief financial officer through its internal controls function are also involved in compliance activities. However, the information security team should avoid being viewed by the organization as auditors. This is because compliance is secondary to the goal of achieving adequate security, and consequently the CISO has the responsibility of assisting system owners and others in the organization in meeting security requirements.

When organizing the information security office to perform security and compliance functions, there are several key positions that should be defined. First, the CISO position should be established as the leader of the office and primary official responsible for management of the agency's information security program. Depending on the total number of employees assigned or the number of separate functional teams established, a deputy CISO may be warranted. Generally, a CISO will only need a deputy or operational assistant when the office is larger than twenty employees, or has more than five functional teams. For each of the separate functional areas, a team leader will be required. At a minimum, this includes one for policy and training, one for compliance and oversight, and one for situational awareness. Team leaders should expect to be working managers, with responsibility for not only managing team activities, but also fulfilling tasks in the delivery of services and support.

Specialists assigned to these teams will include policy analysts, training specialists, compliance specialists, and incident response specialists. Other positions in the information security organization may include security architects, security engineers, and project managers. On the administrative side, the CISO may have the support of an assigned secretary and, depending on the size of the organization, a management analyst.

Grade levels for members of the information security team should generally be consistent with those across the organization. That is, the grade of the CISO should be equivalent to that of office directors elsewhere in the agency, ranging from SES level to GS-15 at a minimum.

Team chiefs should be Senior Level or GS-15 employees, and specialists within the teams should range from GS-15 to GS-11, according to the agency norm. However, because of the specialized nature of the work, the information security function should be allowed to exceed the agency average for nonsupervisory GS-14 and GS-15 positions. In order to develop the necessary skills, the CISO should establish career-ladder positions to permit realistic career progression. For instance, a junior candidate with potential should be allowed to enter the workforce at a lower grade (e.g., GS-7), with the potential for steady promotion to higher grades as he or she achieves competence. Whenever possible, use should be made of cooperative training programs to make use of the services of short-term seasonal employees and interns. This allows highly motivated young workers to gain an entry into government service and into the specialized security field.

Other means of enhancing the performance of security team personnel include cross-training with other elements of the organization for limited periods of time. Sixty, ninety, and 180-day details can provide a means to advance an employee's knowledge, and can benefit the information security team when the employee returns. Rotational assignments in which employees are temporarily assigned to another office can provide an immediate benefit to each agency involved. For instance, arranging for an employee from the incident response team to exchange places with an employee from the operational security team could benefit the information security function in understanding day-to-day issues encountered in the protection of the agency's network, and could help the information technology operations staff understand better procedures of handing security-related incidents requiring investigation.

Authority

In accordance with FISMA, the CIO has responsibility for the entire enterprise information security effort and delegates this responsibility to the Chief Information Security Officer. In his role as the manager of the organization's information security program, the CISO must have the authority to task other elements of the organization to perform certain security functions. For example, he must be able to direct business units to update their security documentation on a scheduled basis, or he must have the authority to craft policies and directives necessary to manage and operate the program. He must have the authority to investigate incidents and security violations when they occur. The nature of an enterprise information security program is that business units do not have the authority to prevent the CISO from investigating security-related issues within their organizations. Normally, the CISO does not have the authority to enforce the requirements of the information security program. Rather, he must rely on the organizational leadership to take corrective action when violations occur. To be effective in this, the CISO must establish good working relationships with business unit management to ensure that proper disciplinary action is taken in response to violations in order to prevent their reoccurrence.

Recent initiatives at the government agency level and in Congress have elevated the enforcement authority of the CISO. These examples give the CISO direct authority to enforce the requirements of the information security program specifically and FISMA in general.

In organizing for security, one must look beyond the information security function alone, and recognize the need for an information security program oversight function. The existence of an information security steering committee or oversight board provides the high-level direction that the information security program requires in order to stay anchored to the organizational mission and strategy. Such an entity is most effective when it is formally chartered, with defined membership, authority, goals, and whose credibility is recognized by senior agency leadership.

Compliance Organization Operations

The CISO should take every opportunity to celebrate successes that are achieved by the organization or by team members. When major milestones are reached (i.e., FISMA metrics are met), when important audits are concluded, or when favorable reports are received, these occasions are to be celebrated and trumpeted across the organization in order to instill pride and to mark success. Awards received by individual team members should be celebrated by the entire team whenever they are received.

Routinely, the information security function will have to cooperate with several organizational elements in the area of incident response.

This includes the privacy function in the case of incidents in which personal information may have been compromised, the office of the general counsel for legal issues, the administration division for facility security and property accountability, the public affairs office for news releases, information technology operations with network and systems controls, inspector general for investigation and forensics, as well as affected business units.

The information security organization must ensure that it meets all the general requirements of other offices in the organization, and must not hold itself apart. It should not be so independent as to not participate in organizational initiatives such as fund-raising, blood drives, special events, etc.

Contractor Support

The information security organization must be structured so as to effectively manage the services provided by contractors and consultants, and to allow their integration into the team to permit their accomplishment of short-term and specialized tasks. The CISO must anticipate the ebb and flow of workload requirements by initiating contracting actions far in advance of when additional manpower is required. The CISO should be able to recognize the advantage of outsourcing certain requirements because of their temporary nature or because of the ability to apply exceptional expertise not immediately available among the full-time staff. Areas where contractors and consultants can most benefit the information security organization are in policy and procedure development, information security and awareness training development and delivery, security architecture, independent verification and validation (IV&V), vulnerability management and situational awareness, oversight of compliance activities, security documentation evaluation and development, performance of security test and evaluation (ST&E), and certification and accreditation (C&A) of information technology systems. When considering the use of contractors and consultants, the CISO should recognize situations where time and materials type contracts are most effective, and when the situation would most benefit from fixed price support. When there is a definitive work product involved, such as a system security plan, security test and evaluation, or contingency plan test, for example, then it is most cost-effective to contract for the work on a fixed price basis in order to reduce the risk to the government. On the contrary, if the nature of the output is less certain, such as identification and implementation of best practice methodology, the contractor support on a time and materials basis is more advantageous.

Scope

To properly establish the boundaries of the information security function, the CISO should clearly define the points where it interfaces with other internal groups that perform functions that impact security. This will include the information technology operations organization, the personnel security function, and the physical security office as examples. These relationships should be documented, and the level of formalization necessary for the relationship should be specified in terms of operating level agreements.

Summary

A centralized information security function that is applicable and relevant to the entire organization is a key ingredient for the success of the agency information security program. Under the leadership of the CISO, and with the support of the CIO and senior management, the information security function, which is properly organized to perform its critical security responsibilities as a member of the integrated CIO team, provides a recipe for success in FISMA compliance.

5

STAFFING CONSIDERATIONS

The most important resource that the CISO has is the staff of the information security function. To most of an agency, the personnel assigned to the office are the visible faces and hands of the information security program, and the manner in which they perform their assigned duties has a direct and immediate impact on the success or failure of the program. Therefore, the CISO must have only highly effective employees and contractors in place performing these important tasks toward the accomplishment of information security program objectives. To implement an information security program that meets FISMA requirements, the CISO must not only establish a well-organized office, but must also fill established positions with people who understand the mission, know how to achieve program goals, and perform their assigned tasks with diligence, common sense, and creativity. Consequently, the CISO must prioritize the staffing of information security positions, and must manage these critical personnel resources carefully and well in order to achieve his program goals.

Key Qualities

When considering the kind of individuals who make effective security compliance personnel, there are a number of qualities that should be taken into account. Security personnel engaged in FISMA compliance must be analytical, with the ability to dissect complex issues related to security controls implementation, and as a result must be able to identify practical, cost-effective solutions. Rather than being strictly technical, they must be process oriented in order to understand business requirements that underlie the technology. Additionally, they need to have auditing skills, yet they must have the maturity to know how to wisely use the authority with which they have been entrusted.

The following table provides a list of the most desired qualities for personnel assigned security compliance responsibilities.

Desired Qualities of Security Compliance Personnel

Business sensibility
Cooperative
Customer service oriented
Risk management focused
Technically competent

Generally, the basic qualities needed fall into the following categories:

- *Business Sensibility*: An individual's ability to understand the business of the organization is one of the most important qualities. An understanding of the agency's mission and how various business units function in support of that mission is key to an individual's ability to understand how information technology systems support business processes, and thereby to identify practical, risk-based security requirements.

- *Cooperative*: An individual's ability to work with others is another important quality for employees and contractors performing the security compliance tasks. A lack of interpersonal skills limits the effectiveness of an otherwise excellent security technician because he is not able to communicate security requirements to others. Security compliance involves more than mere assessment as to the presence, absence, quality, or effectiveness of information security controls. In most cases, there is an attendant need to explain weaknesses in controls, and more importantly the ability to communicate solutions regarding how controls can be improved.

- *Customer Service Orientation*: Security compliance personnel must display a customer service orientation as their primary approach to performing their work. Dealing with people is unavoidable in security compliance. Evaluation of security controls, monitoring remediation of weaknesses, and recommending solutions to security problems all involve working with people, and working with them as customers works most effectively. This requires security employees to have a basic understanding of the customer's needs, empathy for their situation with respect to security compliance, and the ability to effectively communicate with them verbally and in writing.

- *Risk Management Focus*: This may be counterintuitive, but the security compliance employee must have a solid knowledge of risk management principles. Compliance and risk management generally appear to be at odds with each other. While compliance is rather straightforward—either a condition meets a requirement or it does not—risk management requires the practitioner to be able to see varying shades of gray. One must first realize that FISMA mandates a risk management program for security. This entails an ability to understand the role that risk plays in determining security requirements for information technology systems, to understand the organization's business, and to see the big picture. This makes the exercise of sound judgment and the application of common sense essential qualities.

- *Technical Competence*: To be effective in FISMA compliance activities, security personnel must have solid experience in implementing security controls. Not only because they are called to assess them, but primarily because they must be able to recommend practical solutions based on their first-hand experience. This means that they need to have practical knowledge of the wide array of NIST SP 800-53 controls, and know their interrelationships. Additionally, competence in working with various compliance tools is an important quality. Skills with vulnerability scanning, plan of action and milestones monitoring, certification and accreditation, and FISMA reporting tools, for example, permit them to effectively perform their duties and minimize the repetition of manual effort. Technical competence in the FISMA compliance field also implies a mastery of the regulations, guidelines, methodologies, practices, principles, and processes associated with security compliance activities and operations.

Staffing to Meet Compliance Objectives

In assembling a staff that can meet the agency's compliance requirements, the CISO must seek individuals who understand information security based on personal experience. Agency level eexperience in government information security is certainly beneficial. Contractor personnel who have experience working with government agencies in information security have an advantage because of their familiarity with FISMA requirements. Additionally, military experience is valuable because so many information security principles, methodologies, and practices were spawned by Department of Defense organizations. However, a background in security in the commercial world is not a drawback, in that individuals with that type of experience may be able to provide a fresh perspective and knowledge of leading practices that may prove helpful.

Strategies for staffing the information security organization include hiring from within the agency, hiring externally, and growing your own staff. The problem with hiring internally is that the pool of candidates is usually fairly limited, and individuals hired from within bring with them preconceived notions that may have to be unlearned. On the other hand, hiring personnel from within the agency provides personnel who already are familiar with the agency structure, procedures, strategic plan, and culture. Similarly, the use of rotational personnel and short-term detailed personnel from within the agency may be a good strategy for meeting immediate needs as they arise. Alternatively, the CISO can import talent into his organization from outside the agency. By seeking experienced practitioners who are working in the field elsewhere, he can diminish the time necessary for them to learn their duties. He can choose personnel with professional certifications in the information security field. He can identify high-quality candidates through the recommendations of counterparts he knows and trusts.

The CISO must have sound familiarity with the hiring process, and special hiring authority and programs that the agency may have in place—for instance, authority to re-employ retirees for short-term purposes, programs for hiring veterans returning to the workforce, each of which may allow hiring in excess of the number of staff positions authorized. The CISO needs to work with the Human Resources staff to get to know what hiring strategies he can employ, and may find that there are apprenticeships and summer hire programs available to him to obtain the services of young workers training to enter the job market. He should also explore the available alternatives for temporary workers, rotational, and detail personnel as well.

One wise thing that the CISO can do is learn from the experience of others. By coordinating with his counterparts elsewhere in government, he can identify lessons learned, perhaps the hard way, at other agencies. He should talk with other CISOs, and pay them a visit as he seeks out excellence by identifying the proponents of best practices. These may relate to hiring and staffing procedures, the structure of the information security organization or its placement, roles and responsibilities related to the information security program, or the identification of functions that should be included in the security organization.

A successful strategy for the CISO in managing his personnel is to build career-ladder positions in order to foster growth. Positions that are structured to permit regular promotion and career growth allow employees to see where they are headed, how to get there, the pace of their career path, and recognition of where solid performance will lead them. A career ladder allows hiring of personnel who show potential but who have limited experience at lower grades, but then allow them to be steadily promoted to higher grades as they demonstrate successful performance and build increasing levels of experience.

The ideal information security organization will comprise a mix of employees with solid knowledge of the agency's organization, procedures, and culture based on several years' employment with the agency, coupled with individuals hired from outside the agency who are able to share new ideas and new perspectives based on their experiences elsewhere. The CISO must devise means for effectively integrating new personnel into the organization. Assigning them work with experienced partners is a good way to transfer knowledge about work practices and procedures to new employees and permits them to rapidly become comfortable in their new surroundings.

Succession planning is an important aspect of managing the information security team. The CISO must ensure that the sustainability of the organization can be ensured by identifying and preparing successors for each critical position in the team. A successor for each supervisory position, every highly specialized position, and the position of the CISO must be identified, and a plan for preparing that individual to be successful in this position of higher responsibility must be devised. Such a plan would identify the position targeted, preparatory rotational assignments applicable to the targeted position, and training opportunities that would prepare the candidate for the position.

The CISO should not underestimate the importance of position titles. Not just from the perspective of personal pride of the incumbent, but also recognizing that the incumbent in order to be effective must have a job title that is recognized within the organization at the proper level of authority, and must match the culture of the agency. Similarly, the grades of assigned personnel must be commensurate with the level of responsibility expected of the employee. Otherwise, good employees can feel underappreciated and could seek employment elsewhere.

One of the most important skills that members of the information security staff should have is project management. Because of the emphasis on outsourcing in government today, it is vital that information security specialists know how to manage a project, particularly one performed by contractors. The CISO needs to ensure that project management training is available to assigned personnel, and in order to ensure depth, he should train the maximum number of personnel possible.

Cross-training whenever possible is an excellent way to increase the depth of team member skills. Internal rotation programs permit personnel to broaden their experiences within the team, giving them an opportunity to change their normal routines, at least on a short-term basis, and with an external rotation program, gives them a chance to see how other parts of the organization work. This has a benefit to both the gaining and the losing organization. One note of caution, however; the CISO should ensure that a basic level of efficiency and competence is established across the office before rotating assigned personnel to new positions. And, the number of simultaneous moves should be controlled to limit disruption, and excessive drop-off of services. Having a "deep bench" is a key principle of succession planning. Having a prepared successor available to step forward when key personnel retire, transfer, or leave a different job is a critical aspect of ensuring the continued functioning of the information security organization and the success of the information security program. A backup for every key role must be identified and for each a plan for obtaining essential knowledge, skills, and abilities must be established.

One of the key ongoing tasks for the CISO is to ensure that the CIO is aware of staffing requirements for the information security function. The CIO through his control over resources is in a position to support the information security program's personnel needs either through the apportionment of fulltime employees (FTE) spaces or through funding for support contractors.

Job Descriptions

The development of job descriptions is a critical aspect of staffing for the information security organization, and the CISO should prioritize it. Unfortunately, it is not a task that can be done quickly or easily as many might think. This is because each individual position should have its own specific job description that is tailored to the specific requirements of that position. However, because those are subject to change, the job description must balance the need for specificity against requirements for frequent update. The CISO can start with a standard shell for an information security specialist and begin his customization from there, taking into consideration the grade level, the area of specialization (e.g., incident response, awareness and training, compliance), and the particular agency and office requirements affecting the position. Specific job descriptions of this type should be constructed with the full aid and assistance of the incumbent, who can provide realistic inputs to improve its effectiveness. There will also be a need for a process to ensure that employee job descriptions are updated regularly (probably on an annual basis in most cases), and to be able to locate the most current version of the job description in preparing performance plans and evaluations.

Hiring

Hiring individuals to fill positions within the information security organization is one of the most important activities that the CISO and his managers can perform. In finding qualified FISMA compliance personnel, they must seek out individuals who can demonstrate key compliance skills. In other words, they must emphasize compliance knowledge and experience in their search. Since the inception of FISMA, there has been an emphasis on security-related compliance and, consequently, the number of information security personnel having FISMA compliance experience has grown substantially in recent years. Nevertheless, the demand for security personnel with compliance experience is great, and competition for their skills is significant. Therefore, the CISO must ensure that job descriptions for position vacancy announcements are accurate in order to get candidates who can perform the actual tasks demanded of the position. The CISO will be well served to inquire around the community for recommendations on possible candidates or later after application have been received for opinions of identified candidates. Word of mouth is an important means for the CISO to find out about an applicant's competency and credibility, and a fellow CISO's opinion of an applicant's professional reputation may be valuable.

After applications and résumés have been received, read them closely to ensure they match the position being hired for, and try to read between the lines. Today, an applicant for a government information security position will normally highlight their FISMA-related work experience in their application or résumé. Review applications with an eye toward formal certifications, which show competence in the field, professionalism, personal initiative, and knowledge of the rules. One can assume with some certainty that personnel holding professional certifications have broader experience and qualifications and are generally better able to see the big picture. However, the candidate must have more than just a certification. He must also have real-world, practical experience.

Once candidates are identified, the CISO and his managers must conduct in-depth interviews with each candidate to determine if there is a match. The CISO needs to take the time to get directly involved in conducting interviews for the most important positions, and must oversee other hires made by his subordinate managers. This must be accompanied by comprehensive checking of references. As qualifications are evaluated, it is important to factor in the organizational culture to ensure that the candidates will fit in. Try to envision how they will be able to work with customers, and also with members of the information security team. Look for candidates who can function well as part of a team rather than those who appear to prefer to operate independently. Necessary interpersonal skills such as these are best ascertained during the job interview.

Candidates who have contract management skills are particularly valuable when hiring for FISMA-related positions. Such individuals may be able to manage a critical outsourced task. Personnel who have knowledge of risk management principles and experience in the application of risk-based solutions have an advantage over personnel who have only performed compliance tasks. Applicants who have demonstrated customer service experience and skills are more likely to be successful in performing FISMA-related tasks than a technician who cannot relate well to others. Those who have an ability to understand the business wherever they have been are much sought after. A candidate's knowledge of security compliance practices at multiple agencies might also be helpful from the perspective of implementing leading practices.

Acceptable personnel must demonstrate technical competence based on recent experience with applicable software and hardware platforms, as well as security compliance tools being used. Finally, an applicant who has experience as a trainer and with training in general as well as presentation skills has an advantage in performing his tasks.

From the perspective of individuals applying for information security positions in the federal government, it should be readily apparent that a thoroughgoing knowledge of FISMA would at least enhance an applicant's credibility, but may very well be essential. To position oneself for employment in a government information security position, an applicant must understand the risk management principles inherent in FISMA; current reporting requirements for agencies; the primary processes mandated by FISMA (i.e., risk assessment, security planning, controls testing, deficiency remediation, incident response, contingency planning, etc.); aspects of the FISMA roles for the agency head, the CIO, and the CISO; and responsibilities of system owners and authorizing officials.

Working with Contractors

To augment the full-time government staff, contractors are normally used to strengthen the security compliance team. Contractors are well suited for short-term or one-off tasks. They are also useful in responding to recurring, periodic tasks such as ST&E, contingency plan testing, risk assessment, and other certification- and accreditation-related tasks. The CISO should seek to integrate contractor support fully into the information security organization as much as possible in order to achieve unity of effort. He must also establish the proper balance between government and contractor staff, and the agency's view of contractors will establish the level of authority that they may be given with respect to dealing with agency personnel. Contractors and consultants should be given all the authority they need to perform their tasks, and the information security staff must learn to trust them as professionals and partners in the program. The use of contractors and consultants should not be overly burdened by bureaucracy, so that the information security function has flexibility in their use. When dealing with contractors and consultants, the CISO needs to ensure that they are aware of their roles and responsibilities as well as their authority. Be careful with consultants who qualify as loose cannons, and who purport to speak for the CISO. With such people, the CISO can spend a lot of time cleaning up after them.

The CISO should carefully review contractor work plans to ensure that staff hours associated with project management tasks are limited to no more than around 10% of the total number of hours for the project. A better approach is to require project managers to also perform project tasks as the best value.

When choosing a contractor, the CISO should take into consideration the quality of their proposal coupled with the level of experience they are able to substantiate. The CISO must check their references thoroughly and, if possible, speak with his personal contacts as another means of establishing their reputation. Other factors that should be considered when choosing contractors is whether small or large companies are preferred for the given task. Often, small companies can be engaged more quickly, are more flexible, are less expensive, and can deliver more quickly than large consulting firms. On the other hand, large companies normally have a deeper bench of qualified personnel, have more experience in a broader number of areas, and their qualifications can be more easily established. Whatever the size of the company, the one chosen should be able to demonstrate its competence, reputation, experience, and vision.

To validate the quality of work products that contractors and consultants deliver, the use of independent verification and validation

(IV&V) is a common approach. Using either government or contractor personnel to ensure the quality and independence of the work that has been contracted out provides an independent assessment of the quality, completeness, and adequacy of the vendor's work.

Managing Security Compliance Personnel

The primary principle to employ in managing personnel involved with FISMA compliance is to know your people. Know their strengths and their weaknesses. Know their personal and career goals. Know their work habits. And know their history. Knowledge of this type will permit the CISO to balance mission accomplishment with the employees' need for job satisfaction.

Some of the strategies that the CISO can use to effectively manage assigned personnel are to continually promote their professional growth. Their professional development should be documented in an approved individual training plan that both the employee and the CISO agree with. The plan should permit participation in outside training and conferences in order for them to stay up to date with current thought and technology. It should include a path for the employee to achieve pertinent professional certification. Similarly, the CISO should support membership in professional organizations.

When managing security compliance personnel, the CISO should use various incentives to maximize their performance, both formal and informal. Payment for overtime and provision of compensatory time, should be given to make up for the extra time they will probably have to spend in performing their duties. Depending on the programs that the agency may have in place, the use of work-at-home arrangements, alternative work schedules, compressed work schedules, and flexible work schedules should be taken full advantage of, consistent with business requirements. In most cases, remote access can be effectively used by most employees to perform their security-compliance-related duties. Employees should also be encouraged to identify and work with their counterparts in other agencies in order to gain a broader view of security outside the agency and to help them identify best practices that they can apply in their jobs. Along the same lines, they should also be encouraged to establish working relationships across the agency to ensure they have a solid understanding of how the various elements of the organization function and what initiatives they have under way. However, with respect to relationship building within the agency, employees should be able to meet with their counterparts without repercussions, and without being second-guessed for perhaps circumventing normal lines of coordination.

Employees should be encouraged to take advantage of external training opportunities to sharpen their skills and to get up to speed on new technologies and techniques. They should participate in seminars, but only after choosing wisely among all the alternatives available. Participation in webinars is an inexpensive means of staying current with the newest technologies. Whatever training is chosen, it should both comport with an individual's training needs as well as meet program needs. Employees should be encouraged to read widely. Good analytical reports and articles are readily available in journals, news reports, and security Web sites that are highly germane to the individual's job position.

The CISO must be prepared to play a direct role in the development of his staff using his own knowledge and expertise. The CISO's talents as well as that of other staff members as a trainer and mentor can be used to maximum advantage to transfer knowledge to junior staff members. This does not have to be provided in a particularly structured way. Rather, when a need is identified, use this as a chance to train the entire staff in a particular practice or procedure to enhance their skills and give employees and contractors an opportunity to ask questions and benefit from personal experiences.

The accomplishments and successes of staff members must be celebrated to build spirit among the team. Awards, graduations, bonuses, certifications, etc. give the CISO an opportunity to recognize achievement and hard work while building unity and camaraderie within the team. For the same reason, the CISO needs to play a direct role in achievement building by giving cash awards and time-off awards for excellent performance.

Other proven techniques that the CISO should practice in managing his personnel should include giving employees and contractors a stake in the success of the office. This relies on their understanding of what actual success looks like for the organization. This basic team-building principle is important to laying a foundation for instilling an outlook for continuous improvement on the part of each team member. Employees should be encouraged to submit suggestions on improving processes, not just related to their own jobs but processes elsewhere in the office. The CISO should also ensure that his employees know they are free to disagree with him and know that they can be bearers of bad news without repercussions. Employees must understand that they have full freedom of action within their areas, based on the CISO giving them sufficient authority to do their jobs. Finally, the CISO should seek to challenge employees to achieve big goals. He should set high standards to avoid their becoming complacent or disinterested. Stretch goals are just that. They entice highly motivated employees to stretch their own performance to attain seemingly unrealistic goals.

To maintain unity within the team and to avoid disenchantment, the CISO must ensure that the work the office must perform is divided fairly. It must be apportioned approximately equally across individuals according to their grade and experience, as well as by team. The CISO must be on the lookout for those who do not carry their weight, and must take corrective action in such cases. Employees who fail to meet the demands of their jobs are often covered for by other team members who may become disgruntled over having to do this. The CISO must be aware of this situation, and must work hard to identify and to keep the real contributors while sifting out the nonperformers.

The CISO should strive to teach leadership principles to his staff as often as possible. He should communicate his values to his subordinates, and he must demonstrate character traits through his personal behavior. When the CISO leads by example, he can make every observable moment a teachable moment for his staff.

Another principle is for the CISO to make sure that his managers are able to supervise on the basis of their ability to perform the work being supervised. That is, those who supervise the work must be able to do the work. This is another example of leading by example.

The principle of servant leadership works as well in an information security organization as it does in any other work group. Managers as a priority must find a way to support their employees' needs. They must be aware of their employees' needs and supply them so that they can be as successful as possible in their work endeavors. This means ensuring they have adequate work space, up-to-date tools, sensible procedures and processes to follow, and achievable goals for them to reach. It also means that the supervisor must give them his vocal support on issues that may lead to disputes and confrontation.

The CISO's guiding principle should be to initially trust an employee's integrity and competence until proven otherwise. They should be given the benefit of the doubt initially. The qualities of employees who lack integrity and who are less than competent will become evident in short order, generally before much harm is done. The CISO must foster an atmosphere of character and integrity, making it clear there is no room for cutting corners and shoddy work. This quest for quality should be based on an environment of personal accountability where each employee understands that he is responsible for his actions and his performance, and that he will be held accountable when established standards fail to be met.

Newly assigned managers should make it a point to evaluate the competence of their subordinates for themselves. While it is important to hear and respect the opinions of others regarding employees, in fairness, employees should be given a chance to prove their competence through their performance rather than what someone says about them. In other words, do not rely entirely on the assessment of others when it comes to the worth of a given employee.

Performance management is a critical component of an effectively staffed information security organization. Formal performance appraisals document not only highly effective performance, but also record the reasons for successful performance, weaknesses in employee performance, as well as nonperformance. To optimize this process performance, plans must be prepared annually, and standards for performance must be clearly specified. They should specify standards for meeting job requirements, as well as standards for achieving excellent or outstanding ratings. Performance appraisals should be done honestly, and employees should be given feedback on their performance in a constructive fashion.

Know the people who are filling all the security-related positions across the organization irrespective of their level in the hierarchy. This will help the CISO establish the level of trust he can have in the individuals who have the most to do with the success of the information security program.

Staffing Other Positions

As stated in Chapter 4, there are quite a number of positions that lie beyond the direct hiring of the CISO and have staffing considerations. For instance, the authorizing official, system owner, ISSO, and security administrator all have essential qualities that should be sought in an effective candidate. Even though the CISO exercises no hiring authority over such positions, he may be called upon to provide recommendations to others who do have that authority. When asked for his input, the CISO must be able to articulate selection criteria for the following positions that are critical to the success of the FISMA compliance program:

- *Information System Security Officers*: Staffing of ISSO positions should consider an individual's comprehension of the business process supported by the system, their understanding of information technology, and their knowledge of security principles.
- *System Owners*: Those selected to function as system owners must have knowledge of and responsibility for the business process that their system supports. They must have the authority to make decisions regarding the protection of the system, and must have control of the resources supporting the system. System owners should also have an appreciation of risk management principles.
- *Authorizing Officials*: Individuals who serve as authorizing officials must have a broad understanding of the mission of the organization so as to be able to judge the risks that the operation of the system may have on the mission. They must also have some accountability for the business function supported by the system, and must have an appreciation of how systems for which they are responsible support the agency mission.
- *System Administrators*: System administrators must have sound expertise in the technology of the system, and must understand how the security controls implemented with the system function. Knowledge of NIST SP 800-53 controls is particularly beneficial.

An information security organization that is able to implement an agency-level certification program for individuals in these critical positions provides a heightened level of competency and professionalism. This is particularly important in positions that involve security-related roles performed only on a collateral basis. This generally applies to ISSOs and system owners. In these cases, a CISO-sponsored training curriculum and boot camp can be particularly useful. Additionally, because of the criticality of the ISSO position under FISMA, external certification of ISSOs is a very effective approach to building competence and warrants consideration for centralized funding by the CISO.

Summary

A FISMA-compliant information security program that is successful relies on the efforts of a highly integrated team of government employees, contractors, and consultants staffing well-defined, mutually supporting positions, which combine the talents of professionals who perform their tasks with pride, diligence, and technical competence. This is not an ideal; this is essential. A CISO can only be as successful as his personnel allow him to be, and the agency information security program can only be as good as the efforts of the people charged with its implementation.

6
PROGRAM PLANNING

Implementation of a FISMA-based information security program requires multiyear planning that is fully integrated with agency plans for accomplishing its mission. This includes both long-term (three to five years) strategic planning as well as tactical planning for the achievement of short-term objectives. For the purpose of this book, the purpose of strategic planning is to provide a path for the structured and systematic implementation of the information security program and its components, while tactical planning is seen as a means to achieve timely accomplishment of shorter-term objectives necessary for the continued effectiveness of program components, or for achieving subordinate information security program objectives.

Information Security Program Design and Development

The focal point of security planning is the implementation of an information security program that complies with federal requirements and that satisfies agency-specific needs for security. Program requirements are drawn from a number of sources. There are requirements that are mandated externally, for instance those of FISMA and required by OMB, and then others that stem from internal drivers. The agency head will have expectations for the program, which he will fully see from the perspective of the overall agency mission. The chief information officer, particularly in terms of FISMA compliance, will have information security program goals and objectives that must be addressed. And, of course, the CISO will have his own set of program goals and objectives that he aims for based on his experience.

In addition to this, other essential documentation for the information security program should include the mission statement for the information security function or organization and the CISO's vision, which helps set the direction for the program and for its implementation. Both of these documents should be directly related to the program requirements specified immediately above, and should be fully supportive of them.

It is the responsibility of the CISO to design and develop the information security program and document it for agencywide review and approval by the CIO and agency head. In most cases, the information security program has already been defined, documented, and is currently in effect when the new CISO is assigned. However, even the most effective programs require an occasional review to assess the current health of the program and its ability to support actual program requirements. Often, it is beneficial to use experienced consulting firms for this purpose because their broad experience with other similar organizations and their independent view may better enable them to perform the analysis and to have the results accepted by the agency. Additionally, an external entity can often identify program requirements that are hidden in plain sight, and have not been unrecognized by the CISO, CIO, and agency leadership.

Important inputs into the development of the program will naturally include an assessment of what is required by FISMA. An analysis of FISMA is a good starting point for the CISO to begin to understand specified and implied program requirements of this important legislation (see Chapter 1). This could be augmented by a follow-on assessment of NIST guidance as a means of defining specific program components (i.e., system authorization, awareness and training, incident response, policy and procedures, etc.). Remember, however, that the program should not be designed to merely satisfy compliance requirements. While this is an important driver, compliance requirements must be integrated into the overall information security program along with many other types of requirements.

Then, an awareness of how other agencies have designed their programs will prove helpful in that it may result in the identification of examples for possible adoption, either in whole or in part. Coupled with information obtained about other government agencies and other sources, the CISO should use his past experience to further define the contours of the end-state information security program.

Most importantly, the program will need to be designed to support the specific mission of the agency to meet established agency strategic goals. The program can be refined by identifying particular capabilities the program will be expected to deliver from the perspective of the agency head, other senior agency leadership, the CIO, and supported business unit managers. From all of these sources, the mission, functions, role, and responsibilities of the information security program and its various components can be determined and documented. The CISO should sit down with the CIO and obtain his input on the program. Together they should review what the CIO considers to be important for the program to deliver. The CIO's views should normally be documented in the CISO's performance plan, which might serve as a good starting point for this discussion. The CIO can help the CISO understand how he sees the program supporting the documented agency mission and vision, and can share with the CISO his vision for how the agency will achieve mission objectives, for information technology support to agency elements, and the information security program's support to agency information technology. Perhaps most importantly, the CIO can articulate the priority for program implementation by sharing his views on what needs to be accomplished in what order.

The enterprise information security program document should comprise all the primary topics addressed in this book. In particular, the plan will identify who has responsibility for the program, how the agency will organize to implement the program, the primary functions that make up the program, the policies and standards that provide the authority for the program, and the functions that will be performed as part of the program. The information security program design and development effort will result in the definition or redefinition of the information security program and its major components.

The Information Security Strategic Plan

With the program now defined, the CISO must now take the lead in creating the overall plan for implementing the enterprise information security program. The strategic plan needs to set very clear and well-articulated goals and objectives for achieving program requirements. An effective plan must begin with an assessment of the current situation in order to determine where the program currently stands. This current state provides a basis for conducting a gap analysis and a road map for achieving the goal of full implementation of the enterprise information security program. Planning will require identification of short-term, intermediate-term, and long-term objectives, and the tasks, steps, activities, milestones, resources, and dependencies necessary for achieving them. It should be clear that the plan will require application of a structured project management approach to implementation.

When establishing requirements to include in the plan, ensure that management's goals are fully addressed. This means evaluating the agency strategic plan and all information-technology-related plans to identify specified and implied tasks that need to be included in the plan. The CISO will need to look for the security implications of high-level, general, and perhaps seemingly nonapplicable strategies, goals, and objectives to achieve this, and translate them into clear, achievable, and measurable requirements.

In developing the plan, the CISO must consider an incremental approach to accomplishing long-term goals over time. Seldom will the plan be achievable in a single year. Rather, a multiyear approach is a more likely solution, in which critical tasks are performed according to risk and criticality as fully as possible. The definition of time period the plan should span will be a function of knowing how much time management grants you to implement it as well as how much time actions normally take or should take. This implies an awareness of the culture of the agency and the nature of change in the context of that culture.

There must also be a realization that for certain tasks, there will need to be incremental implementation at multiple levels over time. For instance, all training cannot be implemented in year one, but some training has to be initiated in order to show immediate results, to achieve short-term program requirements, and to build a foundation for future training. Therefore, there will be a need to prepare a plan that addresses both tactical and strategic requirements, and that supports concurrent implementation of several related and mutually supportive initiatives.

Often, it will be fruitful to seek input from the CISO community to solicit information regarding the solutions they have chosen to implement and the approaches they have used in implementing their programs. This can provide good ideas about best practices that could perhaps warrant consideration in your agency. However, feedback of this nature must be carefully weighed and evaluated as identified: best practices may not fit your needs precisely.

When identifying requirements to include in the strategic plan, be sure to review OMB memoranda, which establish requirements and initiatives, for example, special requirements for the protection of personally identifiable information or the need for agency breach notification plans. These very often become special issues for evaluation by inspectors general in the annual FISMA audit and other special-focus audits. Most importantly, in creating the plan, the CISO needs to carefully study OMB's FISMA reporting guidance to identify requirements that OMB expects agencies to report on either quarterly, annually, or both. These must be identified in the strategic plan, which should anticipate changes in reporting requirements on an annual basis.

The information security strategic plan can be used as the basis for budget formulation. It is helpful if you are able to quantify each requirement and then to account for the funding required for implementation in the budget. A sufficiently granular plan that identifies discrete requirements by year of implementation will readily support development of long-term budget requirements. Wherever possible, prepare the budget to include direct cross-references to corresponding strategic plan line items. Because of their importance to the long-term viability of the program, budget formulation and execution dates should also be included in the plan. In government, it is normal to work with budgets for two to three years simultaneously. You will manage not only the current year's budget, but also will be preparing to manage the next year's budget, and may be formulating the budget for the year after that too. In addition to this, in some agencies you may be managing the execution of carry-over funds from the prior year's budget. This wide variety of budget information can be difficult to manage and a comprehensive plan lends itself to effective management of budget activities. You must ensure that the plan identifies and supports all budget deadlines, allowing you to manage requirements for commitment, obligation, and expenditure of information security program funding.

To ensure that the plan remains current, a process for updating the plan on a regular basis must be employed. Update the plan at least annually, with regard to input from an interdisciplinary group that includes the information security function, information technology operations, systems development and enterprise architecture, audit, information management, privacy, and legal. Achievement of annual plan review requirements is facilitated by inclusion of plan maintenance requirements as a task within the plan itself.

Another consideration in developing the plan is the need for creating it in such a manner as to allow it to be administered by different individuals in the event that the primary plan manager is not available. Administration of the plan through the use of a software program is an excellent means of providing administrative continuity. Also, when determining milestones for developing processes to support the information security program, be sure to consider the time necessary to ensure process quality.

Achievement of many plan requirements can be enhanced through information technology governance processes the agency has instituted, which can be employed to ensure that regulated organizational elements meet plan requirements and integrate them into their own planning. Existing processes such as capital planning and investment control, budget formulation, information technology project management, and performance measurement can be leveraged to meet other plan goals. Your customers should be consulted during plan development to allow you to fine-tune the plan to better meet their business requirements.

The plan should include requirements for linkage of plan implementation to organization performance measures as well as to performance plans for executives and managers. This normally will require incremental implementation, and support for these requirements could require significant political will.

To ensure the proper level of support for the implementation of the plan, all stakeholders need to know where they are going and how they are to get there. Goals recorded in the plan should be realistic, and should not only be achievable but should actually be set so as to allow an opportunity to exceed them. The CISO may include in the plan tasks and milestones that are important to achievement of his overall goals and objectives, but for which he may have little to no responsibility for or authority over. For instance, he must always ensure that plan milestones related to the implementation of technical solutions are fully supported by and agreed upon by the information technology operations and enterprise architecture staffs.

Another benefit of the executive steering committee is to provide a forum for gaining high-level approval of security activities. This should also include approval of the information security strategic plan.

Implementing the Plan

With the plan prepared and finalized, it is now time to begin implementing it. The tasks identified in the plan can now be performed, and action can be initiated to move toward achieving the end state envisioned by the CISO, CIO, and agency management. In all likelihood, many of the actions documented in the plan will be well underway at this point, and it will just be a matter of updating the plan to record the current status. Nevertheless, it will be important to continue to use the plan to keep the train on the track, and to stay on target with task accomplishment. Military doctrine gives us a term to describe the value of the plan; use of the plan helps you to remember the "Principle of the Objective" to take the long view and provide continuity toward an established objective.

To facilitate implementation of the plan, it is best to manage the plan as a project, as a project manager does. This includes monitoring progress toward completion of plan requirements, interceding when there are problems, assigning responsibility for tasks, identifying resources, and continually reporting on the status of plan implementation. However, in the busy work of managing plan implementation, be careful not to lose sight of the critical path. The CISO, as primary plan manager, will need to work to keep everyone on target. This will require frequent reference to the plan, assessment against its milestones, communication of variances, and dispensing rewards and punishment when necessary. The CISO should not hesitate to celebrate when key milestones are met and successes are achieved.

One of the most important functions of the plan manager is to provide feedback to stakeholders regularly. Let them know how the plan's implementation is going and how it affects their activities, goals, and plans. As fully as possible, this should be related in terms of their own operational missions. Of course, the information security function does not operate in isolation, and the CISO must know what the plans are for other organizational elements and must be able to support them in addition to his own. The CISO should immediately and thoroughly communicate delays in plan implementation that have an impact on stakeholders, ensuring they understand what the impact is, and proposing actions thy can take in response to the delay to keep plan implementation on track. The ISSO community can be effectively used as a vehicle for communicating plan implementation status, and can assist in the development of a short-term plan implementation calendar. The publication of a calendar of this type can assist in the implementation effort by documenting recurring activities, tasks, deadlines, and milestones in such a manner that stakeholders can be aware of them and can plan their own activities in support of them.

The individual the CISO assigns to manage the plan must be flexible, just as the plan itself must be flexible in order to support changes in business objectives and priorities. The plan manager must realize that the plan is not merely a work of art and as such is not sacrosanct, and must permit updating in order to respond to the needs of the agency mission, and be subject to readjustment as the need warrants.

With regard to the information security staff, the CISO must clearly define team member roles and responsibilities and determine if there are overlaps that can prevent efficient accomplishment of tasks recorded in the plan. Overlap of responsibilities can be minimized by ensuring that all position descriptions are fully integrated and mutually supporting. When assigning tasks and setting milestones, the CISO can look for efficiencies by identifying task dependencies and by assigning lead and support responsibilities for the completion of every task. Every position should be identified with both a primary and a secondary staff member to ensure continuity. The CISO must also carefully consider how he will assign project managers, ensuring that proven performers are assigned to manage the most critical tasks or to support the most critical mission area or business unit. He should ensure that he has enough members of his staff who have completed program management training and whose skills have been certified.

The CISO should ensure that requirements related to information security processes he has instituted under his direction are also included in the plan. This allows activities such as continuous monitoring milestones, remediation reviews, contingency plan testing, and annual controls testing to be effectively forecast and monitored. Managing discrete activities such as these through the plan will allow the CISO to be aware of and to provide advance notice when achievement of milestones is at risk, will help him maintain a realistic picture of the status of ongoing projects, and will allow him to assess the impact of short-term delays on other initiatives recorded in the plan.

The quality of processes such as system inventory, the system authorization, contingency planning, or weakness remediation should not be sacrificed; and because of their importance to the overall effectiveness of the program, shortcuts can afford to be taken in their development as it will become readily apparent when flaws in poor-quality processes surface in their implementation. Finally, be sure to obtain input from subordinates. The CISO should rely on their knowledge and insights in formulating the plan, and should allow them to manage the information in the plan that pertains to their area of responsibility.

The CISO can improve the likelihood of high-level performance by providing effective support to officials charged with accomplishing plan requirements. This can take the form of developing methodologies and processes for every task listed in the plan (see Chapter 7). This approach provides assurance that activities such as annual controls testing, continuous monitoring, contingency planning, system authorization, and weakness remediation can be completed on schedule. Additionally, the CISO can develop self-assessment checklists for every information security role to aid agency officials charged with significant information security responsibilities, and increase their performance. When such checklists are provided with no expectation of their review and evaluation by the information security function, their usefulness will be more readily accepted.

The information security program strategic plan requires mechanisms that allow not only assessment of progress toward achievement of its goals, but also the effectiveness of the plan itself. Identification of critical success factors for plan elements provide an effective means for measuring success in achieving discrete program objectives. Examples of critical success factors include performance measures stipulated in FISMA reporting guidelines related to percentage of users who have completed annual awareness training, status of completion of annual controls testing, and performance of penetration testing on an annual basis.

Measuring Performance

To ensure that the strategic plan is implemented in a timely and effective fashion, implementation activities should be continually measured against established and identified plan milestones. This will provide detailed information that can be used to make appropriate adjustments to the implementation schedule and priorities, and can serve to make management aware of the status of the program.

To achieve this, the CISO will need to identify metrics that most effectively measure progress. The measures required by OMB reporting guidance are a starting point, but only that. The CISO must go beyond measures that OMB requires (for example, appointment of ISSOs, inventory reporting/maintenance) and identify those that truly indicate the status of the program. Tracking patch levels of operating system software, having the capability to identify all hardware and software assets in real-time, and having ready awareness of unmitigated vulnerabilities by risk ranking are good measures for individual information systems. The effectiveness of office-level program support can be measured by validating the appointment of primary and secondary information security roles, training completion by individuals performing those roles, participation of assigned users in refresher training, and the number and nature of security incidents involving business unit personnel.

Whether performance is measured by system or by business unit, it will be necessary to break out measurements by organizational element in order to facilitate communication of results and to permit easy comparison. This is because the effectiveness of the measurement process will be directly tied to management's level of interest in taking action by holding business unit managers accountable for performance failures.

When establishing performance targets, there may be a temptation to take risks by setting lofty implementation goals. However, risks should be considered in terms of no more than stretch goals that can be achieved with some bit of extra effort, if the stars align. You should not consciously set yourself up for failure. In fact, it is important to remember to leave room to exceed goals. In other words, your goal should not be 100% achievement of the measure as there is no way to exceed that goal.

When establishing timelines for planning, it would be a mistake to fail to take into account the time it takes to negotiate various agency processes that affect (delay) the completion of plan requirements. For instance, know how long it takes for contract actions to be performed, and the amount of time for administrative processing of major policy documents. In fact, the plan should allow oversight of compliance with deadlines for submission of required documentation associated with these processes.

Performance metrics selected should always be measurable, and should be as specific as possible. Do not measure activities and processes used; rather, measure the outcomes from these processes. Actually, measurements should not focus on the process level except to develop a process, as the output from processes is normally much too low level to be an effective measure.

The CISO should establish a program for conducting periodic reviews of performance against established goals and standards. For instance, quarterly performance reviews can be conducted with business unit leaders or system owners to review the status of implementation in their organization or with their systems according to previously communicated, agreed-upon, and defined measures. There should also be provisions for providing a supplemental briefing of the CIO or agency head on program status on an annual basis.

A scoring system should be utilized in association with these reviews to provide a means of easily understanding review results. As noted previously, linkage of the results of such reviews with organizational or personal performance plans is a highly effective means of ensuring management accountability and program support. Should the CISO choose to use scorecards or "dashboards" to show status of progress toward implementation of plan elements, he must be aware of the intricacies of scoring performance. These must be carefully considered and planned for before their use in grading the performance of agency managers and organizations. Any performance measurement initiative the CISO devises should be thoroughly coordinated, documented, piloted, and communicated to those affected by it. Acceptance of the measurement process is enhanced by the degree to which its creation and functioning is made transparent. Data points to be used in scoring (e.g., number of security controls weaknesses that are behind schedule) should be clearly defined, and the manner in which they are weighted for scoring purposes should be carefully documented.

Related Plans

There are a number of special-purpose plans that need to be considered in association with the development of the overall information security strategic plan. Requirements related to the development, update, and testing of these plans should be included as warranted. For instance, the plan should be linked to plans for implementing new information technology (sometimes referred to as the information technology roadmap). This linkage could include key dates for rolling out significant new technological capabilities (e.g., single sign-on, Trusted Internet Connection, Einstein). Tasks and milestones relating to the agency disaster recovery plan must be considered in the development of the plan, and the agency continuity of operations plan will also have an impact on information security strategic planning, so both should be included. Requirements for system-level contingency plan should be included in the strategic plan, as should requirements for formulating related processes for developing, implementing, testing, maintaining, and monitoring the effectiveness of contingency planning. The following table lists additional plans that should be reviewed for their impact on the information security strategic plan, and their milestones and activities considered for inclusion:

PLANS RELATED TO THE INFORMATION SECURITY STRATEGIC PLAN (ISSP)	NATURE OF RELATIONSHIP
Enterprise configuration management plan	Documents activities and schedules that may need to be included in the ISSP
System security plans	May reflect critical activities that should be documented in the ISSP
Concept of operations (CONOPs) plans	Often record milestones that could impact the ISSP
Information-security-related spending plans	Should be driven by requirements documented in the ISSP
Plans of action and milestones (remediation plans)	In particular, program-level POA&Ms reflect corrective actions and milestones, which may warrant inclusion in the ISSP

Other Planning Considerations

The information security strategic plan is a valuable tool the CISO can use to communicate the status and direction of the agency information security program. The CISO should use it to share information about program activities, milestones, and goals. He should use the plan as a basis for developing presentation materials, which he can use to educate senior agency officials on the program. The CISO can support other agency planning efforts by being responsive to planning requirements that are the responsibility of other offices. Armed with a comprehensive information security strategic plan, the CISO should be well equipped to integrate his requirements into the plans managed by others involved in agency planning when periodic updates are required. The CISO can also promote effective planning for information security activities through the development and dissemination of timely instructions and planning considerations to responsible officials that help them properly budget and prepare for these activities in advance. For instance, instructions for annual milestones to test security controls, complete training requirements, or submit status of corrective actions should be published in the last quarter of the prior fiscal year. Finally, the CISO should ensure that, where appropriate, strategic plan requirements are captured in service-level agreements, memoranda of understanding, interagency support agreements, and contracts, and renewal dates should be recorded for the most significant documents of this type in the ISSP to ensure that evolving requirements are considered in a timely manner.

Summary

Strategic planning for the implementation of the enterprise information security program begins with definition or redefinition of the program itself to include its mission, functions, roles, and responsibilities. This is based on an awareness of requirements from outside the agency, from internal requirements prescribed by the agency head, CIO, other agency officials, business drivers, and on the CISO and his desires, vision, and priorities for the program. The strategic planning effort then results in the creation of a plan for establishing or updating the program as appropriate that satisfies external and internal program requirements and identifies both short-term and long-term implementation tasks, depending on their priority or complexity. This is then followed by the execution of the plan to ensure that plan objectives are achieved according to plan milestones. Finally, the strategic and tactical security planning will require measurement of progress in implementing and maintaining the program, coupled with an approach and an intention to make necessary adjustments whenever necessary.

7

DEVELOPING POLICY
AND GUIDANCE

FISMA assigns responsibility for ensuring the confidentiality, integrity, and availability of sensitive agency information and the agency's information technology systems to the senior agency information security officer or chief information security officer (CISO). The CISO achieves this objective through the institution of policies, development of processes, and implementation of procedures to permit visibility of vulnerabilities in security controls, changes in information systems, and in their security posture; to define security requirements; and to exert influence on the behavior of system owners, managers, and users toward a positive, secure end. It is through these policies, processes, and procedures that a CISO has assurance that systems are in fact secure, and has visibility of vulnerabilities that prevent them from being secure.

In order to serve as a useful basis for the enterprise information security program based on the Federal Information Security Management Act (FISMA), a comprehensive, current, well-organized, and useful enterprise information security policy must be in place, along with an accompanying set of supporting security procedures, standards, guidelines, and documented processes. All of the agency's policy related to the security of information technology systems and electronic information should be fully integrated and consistent. This is best achieved through the development of a single, comprehensive agencywide information technology security policy. In organizations where this is not possible because of structural, cultural, or political barriers, at least for the moment, the primary information security policy should provide at a minimum a framework on which information-security-related policy information from various elements of the organization can be linked.

Documented policies are needed to document the information security requirements for which compliance is required, for without them, there can be no sensible information security program. It is the information security policy that establishes an agencywide information security program, which in turn provides the foundation for assessing compliance with information security program requirements.

Security Policy Considerations

The purpose of the security policy is manifold. First of all, as stated earlier, it defines the organization's information security program. This includes requirements for compliance. It specifies the objectives of the program, the roles and responsibilities for the program, its scope and applicability, as well as including a statement of management's commitment to the protection of its information resources.

The policy is also used to address mission requirements for security. The requirements that the policy specifies must be tied to larger business drivers that relate to security. These normally include legal and regulatory drivers such as FISMA and HIPAA, or PCI requirements. For most government agencies, it is sensible to start by addressing FISMA requirements for compliance and then include other regulatory directives. There may also be contractual drivers for security such as those that a business partner establishes to ensure trust when accessing their information. Operational drivers related to how the agency operates also have an impact on what the policy may need to include, such as the need to operate in multiple jurisdictions, or requirements for emergency response, or high availability needs.

Today, in many government agencies, one will find information security policies that are out of date and do not support the agency's mission, its business needs, or its risk appetite, or are unorganized and difficult to find or use. All of these conditions greatly limit their effectiveness. Often, existing policies are internally inconsistent, conflict with other agency directives, and do not address pressing agency needs for security. In some agencies, one finds that the information security policy does not map to higher forms of agency guidance such as the mission, vision, values, strategic plan, or IT/IM strategic plan. Another often-observed deficiency is that the agency security policy is not written at an appropriate level; that is, it is either too brief and generic to be useful or too detailed to permit it to be effectively maintained.

Most government agencies have some sort of information security policy that one can evaluate across the full spectrum for quality and usefulness. Assessing the effectiveness of existing agency information security policy and guidance is one of the initial and more important tasks that a CISO must address following his assignment. The most typical scenario that the CISO will find himself in is one in which existing policies require updating. The requirement for government agencies to have documented security policies has been in effect for a generation, so the problem is not the lack of a policy but rather the lack of a good policy or even too much policy. At some time in the past, the agency policy may have been adequate, but over time it has become fragmented and no longer meets the business needs of the organization.

The policy development or update task provides the CISO an opportunity to engage authorizing officials and other senior agency leaders in establishing the information security program, and to build support for it. As related in Chapter 3, upper management must become invested in the program, and their support of the information security policy is a means of demonstrating this. The information security policy documents management's and the organization's view of the information security program and is a mean indicator of how much emphasis they have chosen to place on information protection. The CISO should consider the policy development task as an education exercise that can be leveraged to increase management's awareness of critical security goals, issues, principles, and initiatives. As part of the update process, the CISO will need to obtain concurrence on changes in security documentation from the appropriate offices, that is, offices that are most affected by changes in the policy. Their feedback may be useful in assessing the business impact the change may cause, or in determining the difficulties business units may have in responding to the change.

In keeping with the theme of a centralized information security function, the information security policy is most effective when it is implemented agencywide. In fact, FISMA mandates an enterprisewide approach to security requirements and management. The CISO should dissuade bureau heads, regional offices, and other organizations from issuing their own versions of the agency policy. Over time, these can evolve into versions that may be in direct opposition to the actual agencywide policy. This of course must be balanced against local supplementation of the policy to meet specific needs. However, these should be published as supplements and must be clearly recognizable as not having agencywide applicability.

When developing or updating the organization's information security policy and guidance documents, it is important to employ the FISMA-related guidance developed by the National Institute of Standards and Technology (NIST). Of course, the implementation of NIST's Federal Information Processing Standards (FIPS) is mandatory for federal agencies. However, even though advisory in nature, the NIST Special Publications provide highly useful guidance for implementing FISMA and for developing information security policy. In fact, because auditors rely so fully on them, implementation of many of these guidance publications has in practice become mandatory. Since auditors use them as a basis for their FISMA audit standards, it is only reasonable for CISOs to ensure that their agency-specific policies hew closely to them with variations only in the case of justifiable local conditions.

Major policy development or update projects (for example, in situations where the policy is badly out of date or major regulatory requirements have occurred) should be guided by a project plan. The various tasks, responsibilities, timelines, dependencies, and resources necessary for the successful completion of the project must be included in the plan to guide and permit control of the project. The time required to complete a major policy development or update project can be extensive due to the necessity to research, develop, and review, as well as to obtain necessary concurrence and signatures of approval. A project with the objective of updating an enterprise security policy should require between six and eighteen months to complete. In order to maintain necessary control over the project specifically, and all information-security-related policy in general, the CISO should maintain approval over all security policies and procedures. This ensures consistency, provides for maintenance of the proper level of approval, and ensures coherence with the process and with security policies published.

In addition to NIST guidance, the development or update of security policies should consider leading practices too. Every government agency has at least some semblance of an information security policy, some good, some bad. A policy development project is a significant project, and it is worth the time and effort to collect policies and evaluate them for their usefulness in the project. The CISO should plan on reaching out to his counterparts for copies of their policies and then ensure that they are considered for adoption normally in part rather than in total.

One of the larger challenges faced by the CISO is to keep the information security documentation up to date. The documentation must continually be evaluated for the impact of new technologies and business requirements on what has been published. The CISO must also stay informed about new guidance issued by external entities that may have a bearing on security policies and procedures. OMB, NIST, DHS, US-CERT, and other organizations regularly and frequently publish guidance and requirements that could make security documentation out of date. The CISO must decide how to address these external changes and determine what agency documentation needs to be changed in what fashion. Additionally, the CISO must evaluate the results of audits, inspections, and reports that may have an impact on the way the security documentation is written. Similarly, identification of new risks to agency data and systems may also force changes in security policy and procedures. To cope with the problem of keeping security documentation up to date, the CISO's policy team should develop a tracking system for managing policy update actions. This will ensure that all actions to modify security policy documentation are accounted for and not overlooked, and are addressed in policy updates as they should. It is discouraging to develop a policy, to coordinate it, and then to get it approved only to find out that it does not fully address the original need. The CISO should establish a cycle for periodically updating the policy. Normally, the schedule for this includes an annual review, with resulting interim updates as warranted, accompanied by a major update every three years.

Often, it will be necessary to publish policy documentation on an interim basis—for instance, to get guidance out in the field to permit its rapid implementation to remediate a particular vulnerability or to prevent an exploit may require an interim policy update. The interim policy can then be integrated into the main security policy more formally when the next periodic update is scheduled. There must be provisions for the information security policy documentation to be updated in emergencies and for making immediate notification across the organization when such policy changes and adjustments are made. To facilitate this need for updating, the CISO should prepare procedures that are constructed to allow ready review and update of the policy. Another approach that can be employed to deal with needs for changes is to develop procedures in lieu of a policy. Procedures by design are flexible and more easily updated and are therefore better able to address immediate needs than policies, which should require only annual or biannual updating.

As stated in Chapter 3, management must set the tone for security policies to be effective. If management does not place priority on developing and updating information security policy documentation, the program may flounder for lack of a foundation and for lack of direction. Management also plays a role in the development of the enterprise information security policy by establishing authority for enforcement of the policy. The policy should define the consequences of failure to comply with the policy. This warning to users provides the authority necessary to ensure the policy can be enforced, and that compliance can be expected.

The enterprise information security policy must include several key sections that promote acceptance and usefulness of the document. This includes a statement of the authority for the policy (i.e., Department Secretary), the purpose of the policy, the scope of the policy (e.g., security of electronic information or security of all information), the applicability of the policy (i.e., the entire agency), the intended audience for the policy, identification of how waivers and exceptions to the policy are to be handled, identification of the policies and other documentation that are superseded by the policy, primary policy roles and responsibilities, definition of terms and abbreviations used in the policy, references on which the policy is based, and the policy's relationship with other policy documents. The roles and responsibilities section of the policy should document who has the authority to fill each security-related position in the organization. For instance, the CIO will have the lead on naming the CISO, and the system owners will have the authority to appoint ISSOs.

The information security policy should be specific enough to address requirements in several key areas, particularly in light of NIST SP 800-53 requirements for agencies to specify their organizationally specific security controls. These sections include access control, encryption, identification and authentication, physical and environmental security, system development, incident reporting, certification and accreditation, system categorization, security planning, acquisition, system interconnection, continuous monitoring, media controls, contingency planning, audit, training and education, configuration management, and risk management. A good guide for defining these control families is NIST SP 800-12, SP 800-53, SP 800-100, or ISO/IEC 27002:2005. When developing these sections, compliance requirements can be met by weaving in NIST guidance for FISMA, and in particular the SP 800-53 requirements for security controls.

The information security policy is the starting point for a risked-based approach to security in that it codifies the risk tolerance for the organization. However, it is the beginning rather than the end, in that the policy must be viewed through the lens of addressing specific, widely varying business problems, which often require granting of exceptions. Security documentation must make provisions for situations were requirements cannot be met for bona fide operational needs. Normally, this is provided for through a waiver and exception process. Such a process must be based on an assessment of the risk that waiver or exception poses to agency data and systems. The process should include a requirement for authorizing officials to approve waivers and exceptions on an individual, system-by-system basis. To minimize the number of waivers, exceptions, and deviations, the policy should chart a course that ensures that a minimum set of controls is implemented in the overwhelming majority of situations, while providing a mechanism for dealing with special situations.

Another important consideration with security policy documentation is where it will reside or where it will be stored to allow ready access. These days, an agency Web site is where most of this documentation is found, and the days of publishing the policy in a bound volume seem to have passed. Many agencies also manage security policy documentation using a change management system to make it a part of their agency documentation repository. There are situations where extracts of the policy must be made and disseminated as handouts, or embedded in notices and e-mail messages. Additionally, the use of SharePoint sites facilitates easy use of policy documentation. Each agency must find its own best way of communicating its policies across the organization. Effective policy communication focuses on informing all who have a need to know and on providing a mechanism to prove that those who need the information have actually received it.

The sensitivity of security documentation itself must be considered as part of the development and update process. Normally, because it describes controls and how they are implemented vis-à-vis various agency assets, it should be considered sensitive in nature. What the policy does not address provides further justification as to why it should be treated as "internal use only" at a minimum. All pages of security documentation should be marked as sensitive security information or in accordance with agency rules for sensitivity marking.

The trick with turning external security requirements into useful information for guiding agency requirements is to prepare the information security policy with the agency's mission and culture in mind and to translate it using the agency's working vocabulary. Because policy should be written with regard to the user, it is a good idea to make it as easy to navigate and use as possible. The policy should be hyperlinked to supporting procedures, standards, guidelines, etc., to the corresponding section of the policy as fully as possible. One of the key principles of policy writing is to write it so as to be understandable to the target population. If this means "dumbing down," then so be it. Use of layman's terms is preferable to technical jargon that may only be understood by security specialists. The use of a technical writer can be most helpful in ensuring that the policy is understood by the correct audience.

Supporting Security Documentation

There are a number of types of other security documentation necessary to effectively deal with FISMA requirements and ensure that the enterprise information security policy is properly implemented. The basic enterprise information security policy must be augmented with standards, procedures, and guidelines to ensure that the policy's provisions are complied with. All of these various forms of policy documentation must be complementary and consistent. Information security policy documentation should have as a goal the definition of all significant security processes, procedures, and services. A comprehensive view of security documentation such as this will ensure that the entire program and all its components are interlaced, coordinated, mutually supporting, and integrated to the extent required to ensure effective implementation.

Rules of Behavior

An important component of the security policy documentation library is user rules of behavior. These rules are designed to establish requirements—the dos and don'ts—to guide users on how to securely use a single information technology system (system specific rules of behavior), groups of systems (organizational rules of behavior), or all information technology systems (enterprise rules of behavior).

System Authorization Process

When creating guidelines for systems authorization (certification and accreditation), adherence to NIST and higher-level guidance should be given the highest priority. This underpinning gives credibility to the process, and presents a strong argument for the veracity of the agency's certification and accreditation methodology. The agency's C&A methodology must be appropriate to the agency's mission and culture. It must be tailored to match the agency's needs. It must also recognize the agency's risk appetite. This will govern the level of approval of various actions but, most importantly, authorization of systems to operate. The authority of the CISO must be defined in the policy as well as that of the system owner and certifying agent. All of these roles and responsibilities relative to the C&A process must be defined, and must support and complement each other.

The process guidance must also define what particular documents are required for inclusion in the certification and accreditation package. The methodology must include useful templates that are easily understandable, can be easily accessed, are linked into the SDLC documentation requirements, are supported by a mechanism for keeping them up to date, are annotated with useful instructions on their use, and are supported by examples and samples that give users a head start in creating security documentation that demonstrates due diligence, that meets the commonsense test, and that meets policy requirements.

Include in the documented certification and accreditation process how automation is used to support various activities. Automated tools should be used whenever possible to promote consistency of format and content, standardization of procedures, and ease of data entry. However, the utility of automated tools must be judged against their ability to support the C&A methodology. The methodology should be the primary driver of tool selection, and tools should not drive the methodology. It is possible to become overly reliant on a tool that does not actually meet the needs of an agency. No tool will match the agency's C&A methodology precisely, and swap-offs for and boundaries of tool use must be carefully defined and considered to identify the best tool and how it will be used.

Integration of deliverables must be defined in the written C&A process showing the interrelationships between the various types of documentation generated or updated as part of the process or relied upon in C&A activities.

The conditions under which C&A activities must take place can become a contentious issue, and it is therefore very important to define what constitutes a change that is significant enough to warrant recertification and reaccreditation of an information technology system. These can vary among agencies and must be clear enough to provide useful guidance, and should be supported by examples as a priority.

The documented process must also provide definitions of the types of information technology systems that it addresses. These definitions must, of course, comport to FISMA, OMB, and NIST requirements and at a minimum should address major applications (MA), general-support (GS) systems, minor applications, and other terms as necessary.

To help system owners and certification agents to plan for C&A activities in a reliable and consistent way, the methodology should include a standard C&A Work Plan for use in all new projects. This will highlight the milestones, activities, tasks, deliverables, dependencies, and timelines for completion of a C&A project and provides a starting point for building a realistic project plan.

When documenting the C&A process, it is helpful to see things from the customer's perspective in order to make it useful to system owners, ISSOs, and others who are the primary users of the process. One has to ask what information they need to apply security in their areas, and then set about providing for it in the documented process guide.

The C&A process should also address the following areas:

- Instructions on how critical systems are to be defined, and how this guidance relates to the business impact analysis developed before system contingency plan creation. It must also link to an enterprise view of criticality as a context for system-level business impact assessments.
- Guidance on how the security architecture supports C&A activities as part of the enterprise architecture. The security architecture must inform corrective actions identified to mitigate vulnerabilities in information security controls as a matter of efficiency, consistency, and cost-effectiveness.
- Reference to standard contract security language for C&A activities and deliverables, and where possible sample statements of work and requests for procurement, should be included.

Finally, the agency's C&A methodology should be flexible enough for all parts of the agency to be able to follow it. It is important that a single C&A process be in place for the entire organization, but for that to happen, it must accommodate the wide range of needs for the organization without being so limiting that exceptions to policy become necessary.

System Categorization Process

Another key security process to document is system categorization. This should map clearly to NIST 800-60, must take into account agency-specific risk tolerance, and should clearly define how the process is used to define the sensitivity of information systems according to their needs for protection in the areas of confidentiality, integrity, and availability. Clear definition of the concept of the high watermark and use of high, moderate, and low rankings must be included, as well as the types of systems for which formal system categorization is required.

Contingency Planning Process

The CISO must also develop and disseminate guidance for system-level contingency plan development, training, and testing. Assurance of availability is a major concern for most information technology systems, and documenting how individual systems are to be recovered in the event of an outage must be emphasized in the C&A methodology. This guidance document should describe the content and format of contingency plans, requirements for frequency, nature and planning for testing plans, and actions required in response to testing, including documentation of test results and update of contingency plans.

Security Impact Assessment Process

This document provides a structured approach for evaluating the nature and extent of proposed changes to systems that have been previously authorized to operate and are currently in operation. It should be developed in the form of a questionnaire that can be completed by ISSOs for submission by system owners who essentially apply for security approval of their plans for addressing security in their proposed information technology project. It provides the information security team with the information necessary to assess the impact of the proposed change on the existing security posture for the system, allowing them to provide a road map of actions and artifacts the system owner must complete or submit to satisfy security policy requirements. The security impact assessment can serve as the primary tool for determining if reauthorization is warranted, and if so, the scope and rigor of the authorization process with respect to the proposed change. Additional documentation that the CISO should consider in building a mature library of information security policy and guidance include the following.

> *Security Baselines:* The collection of information security program documentation must include configuration baselines for each technology in the organization's portfolio. These allow the information security function to measure compliance of these platforms against published standards, which owners of the platform should be required to implement and maintain. Realistically, the security parameters stipulated in the security baselines should be established to address a known risk to agency data and systems. To facilitate their implementation and maintenance, these configuration baselines should be readily available on the CISO or other Web site, and they

need to be kept up to date by the information security function, and must be consistent across the agency. For example, the version on the CISO Web site should be the same as the version in the SDLC. To ease the burden of implementing secure approved configurations, standard images for each technology should be developed, and their use should be mandated.

Samples and Templates: For every artifact required, the CISO should ensure that a template and a sample are prepared and readily available for use. These greatly aid in the creation of artifacts and ensure consistency of format and content. Primary artifacts for which templates and samples are most beneficial are security plans, risk assessments, security tests and evaluations, contingency plans, contingency plan test plans, plans of action and milestones, and continuous monitoring plans.

Implementation Checklists: One good piece of advice for ensuring policy compliance is to develop detailed checklists for security documentation to ensure its quality. Such checklists also provide a means of documenting how the information security function has exercised due diligence over the quality of the security documentation as mandated, and also can be used to communicate areas of weakness to system owners, ISSOs, and contractors who have produced the documentation. They also facilitate standardization of periodic compliance reviews.

Security Procedures: An important consideration in the development of security documentation is the recognition of the need for system-level procedures to implement established agency-level policy and standards. System-specific procedures provide additional requirements necessary to allow implementation of policies and standards in a manner that will be most effective in the protection of the system's sensitive data, and will best address the system's confidentiality, integrity, and availability needs. The CISO should make provisions for reviewing system-level procedures to ensure they complement rather than contradict agency-level security policy and procedures.

Security Instructions: Security policy documentation must include guidance on the creation of security artifacts and instructions for preparing them. Processes that must be documented include security plan development/update, risk assessment, security controls testing, continuous monitoring, weakness remediation, system inventory, and configuration management. Instruction should take the form of documented procedures, which should be couched in layman's terms, on how to prepare (usually through the use of templates) important security documentation with consistency across the entire agency. Instructions should be available to system owners for the preparation of the system security plan, the security categorization, the risk assessment, the contingency plan, the contingency plan test plan, the annual controls test plan and test results, the system specific rules of behavior, the security test and evaluation plan and ST&E results report, the plan of action and milestones, and the authorization to operate.

Security Function Practices: The information security function must establish practices that provide an opportunity for review of correspondence, written requests, proposals, statements of work, and papers to ensure their compliance with policy documentation. These internal procedures, when documented and followed, provide consistency for the performance of routine functions regularly encountered by information security team staff.

Security policies, procedures, and practices that are documented in writing allow the information security function to avoid ad hoc policy interpretations and decisions by its staff, and serve to guide the advice provided by the CISO staff toward accuracy and repeatability. The CISO should discourage his staff members from making off-the-cuff policy pronouncements and ad hoc interpretations without first referring to documented policies and procedures. This can lead to much confusion and dissatisfaction on the part of customers. Dependable verbal guidance is essential to maintaining the support of customers. And to further support customer service needs, it is important to ensure that customers know who to go to in order to obtain accurate, useful, and up-to-date policy information. Points of contact for policy areas need to be established and need to be communicated across the organization. Then customers can be channeled to the proper source.

For all policy documentation relating to major compliance activities that is being disseminated, there should be a communications plan. This includes plans for information security program planning, initiatives, and new or updated policies that have an impact on the operations of business units. A communications plan provides a means for the information security team to make business units aware of the need for the change, allows them to describe the new process prior to its implementation so as to permit business unit feedback, and to gain acceptance in advance of implementation.

Other Considerations

To keep security policies and procedures in tune with what is going on elsewhere, the CISO must have the capability to track literature, publications, notices, and the like for information that may indicate a need for updates. This could be in the form of NIST bulletins, OMB guidance, US-CERT notices, or other DHS policy-related information. Of course, such information must be filtered and evaluated for applicability prior to deciding to update the policy, and they must further be assessed for the impact of implementing the changes prior to any update.

Contractors and consultants are often used to develop policies, standards, and guidelines because of their experience in best practices and their exposure to various policy requirements elsewhere in government. In contractor-developed policy projects, the CISO should be sure to define requirements in detail, establish required deliverables, and stipulate milestones for when they are to be submitted. The activities of contractors and consultants should be controlled to ensure that they are on the right track. Require them to submit preliminary drafts of the documentation they produce, particularly in the early phases of the project, to allow government review for quality, completeness, accuracy, applicability to the agency, and level of detail. Ensure that you require them to conduct interviews with key government personnel to obtain input, and require them to review and take into consideration existing agency policy documentation. Similarly, the CISO should beware of excessive use of consultant-favored boilerplate material or the use of policies developed for other organizations that may not fit the agency culture or need.

Development of security documentation must closely track with the agency's enterprise architecture. The interrelationship between these two requirements sources is key to ensuring consistency of business needs identification, solution identification, and services provision.

Conclusions

The information security policy and supporting policy documentation can be used to develop an organization's information security culture. This makes it a powerful means of leveraging important elements of the program. Therefore, it is important to include in the policy and procedures the components identified in this section. First, to ensure that the program can serve as a firm foundation for the organization's compliance, it should be used to specify, reinforce, and operationalize FISMA requirements. This would include specifying a set of controls, preferably based on NIST SP 800-53. The policy documentation must also address the most current issues that may have arisen from security incidents, situations, and recent organization experience. Without addressing these current issues, such as use of wireless networks, the policy might be labeled as out of date and less than useful by its intended audience. Additionally, the policy documentation must consider and address the human element. It must be written with the user in mind; that is, it must consider how it will be received by the typical user, and must speak to this lowest common denominator. It must be understandable, without being condescending. A policy that is able to change an organization's security culture will require a high level of authority. It must be coordinated with by all major elements of the organizations to ensure broad-based support, and it has to be accepted, supported, and approved by the organization's highest levels of executive management. Similarly, policy documentation has to be based on the proper coordination in order to be effective and to be accepted by individual users. The concurrence of the human resources staff, the labor union, the office of the general counsel, contracting function, and the office of the chief financial officer, the inspector general, information technology operations, and the enterprise architecture team are necessary steps in building support for the information security program policy and procedures.

8

TRAINING AND AWARENESS

A review of FISMA reveals that there are specific requirements relating to the training of personnel in information security. The chief information security officer (CISO) must be aware of these requirements and must ensure that the information security program complies with these mandatory legislative requirements. More important than the compliance aspects, however, is that effective security training is also simply a good idea in practical terms and just makes good sense. Users play a large role in the protection of information and systems, but are perhaps one of the most overlooked elements of the information security program. Security awareness, training, and education are essential to the ability of system users to perform their security responsibilities. This assertion is based on the influence of users on the secure operations of an information system and data. Irrespective of the nature and number of controls that are implemented to reduce the impact that users have on a system, in the end, the user is still there, and the protection of the system and its data has to rely on the right behavior of the common user to a greater or lesser extent. Most practitioners readily accept that the number-one threat to data is trusted users.

The importance of training is overlooked because it requires soft skills, unlike most information security program components, which tend to be more technical in nature. In developing an information security awareness and training program, the CISO must address who is to be trained, what they are to be trained on, how they need to be trained, who is to provide the training, and what are good sources of training and materials.

The training role of the CISO is normally one of oversight and marketing. In terms of oversight, the CISO is responsible for selecting and managing the information security staff who exercise day-to-day control over training and awareness efforts; he establishes goals for the team and provides direction, and monitors the effectiveness of the program. As for his marketing responsibilities, the CISO must market security awareness as a central part of the enterprise information security program and likewise see himself as the agency's chief trainer and act accordingly. He must use every opportunity to emphasize the program, to articulate proper courses of action in response to current issues and in the face of new threats, and to be the lead salesman for and face of agency awareness efforts.

Components of the user awareness and training program must include training for new users, periodic refresher training for all users, ongoing user awareness and training on topics of need, including provision of immediate user alerts as necessary, role-based training for users assigned specialized security responsibilities, security staff education/certification, and communication of information on the security organization, functions, goals, plans, and security posture, and program status. We will explore each of these in more detail in the following paragraphs.

New User Training

There is no more important time to introduce users to good security habits than when they first join the agency. This early conditioning permits good habits to be learned before bad ones can take root. Of course, new employees can learn bad habits elsewhere, but that cannot be resolved through new user awareness training alone. Providing security training to users early on in their careers with an agency demonstrates that the organization considers it a priority and sends a message to the user that it is important. Normally, an agency will have a process for orienting and familiarizing new employees with the organization, which includes indoctrination within the first week on the job. The most effective approach for the CISO is to ensure that computer security awareness is included in the agenda. However, new employee training is normally restricted to full-time and part-time employees only, and is not designed to meet the needs of consultants and contractors. Therefore, the CISO must determine an alternative means for addressing them. I will discuss this topic in a moment.

The best approach to new user training is to provide them only the information that will be most beneficial to them in the first hours and days of their assignment, in order to avoid overwhelming them. The training should focus mainly on the rules of behavior applicable to the vast majority of agency computer users. If rules of behavior such as these have not been developed, then a top-ten list of good security practices should serve as the centerpiece of the training content. It will be important not to load them down with too much or overly detailed information at this early stage because they will be inundated with information on health care, insurance, leave policy, hours of operation, ethical standards, the employee grievance process, and the like. Limit the material that you provide them, but make it hard hitting, of high quality, and to the point. They should know what to do if they become aware of a security incident (notify their supervisor, help desk, or incident response team), the most common threats they must be concerned about when using the system (social engineering and malware), and where they can obtain more information about security (the security policy and the computer security Web site). Avoid the temptation to describe the organization and mission of the security organization, the identification of the security staff, and the penalties for noncompliance. This information is best presented at other times in other forms. Much of this, if not all, can be shared with participants in the form of handouts to highlight the most important information they will need immediately. Consider the use of laminated cards containing key information that users can carry in their wallets or on their badge lanyard. When presenting training material either live, via video, or in written form, try to present security requirements in the context of the overall agency mission so that the new employee sees security in the broadest possible light. Speaking of video, security training for new users is ideal for presentation in this manner. Because its content is relatively stable and is broadly applicable to all new users, video recording of the presentation is especially effective. This is particularly true for agencies whose employees are widely dispersed in regional offices and other field locations. However, the content of new user training should be reviewed at least annually to ensure that it remains accurate, appropriate for its intended purpose and to the target audience, and effective in communicating important computer security messages to the intended audience.

Ideally, completion of this training can be enforced by linking it to initial system access. That is, new users should not be permitted to gain access to the network, e-mail, intranet, etc. until they have attended awareness training or have completed that training through some other form, such as review of the materials with a supervisor. It may be possible to implement automated delivery of training to expedite and lessen the impact of meeting the requirement for training before granting access. Similarly, there needs to be a process implemented at the individual system level to ensure that first-time users complete system-specific security training prior to being granted access. This is important because the unwise actions of an uninformed user can be readily exploited by an adversary. This system-specific training should also be linked to standing rules of behavior that are specifically designed to address the security of the system and user responsibilities for its secure operation.

As mentioned earlier, new user training must not be limited to new employees only. It must cover all new users, as well as contractors and consultants. Typically, the process for "on-boarding" short-term workers is less centralized than for full-time employees, often because contract specifications are not standardized and due to the nature and timing of the work being performed under contract agreement. Months can elapse before a new contractor begins work, and he may very well start work individually rather than as part of a larger group. For these reasons, responsibilities for training new users who are contractors usually reside in the hands of the project manager for the work the contractor supports. This is why the program management methodology and instructions must be very clear about the importance of this requirement, or else it will be minimized and its impact will be reduced. Automated monitoring of training completion can help ensure that a contractor does not slip through the cracks due to lack of oversight. Note also that it will be difficult if not impossible to force contract personnel to meet requirements for training and to follow specific processes unless these requirements are specified in governing contract language.

Training of business partners and public users presents a related issue that requires careful consideration. Users of this type engage with the agency almost exclusively through the agency's information systems. This presents a particular difficulty in that although they cannot participate in training on-site, they have just as much need for the training—if not more—than users who are on-site. Therefore, completion of an online training module that is related to the system or systems they will be accessing is the only practical solution. System access must therefore be managed in a phased approach in which limited access is granted initially, followed by full access once the security module has been successfully completed.

Refresher Awareness Training

Government agencies have been emphasizing user awareness training for over twenty years. Ever since such training was mandated by the Computer Security Act of 1987, agencies have been required to ensure that users of federal computer systems are reminded of their responsibilities for the protection of these systems and data. Refresher training is important in ensuring that users are made aware of changes in the processing environment, in security procedures and policies, and in threats to agency information over the past year. Unfortunately, the efforts of government agencies in meeting these goals have been generally uneven in their application over the years, and in many cases have proved ineffective in reducing the vulnerabilities that users present to a secure processing environment. Many programs have focused on simply meeting the regulatory requirement without truly delivering effective training that is useful to most users.

Since annual refresher security training is just that—annual, the challenge is to keep it fresh and new, and something more than just an annual drill for users who have to meet mandatory agency training requirements. A few approaches can help achieve the freshness goals. It needs to be useful; that is, it has to address real needs. This can be achieved by keeping the focus foremost on the user and his job responsibilities. Construct training that will help users understand the importance of computing securely. Because the requirement must be met annually, it is important that the training content and method of delivery is varied year to year or as frequently as possible within resource contraints. The use of guest speakers and live presentations breaks up the monotony of computer-based training, and is often worth the additional cost and time required for such training for this reason. Also, try to create content that takes advantage of what is hot in the news to realism to the training. If you can make the refresher training pertinent to the user's needs as a home user, it is a big advantage. It must be challenging. It should tax the individual's ability to solve the problem.

The training must not be so cute as to be counterproductive and so simplistic as to be a joke. The training can be livened up through the use of games, puzzles, quizzes, and practical exercises. Whatever you decide to do, you must deliver training that is of high quality, and in the case of computer-based training, training that is visually pleasing.

One of the primary challenges the CISO has is tracking compliance with the refresher training requirements he establishes. Even the simple measurement of completion by name and by office can be difficult in the beginning. However, tracking who completes the training by what milestone is seldom enough. Normally, the effectiveness of training must also be tracked in order to ascertain whether realistic goals are being achieved for the training. The degree to which users comprehend the course materials can be evaluated through the use automated quizzes interspersed throughout, and at the end of, the course. This must be accompanied by an effective means of recording completion, scores that normally include the ability to periodically report completion status by user name, organization/suborganization, by course/module completed, as well as the ability to generate a list of users who have not yet completed the training, which with some learning management systems may not be as easy as it sounds. To help with the task of getting all users to complete annual refresher training on time, it is necessary to obtain and maintain the support of business unit managers. This will require giving them continual feedback on completion status for their organizations in a useful form. Where possible, the CISO can try to build on the natural sense of good-spirited competition among managers, without it becoming a form of punishment. In this effort, the CISO can recognize early goal achievers and can reward exceptional support without openly calling out those who are falling behind. That is a matter best resolved behind the scenes. Work closely with business unit managers to meet training deadlines; grant exceptions to individuals for various reasons (no access, limited access, seasonal access, maternity, illness).

However, to go beyond this, to determine a user's retention of the information and his ability to apply it in realistic circumstances is more of a challenge. Even so, the refresher training program must be augmented with the capability to validate the effectiveness of training and the adequacy of training content in meeting current security needs. This should include a process for testing the behavior of user susceptibility to social engineering attacks, and a process for conducting after-hours walk-through checks and inspections. The CISO should focus on developing well-thought-out test scenarios that will allow him to determine the effectiveness of security training. This could take the form of attempts to social-engineer groups of users to see if they respond to phony telephone calls and e-mail messages asking users to provide their log-on information. After-hours walkthrough inspections can reveal the effectiveness of training on physical protection of sensitive media, and compliance with log-off procedures. Dumpster diving or looking at the contents of trash receptacles may be employed to determine if sensitive documents and media are being properly disposed of. Other tests can be used to ascertain compliance with physical access controls, including attempts to gain physical access to controlled areas by "piggybacking" behind an authorized person, or testing escort procedures to see if employees are actually maintaining control over visitors. For each element of the training content, the CISO's team should attempt to construct a test that will demonstrate the effectiveness of the training. Be careful that exercises and tests do not get out of hand and have unintended consequences. For example, in one case a federal agency did not foresee the effects of an exercise message being forwarded outside the agency and causing a mild panic in another agency not involved in the exercise. Testing of user behavior must be coupled with a process for fixing accountability, and permitting follow-up on necessary corrective action. Communication of results of testing to managers and to the individuals is an effective means of changing user behavior.

Another challenge for the CISO is the identification of the user population to be trained. It is important that the information security training team identify the target population (e.g., information technology users only, all employees, contractors, customers, etc.) by coordinating with offices that have the most accurate data such as Human Resources, Contracting, and those offices that have responsibility, that is, business units. A master list of personnel to be trained must be constructed to provide a baseline. Because the training is most often focused on computer users, a user database such as Active Directory is normally used. Further coordination with the personnel or human resources staff is necessary to cross-check for departed employees, and coordination with the contracting office will be required to validate the names of contractor users and eliminate those who no longer require access. In some cases, business partners will need to be included in annual refresher training. Additionally, a form of annual training will need to be developed for workers who may not have computer access, but who may come into contact with agency information and therefore will require training in the security and privacy of information.

Topical Training

In addition to awareness training for new users and annual refresher information security training, there is a need to provide training on various information-security-related topics to agency personnel. Training of this nature normally takes two forms: in-depth how-to classes on information security processes and procedures to agency personnel involved in their implementation, and short, targeted information disseminated on short order in response to a given situation.

Training on specific topics is necessary for personnel who are responsible for conducting a business impact analysis, developing system-level contingency plans, and in performing testing of contingency plans. Also, such training can enhance the ability of agency personnel in their performance on annual self-assessments of security controls, development and update of risk assessments, security categorization activities, development and update of security plans, and performance of eAuthentication risk assessments. The primary principle to remember is to base this training fully on current agency security policies and procedures. If those policies and procedures are not up to date, then they need to be, otherwise the training will result in confusion rather than learning.

Another type of topical training results when security information needs to be disseminated immediately in response to some security-related situation. When necessary, short messages and notices will need to be prepared for communication to all users or to a specific group of users, depending on the nature of the situation the message deals with. If a particular threat has been experienced (e.g., a phishing attack), or if a new policy or procedure is about to be posted, a short topical message should be communicated immediately to the user community to announce the change, or to remind them of proper behavior when responding to the situation. For this to be effective, the computer security awareness function will need to have close and frequent contact with the organizational elements that monitor threats, vulnerabilities, and risks, as well as develop security policies and procedures that impact system users. A process is necessary for disseminating mass e-mail broadcasts, for publishing daily notes on security topics, and for posting information on the front page of the agency internal Web site. All are effective means of getting out the word quickly. Often, when security incidents have been resolved and lessons learned have been developed, it is useful to extract pertinent user information and communicate it across the agency to enhance user awareness. The same approach can be used to share results of security-related audits that have implications on user behavior.

Role-Based Training

Another training requirement mandated by FISMA is specialized security training, which has come to be known in government today as role-based security training. Training of this type is targeted toward the security responsibilities of specific positions. Role-based security training should be created for actual roles and positions used within the agency. For example, this normally includes authorizing officials, system owners, information technology coordinators, office technology coordinators, application system security administrators, ISSOs, office information security officers, developers, information technology professionals, executives, and project managers. Often, the requirements for each role are similar for most agencies. However, the training material developed for each role must be responsive to actual agency needs. That is, it needs to be tailored to the actual organizational environment, culture, terminology, and situation. The task of identifying which agency roles exercise significant security responsibilities belongs to the CISO, who should rely on solid knowledge of the organization. As far as possible, he should use actual position titles accepted by the organization. The identification process should also result in a prioritization of the content development effort by role. In most cases, the most important roles requiring immediate attention will be those of the system owner and the ISSO. The application of risk-based principles may have to be used in cases where training contact will have to be developed over an extended period of time. The CISO should consider creation of a training development plan in which the most important training is developed as a priority, while targeted but limited incremental training is offered until resources are available to support creation of content for less significant security roles.

Once the roles are identified, and are documented with clear definitions, business units can be tasked with the identification of their personnel who perform established roles. Realize that personnel reassignments and other changes will occur frequently and business unit managers will need to update the collected information whenever these changes occur, and an annual validation process will have to be instituted to ensure the accuracy of the role-based training rolls. A security role database should be established and maintained with close linkage to human resources information systems. Similarly, a database of contractors assigned to security roles should be linked to systems maintained by the agency contracting functions. Naturally, there will need to be clauses in contracts requiring the contracting firm to provide this information to the government and to keep it up to date. If possible, personnel with security roles should be flagged in these databases when they are used for multiple purposes. This will allow the information security staff to readily identify individuals who require role-based training tuned to the requirements of their position.

With the audience to be trained now defined, the type, manner, duration, frequency, content, and delivery method can then be determined. Under most conditions, role-based training need only be completed every two to three years.

The CISO can also consider professional certification as part of the role-based training curriculum or perhaps even in lieu of role-based training; depending, of course, on the role as well as the rigor of the certification. For instance, an ISSO or system administrator should be encouraged to obtain formal security certification for the components comprising the system offered by the product vendor (e.g., Oracle, Microsoft).

Security Team Professionalization

The CISO's efforts in the area of security training must also extend to the skills and qualifications of the security team. Given the responsibility of planning, developing, and overseeing the enterprise information security program, the CISO himself and his assigned personnel and supporting contractors must undergo position-specific training that will help them stay current in issues affecting their areas of responsibility. This could include technical training in the areas of network defense, prevalent attack vectors, and advanced security technologies.

The CISO should be able to rely on his professional staff to seek out high-quality specialized information security courses, conferences, workshops, and seminars that support their job functions. While it may be tempting to limit these opportunities only to those that are directly germane to their jobs, the CISO should permit staff personnel to also participate in cutting-edge sessions that might expand their thinking and that could offer useful best practices from organizations that have little in common with a government agency. The CISO must work with assigned personnel to develop career objectives and document them in a personalized learning plan that addresses both short-term job requirements as well as long-term career objectives. Professional certifications should certainly be included in individual learning plans.

While supporting contractors are seldom provided training other than role-based and refresher training at government expense, the CISO must ensure that the knowledge, skills, and abilities required to perform assigned work are clearly defined in contract specifications. However, the CISO should establish an internal training program for both assigned staff and full-time, on-site contractors to enhance their skills. Such a program should build on the expertise of assigned personnel, which can prepare and present training on subjects in which they have particular expertise using a knowledge-sharing approach. "Brown bag" training sessions of this nature also serve to sharpen their instructional and presentation skills. It also serves to ensure that assigned staff are able to stay on message, and are consistent in the information they share with customers. Additionally, the value of opportunity training should not be overlooked. Taking five minutes or so to explain a security concept, issue, or process should be a regular part of periodic gatherings of the staff such as weekly or monthly staff and team meetings.

The CISO as Chief Security Trainer

The CISO must consider training to be one of the primary responsibilities of his position. He can best do this by considering himself the chief information security trainer for the agency. In this role, the CISO must train personnel assigned to his staff, he must provide training to senior leaders of the agency, and when necessary he must educate his boss (the CIO) on security principles. He is responsible for providing training to his customers and to system owners; to OIG, other auditors, and to OMB on the organization, operations, and planning for his security program; as well as to users in security of the systems they use. He must continually seek out opportunities to train using all resources and opportunities at his disposal.

The CISO in his role as chief security trainer would be well served to create a series of presentations that are mutually supporting and which address key issues and topics that are important for him to communicate. In a moment's time, he should be able to tweak them to fit the needs of any given audience. For instance, he should have a targeted message for the configuration control board, for the information technology business committee, for the information technology strategy board, for all-hands meetings, for off-site events, and for periodic staff meetings. The CISO must have a standard presentation on his organization, program, goals, and initiatives to present deskside to executive-level officials along with handouts for use as leave-behinds of very high quality that he can share with his subordinates. Also, the CISO can communicate his training message through the publication of a periodic newsletter that draws attention to a particular issue or aspect of the information security program and conveys a beneficial security awareness message.

Training Methods

There is no single right answer as to which training method is best for computer security training. The better question is, "What is the best method for this specific training need that I've identified?" It must meet the current need in terms of reaching the right audience, in the right way, at the right time, and these are all highly variable. At various times with varying audiences, computer-based and lecture-based training may be warranted. Use of both internal and external sources for training may be required in the given circumstances. Other occasions will require the need for subject matter experts to present the training, or use of training materials available for governmentwide use may be appropriate.

Consideration of training methods must include development of an approach to using external training resources, such as off-site training, participation in conferences, vendor-provided product-specific training, as well as training provided by organizations that specialize in security training (e.g., MIS Training Institute, SANS, etc.).

The CISO has a number of resources available to him to assist with security training. He should identify assigned personnel who have particular skills and expertise as well as top-notch presentation skills and use them to get out the message. Look for similar capabilities and qualities among the supporting instructor staff, elsewhere in security positions in the agency, as well as from nonsecurity personnel assigned to other offices and departments. Consider also using security personnel from other agencies to supplement the training staff on a limited, guest-speaker basis. The CISO must carefully evaluate the effectiveness of the training presented, including those presenting it, in order to identify instructors who are not good at it, thereby preventing undesirable situations.

To augment other means of training, open houses and computer security days are other means that can be used to focus user attention on security. Along those same lines, some larger organizations host annual security conferences.

Best Practices for Training and Awareness

In my experience with information security training, I have identified a number of considerations and thoughts that fit under this heading. Here are some key ones that might be helpful in establishing and maintaining an information security training program:

- Identify new, interesting issues to provide training on (FDCC, TIC, wireless security, etc.).
- Know when to use face-to-face training versus courseware.
- Ensure that presentations are vetted for adherence to policy before they are presented to an audience. Often, it is far more difficult to undo the damage than to prepare the training in the first place.
- Always seek ways to reinforce security principles, which should be simplified and repeated often. Concepts and principles such

as separation of duties, least privilege, need-to-know, access control, confidentiality of log-on information, etc., should be emphasized frequently and regularly. Redundancy and repetition of these concepts can become the bedrock of a user's understanding of security.

- Continual care should be taken to ensure that training content is both accurate and consistent. A process for continuous review of training content is necessary to make sure it conforms to current policies, particularly with new ones, and that various training materials are consistent in the message they communicate. Training cannot refer to the authorized use of an eight-character password, when in fact the current policy calls for twelve-character passwords. The process should also extend to review of "nonsecurity training" content to ensure that it is consistent with information security policy and practices. For example, training on privacy and physical security often touches on information security issues and should carry a consistent message.

- The CISO should listen to customers for their feedback on the quality, duration, complexity, and usefulness of course content, and then make appropriate changes. Feedback on training effectiveness can be gained through surveys and provision of opportunities to provide suggestions and recommendations. Additionally, security training effectiveness should be an item of discussion in the CISO's outreach efforts.

- Creation and operation of the information security training program in isolation should be avoided. To prevent this, one can maximize the use of existing organizational training resources. This may include learning labs and facilities, training catalogs and curricula, learning academies, specialized training software (learning management systems), and audio/visual facilities and systems. This will permit reduction of program costs and will enhance integration of security training into the larger enterprise training program. This has the added benefit of lessening user confusion regarding completion of mandatory training courses with which computer security training is included. To further lessen the training burden on personnel, ways to combine training that is at least somewhat related should be considered. Integration of privacy training into annual security awareness training provides efficiencies in this area that make the effort worthwhile, as can integration of information-security-related training across the entire organization to include training on the protection of classified information, physical security training, privacy training, and information security.

- The effectiveness of training should be included as part of Security Test and Evaluation (ST&E) efforts, in annual security controls testing, and in other continuous monitoring efforts. The manner in which the system owner plans on training the user staff in system-specific security requirements must be documented in the system security plan for each information system as well.
- To provide proof that annual training meets FISMA requirements, it will be necessary to maintain accurate records of attendance in both annual awareness training and in role-based training. This information must normally be provided to auditors for their review as part of the annual FISMA audit. Additionally, the results of tests and quizzes recorded for each user may also be requested. It is advisable to involve OIG audit staff in training activities throughout the year rather than just during the annual audit. This permits them to see the process for developing training in action, how the program responds to organizational needs to include the need for FISMA compliance, and could provide the security staff with information that will help them better prepare for the annual audit.
- To support enterprise information security training efforts, the utility of the CISO Web site must be maximized. The site itself must be readily accessible to users, must be attractive and easy to navigate, and the information posted on it must be both useful and beneficial to users. Information security policies and procedures must be laid out on the Web site in a manner that makes it very easy for users to access and use them. An index by topic is an effective way to do this. In fact, providing hyperlinks from the index to various sections of the actual security policy is the most reliable way to

facilitate user ability to access authoritative security material. To assess the effectiveness of the site in supporting user needs, one should consider monitoring user activity on the site as fully as possible.

- The CISO must also ensure that his efforts in the training area address the requirements of FISMA. This is best approached by ensuring that NIST guidance is used for this purpose. A good place to start would be an evaluation of NIST Special Publication 800-53 and control families for training and the information security program.

- The security awareness and training requirements mandated by FISMA and addressed in NIST SP 800-53 should be addressed in terms of a hybrid control. That is, certain aspects of training must be viewed from an enterprise level as a common control (e.g., annual awareness training), while other aspects (e.g., system specific security training) must be viewed as the responsibility of the system owner. Taking this approach permits cost-effective provision of training on both an enterprise level and system level.

- Good sources for information security training that satisfy current requirements for government agencies include NIST Special Publications and bulletins, solutions offered by the Department of Homeland Security through the Information System Security Line of Business (ISSLOB), information published by the U.S.-Computer Emergency Readiness Team (US-CERT), DHS' Essential Body of Knowledge (EBK), training developed by SANS, training from ISACA, as well as security-related Web sites, journals, and periodicals.

- To obtain support for the accomplishment of security training goals, ensure that training-related objectives are built into performance plans for offices as well as for agency executives. Obviously, before you can expect acceptance of these training performance measures, there is a need to clearly communicate to management all plans for training through the use of a communications plan, and whenever there are changes in plans. The personal involvement of the CISO in developing the communications plan and sharing its contents will solidify ownership of the initiative, and will help ensure it reaches the correct audience with the proper degree of emphasis, and will offer business units leaders an opportunity to obtain answers directly from the source.

- When organizing for performance of the training function, consider that it is most closely aligned with the security policy function, as training content is primarily made up of policy- and guidance-related information. It is most efficient if the same manager has responsibility for both. This also facilitates consistency of training with policy, with awareness information posted elsewhere, and ensures that training meets the common-sense test.

- Whenever they are included in training materials, make sure that referenced links/URLs work. An out-of-date, dead link is more than distracting; it indicates a lack of attention to detail and can sour a user on the training overall.

- To accommodate user learning styles and availability, build a video library or preferably an online library of training content that can be accessed on demand at any time.

- Make training in face-to-face sessions as interactive and participative as possible. Otherwise, one of the primary benefits of such training will be lost. Giving training participants an opportunity to ask and get answers to their questions is a highly effective means of reinforcing training objectives.

- When a learning management system is employed, ensure that the LMS has a robust reporting capability that will allow the staff to quickly and reliably identify who has completed training—by topic, when it was completed, and who has not yet completed the training. Also, permit the information to be broken out by office and by role. Also, with respect to the use of LMS for security training, the security training team should be prepared for difficulties that may arise regarding the compatibility of automated training content with LMS requirements. These could lead to aggravating delays in having training content available to users. Such difficulties should be anticipated and planned for when developing implementation milestones. Working through these issues will require intensive coordination calls and meetings as well as identification of potential work-arounds, and possible implementation of

less-than-optimal solutions to meet training requirements.
This process can be frustrating, can try the patience of training personnel, and must be planned for.

- Whenever possible, supporting consultants and contractors should be required to complete the identical training
that agency personnel must complete. This reduces the burden of administering security course content and completion. However, in many cases this will not be possible, and
special provisions for contractors such as providing them
access to the training on DVD or other media will have
to be made. Often, corporate staff of the contractor firm
will have to provide verification that their personnel have
completed the training, and will need to be able to access
government systems in order to complete the training. If
such provisions are not addressed in the contract, there
could be difficulty in arranging timely completion of training requirements.

- Consider implementing a message-of-the day capability that
highlights a particular security awareness message for users
upon initial log-on each day. This can be augmented with
implementation of automated training upon log-on, which
requires the user to answer a multiple choice or true-or-false
question related to the material presented to enhance user
comprehension of training information. The capability to
track a user's success or failure can also be used to address
potential problems in their behavior.

- Pay great attention to social engineering as it provides attackers a ready means to bypass costly and sophisticated security
controls. These controls may actually be providing only a false
sense of security when users render them ineffective through
their thoughtless acts or omissions.

- Ensure that security is addressed when system-specific training is offered when new systems are deployed. This level of
training should not only address system-specific security
capabilities, controls, and procedures, but can also be used as
a means of reinforcing general security responsibilities that
all users have.

Summary

It is the CISO's responsibility to establish a security awareness and training program to inform users of their security responsibilities, awareness of threats to government agencies and their information, knowledge of safeguards used to protect systems and data, and vulnerabilities in protective controls. The CISO is responsible for establishing a role-based training program to offer specialized security training tailored to a user's particular job needs. Additionally, he must provide training on other security-related topics according to the needs of the information security program. The CISO must be prepared to dedicate resources to security training to include his own time, interests, and efforts, with the goal of creating a culture of security awareness that matches that of the overall agency culture.

9

AUDIT LIAISON

Government inspectors generally play a significant role in ensuring agency compliance with FISMA. Agency-level Offices of the Inspector General (OIG) are required by FISMA to conduct an audit of the agency compliance with FISMA each year. Just as CISOs are provided with guidance each year on what is to be reported, agency OIGs are provided related guidance on areas where they should focus attention, and specific questions they must address in their audit report. One should recognize that the annual FISMA audit may be used by OIG to support other ongoing audit and evaluation efforts they may have planned or that may be under way (i.e., annual financial statement audit), and the results can be reflected in other audit products. The scope of OIG's annual FISMA audit is to measure compliance with FISMA itself, with NIST guidance related to the information security program and its implementation, as well as agency policy that has been published relative to the information security program. Additionally, the Government Accountability Office (GAO) is regularly asked by Congress to assess specific aspects of agency information security efforts that touch compliance with FISMA and other legislation and OMB directives as part of governmentwide audits. There are examples where an Inspector General (IG) audit will be conducted on the basis of findings of a GAO audit, whether or not the findings specifically relate to the agency.

This chapter will concentrate on actions necessary for the CISO and staff to build good working relationships with both internal and external auditors. There are two things that make this important. First, within an agency, audits provide an independent view of the health of an agency's enterprise information security program, and allows the agency to measure its progress year over year in the case of the annual FISMA audit. Second, the results of audits are a primary means of judging the relative effectiveness of information security efforts among government agencies. Consequently, the CISO must seek to perform well on any audit relating to the enterprise information security program. Often, one will hear complaints about audits, their value, and the amount of work that is required to deal with them, particularly if the results of the audit are unfavorable and show the program in a bad light. However, every CISO can appreciate a positive audit result that shows progress over the previous year's report, and comparative superiority of his program over those of peer agencies.

To understand the nature of the relationship between the CISO and the agency Office of the Inspector General, the CISO is well served to consider OIG's role and recognize that the OIG is also a charter member of the organization. In other words, both the CISO and the IG serve the same agency head. The CISO must check his mindset to ensure that he approaches the relationship in a nonadversarial manner. The CISO should remember that just as he does, the IG is also concerned with the agency's performance in accomplishing its mission, and is also interested in the effectiveness of the agency's information security program supporting that mission. Information technology can help one realize that the agency audit function and the information security function have much in common on this score.

To build on this principle, the CISO must ensure that his staff knows how to deal with auditors too. They should seek to be helpful, and not confrontational or adversarial. The staff should know how to be persistent without being defensive. Most importantly, they must know the importance of the audit and the auditor's role. Not everyone is capable of mastery of these points, so the CISO must avoid putting those who do not understand in positions where frequent contact with auditors is required. Select personnel with good interpersonal skills as well as technical competence, and groom them in the audit coordination skills.

Audit Preparation

Prior to the audit and even during the audit, the CISO should make sure the IG knows what is happening with the information security program. Share information about your plans and initiatives so that the OIG is aware of them and can position his staff to observe your activities and accomplishments as an indicator of what is being done to improve the effectiveness of the information security program. This is particularly important with regard to corrective actions for findings from prior audits. You can facilitate this by providing complete documentation in the correct format in accordance with the schedule OIG has established. This can only be effective if the CISO prioritizes efforts to respond to IG requirements. This priority requirement is facilitated by the establishment of an audit liaison capability for effectively managing the agency response to OIG requests, which includes effective tracking of the status of requested information, provision of support to OIG requests for interviews and the like, and resolution of open issues in a timely fashion. Assignment of this responsibility to one mature, reliable individual armed with a comprehensive tracking tool will do wonders for making this happen in a timely fashion. A centralized response to OIG requests is also facilitated through the establishment of a clearing house for OIG information requests. For instance, all requests for information from the OIG are channeled to the audit liaison staff member, who then records the request, forwards it to the appropriate staff office, and maintains an open tracking ticket on the request until it is filled. All security-related documentation is then packaged, marked, and provided to the OIG once it has been evaluated to ensure it meets the parameters of the original request. This approach provides assurance that the information security function responds to requests as quickly and as thoroughly as possible. This single point of contact for a security-related audit must also coordinate the response to all requests, even if it has little to do with security. This ensures the proper level of control and oversight of the response and makes the request process transparent for the OIG. Your tracking mechanism should record the nature of the data requested as well as the actual data delivered to the IG, and should include all associated file names, report titles, report dates, etc. Because of their importance, most government organizations have assigned a dedicated audit liaison officer or have established a staff office. It is important for the CISO to coordinate his audit-related activities with this function whenever possible, relying on the rapport and working relationships they have established with OIG and GAO. In any case, the CISO should always seek to keep them informed, respond to them promptly, and use them as a resource.

On a routine basis, the CISO should seek to make the OIG aware of what he is doing—not for approval, but to build bridges and provide them an opportunity to ask questions about process and procedures to help their understanding. Do not expect the auditors to "approve" or bless what you are doing. Send them copies of reports, minutes, etc., that you think might be of interest to them or might assist them with the FISMA audit.

One key to audit preparation is to ensure that you have done everything possible to address each finding of the previous year's audit. the OIG does not typically look favorably on the CISO and his staff when prior recommendations have gone unheeded. If the finding from the audit has not been closed, then you should be able to provide documentation that progress has been made since the last audit and a realistic closure date has been identified. Priority for remediation efforts prior to the audit should be aimed at correction of all prior findings but especially on those having an impact on the broader computing environment rather than on those that affect a single system. Those that are broad based and that affect multiple information systems are more likely to lead to a material weakness in a financial statement audit than those whose impact is more limited.

Your preparations for information security audits should include regular meetings with the OIG's chief of information technology audits. This gives you an opportunity to discuss information-technology-related issues that could have an impact on upcoming audits, and allows you to work with the audit staff toward a common understanding of what is happening, and how to interpret external directives affecting the information security program. It also affords you an opportunity to share with the lead auditor what actions you are taking to improve the program and make progress in correcting identified deficiencies.

The CISO should also recognize that the OIG will assess compliance with the agency's own documented policies, no matter how out of date and superfluous they may be. Be sure that you review your policies with a mind toward the agency's ability to implement them and to enforce them. For instance, there is no requirement for an eAuthentication risk assessment to be conducted for all information systems. Such a policy is not only unnecessary but also serves no purpose. So, you should modify or eliminate all policy requirements that do not meet common sense, knowing they may only attract unnecessary attention during the audit.

Similarly, you need to ensure that you are following your own policies. OIG will not just be looking for compliance with FISMA, OMB, or NIST directives and guidance, but will also hold you accountable for compliance with agency-specific policies. So, ensure that practices, activities, and processes are all being employed in accordance with the agency's policy. If, however, they cannot be followed or do not make sense for any reason, then once again modify or eliminate them before the audit begins.

The information security organization should maintain a comprehensive, well-organized repository of all security documentation under its control. This allows an efficient response to data calls, particularly from auditors. This capability is enhanced through the implementation of a process for authorized users to access this information on the basis of need to know. This lessens the burden on the information security staff. Additionally, making images of signed document pages can support many and varied requests from auditors for proof that proper authorities have approved the security documentation in question. A good repository of security documentation is essential to the success of the annual FISMA audit.

Other considerations for ensuring the organization is prepared for the annual FISMA evaluation include the following:

- *Incident Reporting*: For the FISMA audit, be sure to maintain complete incident-reporting data for the auditor team to review. There are specific questions related to incident reporting that OIG must answer on the annual report. For each incident, records of who, what, when, etc., must be maintained and should be readily available for review.
- *Security Awareness and Training*: The OIG section of the report requires an evaluation of completion of awareness and training. To support this need, you will need to maintain records of training completion of all training given, both user awareness and role-based training. This includes minutes of meetings showing topics covered (ISSO forums, presentations, etc.), attendance rosters, and the like.
- *Contractor Oversight:* One key area of focus for OIG in the annual FISMA audit is the agency's process for ensuring that its support contractors comply with FISMA requirements.

Be sure you are able to provide proof that requirements have been documented in service-level agreements, memoranda of understanding/agreement, interconnectivity agreements, etc. And, you must also be able to show that you have exercised due diligence in ensuring that these requirements have been met.

- *System Inventory*: The CISO needs to realize the importance of the system inventory and the quality of the system authorization process in the overall scoring of the audit results. He should therefore prepare well in these two areas, and place emphasis on achieving agreement with OIG on these two areas in particular.

- *Certification and Accreditation:* While you may have documented and implemented a satisfactory process for certifying and accrediting the agency's information system, the IG may not give you credit for the quality of your process if only a limited number of systems have been certified and accredited at the time of the audit.

- *Information Systems:* The IG will likely sample information technology systems because there is not enough time or resources available to them to look at all of the systems. Ten percent is probably a good rule, although up to 50% of systems is possible.

- *Scheduling:* The CISO should prepare for the FISMA audit by locking it in on the calendar and synchronizing documentation update and other key activities to established audit dates. The CISO should recognize that auditors out of necessity must focus on fairly inflexible completion dates. In order to complete the audit on time, they have to establish a cutoff date for when they will accept data that will be included in the report. These dates do not always match up with the dates you have set for compliance with annual requirements. As much as possible, you need to establish annual dates for compliance to comport with the expected dates of periodic audits such as FISMA. This will ensure that all systems will have completed contingency plan testing before the completion of the audit, for example. To complete the annual FISMA evaluation in time to submit the report to OMB on time, the OIG normally has to begin his audit work no later than May. This schedule allows field work to take place for approximately four to five months before the draft audit report is prepared for release on or about September 30th. This allows thirty days to finalize the report and submit it with CIO concurrence by November 15th.

- *Areas of Emphasis*: The CISO will need to ensure the OIG is aware of the information security program areas he considers most important. For example, security of particular critical systems or the effectiveness of security controls for personally identifiable information. You should relate this information as early as possible, so as to allow the IG to tell you what you need to do to do well in these areas.

It may be that there is more than one audit taking place at a given time. This is particularly true if both internal and external audit organizations are involved. This may tend to dilute or fragment the CISO's ability to support each of them effectively. However, your priority efforts should be directed toward support of the FISMA audit as much as possible. This is primarily because of the breadth of the audit and the fact that it targets the effectiveness of the agency information security program. Therefore, it makes good sense to dedicate a member to serve as the point of contact for the FISMA audit for its duration.

In all activities related to the development and implementation of the information security program, it is important for the CISO to stress due diligence. In other words, all information security personnel should think like an auditor. Develop processes, provide advice, record information, and implement solutions with the recognition that all actions are subject to scrutiny and should be provable by means of verifiable evidence. Do not make assumptions about the acceptability of an action on good faith. Rather, all actions must be traceable and documented.

Kicking Off the Audit

One should not underestimate the importance of the entrance or kick-off briefing for the audit. When given the choice, always request an initial meeting prior to the start of audit work. This permits you to find out about the objective, scope, timing, and methodology to guide audit activities, and perhaps even to establish rules of engagement for the audit. The CISO who is able to maximize the usefulness of the audit entrance briefing can avoid the development of misunderstandings during the course of the audit. Here, he can determine who will be doing the audit. He can also find out what areas of emphasis there may be. Knowledge gained from the kick-off presentation can be used to determine how the audit will compare with the prior year's effort. The CISO can ask questions to determine the method of data gathering, milestones for the audit project, and he can share information regarding points of contact and can reach agreement on the process for data gathering, as well as deadlines for key activities. For example, on what date will the auditor assess the number of systems that have been authorized to operate, and the percentage of users who have completed security awareness training? Finally, the kick-off meeting allows discussion of the proper sources of data the auditors are expecting.

At some agencies, the FISMA audit will rely on audit work done on other audit engagements. This should be clarified during the kick-off meeting. Also, when discussing the timelines for the audit, ensure there is enough time to respond to draft findings built into the schedule. At least a week should be set aside for this activity in order to do it effectively without rushing and to effect proper coordination with other agency staff.

The annual FISMA audit is made up of two distinct parts. One part consists of OIG's direct input to the FISMA report itself, which consists of a formatted spreadsheet in a preapproved format. The other portion is the written portion of the report, in which OIG documents findings and recommendations. You will need to conduct a careful review of both parts to make sure they match and are not in conflict.

Another goal for the CISO at the kick-off briefing is identification of the individual auditors who will be participating in the audit. It may prove helpful to attempt to find out something about them. Try to determine their track record, the skill levels, areas of emphasis, and history at your agency. A good place to start is prior years' audits. Being aware of the skills of the audit team and their technical capabilities will help you better prepare for the audit and can help you focus on areas they may tend to concentrate on.

During the kickoff meeting, determine if the audit team will be performing technical scanning, and if so make it clear they need to coordinate those activities in advance. This will minimize the potential for interference with systems in production. During periods when you know that scanning is taking place, be extra vigilant for those telltale symptoms and for the success of intrusion detection and intrusion prevention tools in detecting their activities. It is more than embarrassing to fail to detect IG scans of your network when you know what they are up to.

Before the FISMA audit begins, it will be worthwhile to try to find out the manner in which the audit team will be assessing compliance in key areas that are central to the FISMA report. For example, determine what proof they will be seeking and what process they will be using to evaluate agency controls in the areas of configuration management, incident response, training, systems inventory, certification and accreditation, contingency planning, etc. Will they will be conducting scans to identify systems, or will they rely on the inventory you provide them? Will they review C&A artifacts in order to assess compliance with the process you have defined or against federal guidance?

During the Audit

Once the audit is under way, you should aim for effective coordination of effort and activities and to obtain advance notice of findings. This is a role for the CISO, who should seek to meet regularly with the OIG audit manager. The CISO must continue to have direct involvement with the status of the audit throughout the term of the audit. Actually, another good approach is to engage the OIG audit team at multiple levels, using the appropriate counterpart. For instance, the CISO should meet at least monthly with the manager of OIG's audit function, while the CISO's lead compliance manager should interface with the lead auditor on a weekly or biweekly basis. Functional specialists in the information security function should pair up with the respective auditor in their areas of expertise and responsibility. Naturally, it will be important to speak with the same voice and to coordinate information received from the audit team to maximize the effectiveness of audit support efforts.

How you perform your mission should not be a mystery to the auditors. While there is no need to go out of your way to describe every last aspect of a process or procedure, your operations should be transparent enough to avoid hiding the ingredients of your secret sauce.

When the auditor brings deficiencies to your attention, you should take corrective action immediately, particularly if the auditor says he lacks sufficient information or has not yet verified them. At best, this could result in a possible finding being left out of the report, or at worst, it could be put in a more favorable light. However, you must be prepared to fully validate closure of audit findings. To maintain credibility, ensure that you can provide documented proof that a finding or potential finding has been closed before saying as much.

Often, auditors will be reluctant to share their findings during the audit itself. Therefore, it will be important to understand that the auditor may be telegraphing through the data requests. If he continues to ask for more information about a given process, then he is not satisfied about the information he has been provided so far.

In response to auditor data calls, provide data to the auditors in a form that shows due diligence. For instance, give them proof that weaknesses have been closed on POA&Ms, or provide them extracts of policies and procedures as evidence that they have been documented and published. However, do not expect to be given credit for draft materials that have not yet gone into effect. There is normally little inclination on the part of auditors to give constructive credit for your good intentions. You should clearly understand that auditors distinguish between draft and final documentation (i.e., policies, security plans, risk assessments, contingency plans, etc.). Therefore, ensure that documentation is signed as a measure of its authenticity.

During the audit, the CISO must be careful to monitor the conduct of his staff to ensure he knows if they are unnecessarily argumentative in their dealings with the auditors. The staff should know to escalate issues to the CISO, with an understanding that there will be an opportunity to address disagreements and contentious issues later using well-constructed and well-researched information as a basis for countering the auditor's view. Most information security organizations consist of a mix of government personnel and contractor personnel. While the competence of contractors cannot be denied, government employees should always control the activities of contractors as they interface with auditors during the audit.

As information about the status of the audit begins to come in, the CISO should prepare management for the results. First of all, senior management should be well aware of the importance of the annual FISMA audit and aware that the audit is under way. They should therefore be interested in finding out about indications of how the audit is going and how the information security program is stacking up. Informing management in advance of receipt of the draft report or the exit presentation eliminates the element of surprise and prepares management for the results. At the same time, it is good to be able to share good news at the same time that bad news surfaces. Management is wise enough to know that deficiencies are almost always going to be found in an audit. Nevertheless, their impact can be reduced if the auditor comments about what is being done correctly and points out where progress is being made.

When meeting with the OIG to discuss system-level issues, be sure to include key system owners or representatives. They are the rightful assigned owners of the systems and have a vested interest in defending their activities and security posture before the OIG. When the auditors share a deficiency or potential finding with you, immediately brief the system owner and his staff and then work together with them to either correct the problem right away or on a plan for remediation of the weakness at a later date. If the finding is disputed, the CISO should be prepared to serve as intermediary in these potentially contentious situations.

While it is important to respond to OIG requests for information as rapidly as possible, a rapid response must be carefully balanced against ensuring that the documentation to be provided is accurate, complete, and meets the parameters of the request. Therefore, ensure there is a thorough review of the documentation prior to its being sent to the audit team in response to their request. Do not send it over in a hurry just to show that you are exceedingly responsible, to prove that your repository is well organized and useful, or just because the IG is looking for it and their previous calls for the reports have fallen on deaf ears. Do not be tempted even in these cases to sacrifice quality for quantity or accuracy for speed. Instead, ensure that the file being sent is actually for the system for which the data has been requested. This example can lead to a credibility issue.

Also, you should ensure that the IG knows you are considering security in your maintenance and dissemination of sensitive documentation.

Do not automatically volunteer direct access to information without considering the security sensitivity of the information. Follow agency rules for maintaining access to sensitive information even when the OIG asks for it. Require the auditors to follow these rules, and encourage them to coordinate through the single point of contact to ensure that security protections against disclosure are maintained. Make sure audit reports are labeled appropriately to protect the information that shows a vulnerability in agency security controls. Direct access to sensitive information by auditors should be carefully considered before granting it. For instance, auditor system access should be limited to the scope of the audit, and should be restricted to the duration of the audit.

The Audit Report

Normal protocol is for the OIG to issue a draft report for agency review before the annual FISMA report is finalized. The CISO must be prepared to closely scrutinize the draft audit report as soon as it is received. He should prioritize the review and should assign several people to review it. Work together with all organizational stakeholders (i.e., system owners, ISSOs) to prepare the response to the draft audit and to begin coordination on remediation of findings.

Where possible, the CISO should seek to provide additional input or documentation to the OIG to permit adjustment of findings appropriately if the OIG concurs. In some cases, it will be necessary to provide alternative wording to make the finding more accurate. Do not assume that findings in the draft are set in stone, and try to determine from the OIG what is needed to remove a finding or improve the results reflected in the report. The CISO must be able to recognize the limits of this discussion, and must recognize how far the OIG is willing to go. At that point, negotiations must of necessity stop in order to avoid either wasting time or ill feelings. Often, the CISO will have to seek to achieve the best possible rather than the optimum outcome. He should aim to create the best situation for next year by getting the auditor to give credit for having partially complied with a requirement.

The draft report must be reviewed for any factual inaccuracies as they could present problems later. Perhaps the auditors have mischaracterized a situation or inaccurately described a control. Take what the auditor has written seriously, and do not assume that the inaccuracy will be corrected. Respond to the draft audit report by making the auditor explain the basis of his findings. Auditors should be able to justify each finding documented in the report, and if not, the finding should be removed. This also includes the accuracy or wording of recommendations related to the finding.

You should ensure that audit recommendations are written as generically as possible. To allow you freedom of action on responses to their findings, do not allow the auditors to dictate specific solutions for the deficiencies they identify. Failing to do this makes it more difficult to respond to audit findings once you have come to realize that the recommended solution is not cost-effective, or has significant side effects. For each finding, consider the long-term consequences, and remember that you must live with them in the months and perhaps years ahead. If you accept the wording of the draft report, you do not get a second chance to change it if you find out later that it is problematic. To do this, it will be necessary to get together as early in the process as possible—preferably before the finding is even drafted—to discuss the auditor's interpretations, trying to understand how they view the situation and to understand why they see it as a deficiency.

Another potential problem can be avoided by ensuring the auditor uses language that promotes effective corrective action to address the findings. For instance, there is clearly a difference between responsibility for establishing a policy to address a finding and taking action to implement the policy. Different organizations are responsible for policy and implementation. When this occurs, work with the auditors to clarify who has responsibility for correction of the audit, and convince them to reword the finding to permit the appropriate corrective action to be taken.

In the case of the annual FISMA audit, the CISO and the OIG must work closely together to obtain agreement on the audit report and findings. They must reconcile any differences in opinion or fact prior to the report being submitted to the agency head for signature. OMB does not desire to play the role of umpire, and agency-level disagreements that result in addenda to the report stating areas of disagreement do not show the agency in a favorable light. This means that all parties to the audit must seek common ground and areas of synergy. You should seek to come to agreement on the findings as quickly as possible. Since the goal is to submit an annual FISMA report that is internally coherent with both the CIO and OIG in alignment, it makes sense to shoot for achieving this goal early on. The report must be submitted by a preestablished deadline; the longer it takes to agree on the findings, conclusions, recommendations, and scoring of the OIG section of the report, the more pressure builds, adding to the tension and possibly creating animosity.

Also, since the CISO and the IG must agree on the consolidated FISMA report before it is submitted, this means that OIG must be given the opportunity to review the CIO portion of the report. So, provide the draft to OIG as far in advance as possible and then maintain a record to be able to demonstrate that OIG was given a copy, and that the IG has accepted it. You should also recognize that the OIG staff also has as an objective attainment of agreement on their findings and may therefore be willing to work with you on their report to a greater degree than one might suspect. This may give you the latitude to ask for refinement of wording, recognition of progress made, and addition of notes to clarify other information in the report.

Remember that the annual FISMA evaluation report will be made public. This should inform your view of the findings and how they are apt to be read. Try to imagine how the results might appear in a news article or on a Web site catering to government readers. Because the FISMA report will be a public record, be sure you carefully review it and coordinate closely with OIG to ensure that any information identifying specific vulnerabilities in protective controls is not included in the report. Other audits may indeed require the documentation of specific vulnerabilities, and should be marked as security sensitive; they should be handled so that this information will not be disclosed.

Conclusion

The results of the FISMA evaluation report will not only have an impact on the agency's FISMA grade, but will also be the starting point for next year's audit. A favorable assessment with few findings makes it easier to deal with next year's audit. Obviously, a good audit result builds goodwill that can be banked upon in the future. Productive efforts by the information security function to make improvements in the information security program in response to audit findings establishes a degree of goodwill, and serves as a positive point of departure for future encounters with the agency audit staff.

As described in Chapter 2, the Office of Management and Budget has significantly revised requirements for annual FISMA reporting, which impacts the associated annual inspector general's evaluation. Although adjustments in the guidance have been made, OIG responsibilities for FISMA evaluation remain largely intact. Consequently, the CISO's need to closely cooperate with OIG for the annual FISMA evaluation is just as important as ever, reinforcing the fact that there is a continuing need for good rapport between the OIG audit staff and the CISO's staff, and the importance of the relationship-building considerations addressed in this chapter is undiminished.

10

MONITORING MECHANISMS

This chapter will concentrate on what is necessary to build mechanisms to not only monitor compliance, but also monitor the viability of system security controls. In the early years following the enactment of FISMA, agencies tended to concentrate their efforts on certifying and accrediting all their information systems, or in other words, a static assessment of a system's security controls at a particular moment in time. This focus led to a situation in which most security controls protecting government systems were reviewed only every three years. Of course, the effectiveness of many security controls cannot be assumed even in three days, much less in three years. Consequently, the importance of continuous monitoring has grown since those early days of FISMA implementation, and it is an area that has seen substantial change over the past three years in particular. NIST has focused more attention on the continuous monitoring phase of the system authorization process in recent updates. Additionally, publication of the Consensus Audit Guidelines (Appendix A) has given greater emphasis to the importance of real-time monitoring of security controls through the identification of what is thought to be the most critical controls agencies should implement in priority order to secure their information systems.

Yet, it is up to each agency, based on its particular mission needs, to establish a realistic plan for continuously monitoring controls to ensure their continued effectiveness. The truth is, every control must be monitored, yet every control is not subject to the same degree of change and need for monitoring. The approach the agency takes to addressing its controls monitoring needs will range between static monitoring on a periodic basis at one end of the spectrum to fully automated, real-time monitoring at the other. The balance achieved will result in a cost-effective, risk-based approach that is tuned to the needs for protecting the system and the data it processes in the context of the protective needs of the enterprise itself. Monitoring efforts must support external requirements such as OMB's FISMA reporting guidelines as well as internal monitoring requirements that address agency-specific risks. The approach to achieving this should be to review internal and external requirements for monitoring the effectiveness, adequacy, and viability of security controls in order to determine the most effective strategy for monitoring at the level required.

Compliance Review Process

An important element in an agency's monitoring program is a process for engaging system owners and business unit leaders to review the status of their security efforts. There is a need to meet face to face to discuss their remediation efforts, determine areas and issues with which they may need assistance, and to gain assurance that they have achieved or are on track to achieve established information security program requirements. If the agency has implemented a performance measurement program, this would provide a good opportunity to assess where the executive or organization stands with respect to information security-related measures. Also, if there are other processes that affect organizational elements, it is wise to combine processes as much as possible to reduce the impact on business units. For example, if there are privacy, FOIA, enterprise architecture, CPIC, and 508 compliance requirements that business units must demonstrate compliance with, a unified compliance review process can provide significant efficiencies and can limit the impact and disruption caused by organizational compliance efforts. The annual review should include business cases to ensure that security activities and the resources for performing them are included and to determine if business unit estimates are realistic and have been comprehensively addressed.

The information security function must establish a documented plan and procedures to coordinate this component of the overall program. The scope and the applicability of the effort must be determined. It should apply to all business units for the purpose of assessing compliance with information security program requirements such as completion of annual awareness training, identification of personnel assigned significant security roles, completion of role-based training, and appointment of business unit ISSOs (primary and alternate). It must also be designed to assess compliance of information systems with established requirements. This includes plan of action and milestones (POA&M) management, security documentation update and accuracy, completion of contingency plan testing, incident response plan testing, and accomplishment of annual security controls testing for their systems. The schedule can be constructed in several ways. It can aim to assess a portion of an element's systems according to risk, a portion of its existing weaknesses, or all weaknesses, depending on their number and nature. For large and complex systems, a viable alternative is to review 25% of open weaknesses each quarter.

Instructions for the review must be published following concurrence of those business units most affected by the review. This should include publication of the review schedule prior to the beginning of the review year to give business units as much advance notice as possible, particularly if areas of emphasis are revised year to year. The success of the effort relies on consistency in the application of the process across multiple elements, individualized review results, and fully documented results that the subject business unit has been given an opportunity to comment on prior to their submission to senior management. This type of monitoring approach is greatly enhanced through the use of graded measurements of performance and compliance that allow the business unit, system owner, and senior management to clearly understand the security posture relative to other business units and systems. A grading system that is clearly explained and documented and fully coordinated with affected managers is the one that is most likely to be effective. The effectiveness of reviews of this type is further enhanced when automated compliance baseline scanning and vulnerability scanning of systems being reviewed is performed by the review team as part of the process. This provides a more comprehensive view of system status, gives the system owner and management a more detailed picture of weaknesses in system controls, and can be used to verify the quality of similar scanning the system owner may have performed.

Annual Controls Testing

The OMB requirement to test controls annually has come under scrutiny in recent years because of the focus of the requirement on evaluating controls' effectiveness at a particular moment in time. This is in contrast to the concept presented in the Consensus Audit Guidelines, which tilts continuous monitoring toward real-time monitoring of security controls. However, in the overall approach to an agency-level continuous monitoring program, the place for annual testing of security controls has a secure place. This assertion is based on the fact that not all controls can be monitored through technical means in the manner prescribed in the Consensus Audit Guidelines. This is true for most all management and operational controls, and even some technical controls. Hence, controls that cannot be tested continuously by technical means must be tested by other means. Here is where annual controls testing comes into play. But it must be added that a robust continuous monitoring program takes advantage of the concept of testing controls on the basis of risk while complying with NIST guidance prescribing testing each control at least every three years.

Therefore, the approach to development of an agency-level continuous monitoring program must include annual controls testing that ensures the most critical controls (e.g., Consensus Audit Guidelines controls or agency specific core controls) are tested every year according to risk, that all controls protecting a given system must be tested over a period of three years, and that both system-level and program-level controls require testing. This requires that an established plan be developed to document testing requirements to ensure that testing of every control of every system is accounted for. Normally, this is best achieved by first developing an enterprise-testing strategy that provides direction and details how program-level controls affecting all systems will be tested, which is then supported by a system-specific, three-year test plan that documents which controls are to be tested by year. The agency plan will outline those core controls that system owners are required to test every year, and will also specify that a combination of management, operational, and technical controls will be tested each year. The agency-level testing strategy should also provide for adjustment for annual controls testing selection by emerging threats, impacts of security incidents, and known vulnerabilities in existing systems. For instance, system-level testing should include testing of all controls reported as closed during the previous year to validate actual closure. Also, the agency-level testing approach should provide instructions to facilitate coordination between owners of supported systems and supporting systems to ensure that inherited controls are tested and the results of testing are shared with the staff of the dependent system.

Monitoring in Real Time

Current thinking is that for government agencies to achieve real security, they need to implement real-time monitoring of the controls that protect against the greatest threats to government information systems. As a result of a significant public-private study conducted at the beginning of 2008, the most critical controls have been identified and are documented in what is known as the Consensus Audit Guidelines. An extract of Version 2.3 of the guidelines is provided in Appendix C. The guidelines prioritize fifteen discreet controls that agencies should implement to protect their internal information systems against external threats. The controls identified to support real-time monitoring capabilities are as follows:

- *Inventory of authorized and unauthorized devices*: This is the capability of an organization to identify at any time not only the hardware assets approved for use, primarily with respect to the agency's infrastructure, but also devices not attached to the network. From this inventory, the agency will also be able to identify all hardware that has not been approved for use within the agency.
- *Inventory of authorized and unauthorized software*: Similarly, agencies need the real-time capability of identifying all software assets in the form of common applications approved for use within the agency, and through the development of such an inventory, have the related capability of identifying unauthorized software that is in use.
- *Secure configurations for hardware and software on laptops, workstations, and servers*: This capability relates to the agency having established approved configurations for all approved hardware and software installed on laptops, workstations, and servers, which provide a baseline level of protection. It is

further enhanced by the ability to continuously monitor compliance with established secure configurations through the employment of automated tools.

- *Secure configurations of network devices such as firewalls and routers*: Agencies must establish secure baselines for network firewalls, routers, and switches, and then must implement automated tools that permit these filters and rule sets to be checked for compliance and consistency.
- *Boundary defense*: This capability is necessary for agencies to be able to identify attacks on both public-facing and internal systems, as well as attacks originating from inside the agency infrastructure. This ability is based on the use of sniffers, intrusion detection systems, and vulnerability scanning tools to test sensors to verify their ability to detect such attacks.
- *Maintenance and analysis of complete security audit logs*: Agencies require the ability to capture audit trails from operating systems, network services, firewalls, etc., and to collect them in a central repository. Regular review of audit trails generated by information technology systems or platforms is enhanced through augmentation with correlation tools and employment of trained and experienced information security personnel to analyze this data.
- *Application software security*: This capability provides an agency assurance that application code is free of programming errors that lead to security vulnerabilities. This is achieved through a combination of automated source code testing, scanning of Web applications, object code testing, and performance of penetration testing by trained security personnel.
- *Controlled use of administrative privileges*: This capability ensures that the accounts of users who have been granted administrative privileges are limited to the absolute minimum number according to operational needs, are protected by more stringent than normal security measures, and are not used to carry out routine, nonprivileged tasks. Automated controls can be used to restrict the use of administrative privileges according to established policy and operational needs that system administrators may require.

- *Controlled access based on need to know*: This important capability is necessary to ensure that separation of functions is implemented with respect to privileged accounts vis-à-vis non-privileged accounts and is achieved through operating system controls complemented by documented policy and procedures.
- *Continuous vulnerability testing and remediation*: Agencies must establish the capability of performing automated scanning to identify vulnerabilities in system security configurations. This is done periodically, the frequency (weekly, monthly, quarterly) of testing depending on the risk to the platform to be scanned. A wide variety of vulnerability scanning software and services are available to agencies to support this security need. This capability also provides for linkage of vulnerabilities identified in scanning activities with established trouble ticketing systems or remediation planning (POA&M process).
- *Dormant account monitoring and control*: Agencies must have a process that provides detailed information about account access and the capability for its evaluation to ensure that unused or seldom-used accounts are not exploited by unauthorized personnel to gain access to agency systems, and to ensure that the activities of authorized users comply with agency policies and norms. This can be achieved through the use of native operating system account management capabilities augmented by custom scripts and third-party log analysis tools. Although this process is enhanced by the use of automated tools that identify accounts that have not been access within established parameters, it must fall on system owners and information owners to review access lists to verify that those currently granted access have a bona fide need for continued access, and this must be performed by manual review of access control lists and authorization lists.
- *Malware defenses*: Agencies must provide protection against malicious software. This is normally provided by means of signature-based blacklisting solutions, but also may include "whitelisting" or a combination of both. Automation is most effective in keeping anti-virus signatures up to date and ensuring that antivirus, antispyware, and host-based IDS are

active on all managed end points, and assess the protection antimalware solutions provide. The results of these activities must be reviewed to identify systems without protection and vulnerabilities in systems that do have protection. Network access control is used to supplement malware protection to restrict systems from accessing the network until compliance with the agency security policy has been tested and verified. When weaknesses in malware protection are identified, malware defenses include capabilities for collecting essential information to permit investigation.

- *Limitation and control of ports, protocols, and services*: Organizations must control ports, protocols, and services allowed to function on their networks through the use of port-scanning tools. Such tools permit identification of open ports, as well as protocols and services found on each open port. Security personnel can compare this information with an approved list of authorized services and protocols needed for each server and workstation.
- *Wireless device control*: To control wireless devices, agencies should employ automated scanning tools along with wireless intrusion detection capabilities. Other tools can be used at agency facilities to periodically identify wireless transmissions that do not meet agency-approved protocol and encryption standards. Such devices when discovered should be either upgraded or denied network access.
- *Data leakage protection*: This capability allows agencies to monitor and prevent unauthorized attempts to exfiltrate sensitive data from agency systems through the use of automated DLP tools. This automated capability must be supported by a process that allows the information security team to follow up on suspicious activities.

The implementation guidance relative to each of these controls is also provided in Appendix C. As we saw in Chapter 2, OMB's current FISMA reporting instructions reinforce the necessity for implementation of the Consensus Audit Guidelines (CAG). The approach that most agencies should apply in implementing the CAG controls is to begin by assessing their agency's current capabilities with respect to the individual CAG controls, and then identify gaps that must be filled to provide the CAG target architecture.

Weaknesses identified through real-time monitoring of security controls must be converted into effective corrective action. This requires escalation procedures that permit timely notification of entities responsible for incident response, investigation, containment, reporting, and remediation. The information security function will need to establish procedures that allow determination of what to do with the findings once they have been identified, categorized, and verified. If they cannot be remediated immediately, they will need to be included in the POA&M for the system to which they apply. A process for communicating the weaknesses in inherited infrastructure controls needs to be created to ensure that system owners are made aware of weaknesses that affect the security of their data. Likewise, risk-based response mechanisms to address the most critical weaknesses must be in place to allow priority response when immediate remediation is warranted.

Remediation Tracking

Most monitoring activities are aimed at identifying vulnerabilities in security controls to ensure the effectiveness of the controls that have been implemented. However, monitoring must also include activities that permit tracking of the status of actions to correct identified weaknesses. In fact, vulnerabilities identified as a result of other continuous monitoring activities must be tracked to the point of either full remediation, compensation by other controls, or acceptance by an authorizing official. A POA&M is the primary vehicle used in government for recording the results of monitoring activities in which vulnerabilities in security controls are identified. System owners must create POA&Ms for each of their information systems, in accordance with OMB and NIST guidance, to record vulnerabilities in system security controls. The system owner is assigned full responsibility for addressing identified weaknesses in the controls protecting his system. Consequently, access to POA&M data should be limited to the system owner and his staff, primarily the Information System Security Officer, in order to ensure accountability for the content of the POA&M.

The POA&M process allows the information security function to track and assess the status and effectiveness of remediation actions that are planned or are under way. It provides key information that at a minimum describes the vulnerability and the associated remediation action, identifies the party responsible for correcting the weakness, records the evaluated risk of the vulnerability, lists milestones for corrective action, and documents the current status of the remediation. The information security team can use this information to validate whether or not realistic progress is being made in dealing with the weakness and eliminating the vulnerability before it can be exploited. Remediation activities for all systems should be reviewed at least quarterly. OMB for several years required submission of POA&M summary data each quarter; however, this practice is being phased out in lieu of agency submission of real-time data feeds, as described in Chapter 2.

In performing periodic monitoring of POA&Ms, there is a need to validate the effectiveness of corrective actions according to the criticality of the system and the assessed risk impact of each vulnerability. This review should include validation of the identity and level of involvement of the listed point of contact for accuracy, assessment of the status of remediation action with respect to approved milestones, and evaluation of the viability of corrective action in the context of its current status. To assist the system owner in managing his remediation activities, the CISO should establish benchmarks for the closure of weaknesses according to risk. For instance, correction of vulnerabilities ranked "high" should be completed within thirty days, moderate vulnerabilities in ninety days, and those of low impact in no more than six months. However, it should be clear that these best-guess recommendations will serve only as a starting point for determining target completion dates, and that they are subject to negotiation based on operational and resource constraints with which the system owner must contend.

Periodic monitoring of POA&Ms should also aim to validate corrective actions that are recorded as complete to ensure that they are in fact complete. Systems owners must be made aware of what proof is required to demonstrate closure. NIST SP 800-53A can be consulted to make this determination, and in many cases requirements will be established by the OIG. As a result of these activities, it will be necessary to maintain documentation to demonstrate that due diligence has been performed. Another element of the review will be to ensure the results from external audit efforts are integrated into the remediation process by being recorded in the POA&M of all systems to which the finding is applicable. The review process should also aim to ensure that POA&M weaknesses are addressed in business cases and funding requests so that resource requirements are addressed in capital planning and investment planning.

The review elements described earlier focus on the activities of the system owner and his staff. Additionally, the review should include an element from the perspective of assisting the system owner in performing his remediation tasks. The CISO in the performance of his capacity of the risk executive must take an enterprise view of corrective actions, and remediation monitoring efforts support his capacity to evaluate the remediation level from an agencywide perspective. For instance, corrective actions should be cross-checked to identify resources needed and to facilitate forecasting funding requirements from an agency-wide perspective. The review can reveal opportunities for combining corrective actions across multiple systems to reduce implementation time and costs. The review could lead to a need to apply the results of new or recent research on new technologies and methodologies that may have an impact on current plans for corrective action. Through the review of remediation activities of multiple information systems, trend analysis of weakness can be performed to iden tify remediation efficiencies and economies of scale. This will allow the CISO to provide value to the system owner community through the identification of solutions that span multiple systems.

Finally, the review can be used to verify responsibilities for remediation. That is, it can clarify responsibility for actions for which the system owner has the lead (e.g., system-specific controls) versus corrective actions related to inherited or common controls for which other entities are responsible. The review can facilitate application owner coordination with these other entities, such as the owners of infrastructure systems on which their system depends. The review can assist them by ensuring they are made aware of the status of remediation of weaknesses affecting their system, and by supporting efforts to include proper coordination on remediation activities in service-level agreements.

The remediation review can greatly benefit by the use of automated tools to manage POA&M data and allow performance of trend analysis. Software products of this type can provide a means of holding system owners accountable for their remediation activities, provide increased confidence in the reliability of data, implement work flow activities, and ensure approval of all changes to POA&M data. Automated tools can support requirements for export of data to OMB and other external entities. Also, their use can assist in the preparation of automated reports or dashboards that visually display the status of remediation for each system and across the entire organization.

Other Monitoring Activities

There are several time-tested security activities and processes that should also be considered in addressing identified requirements for continuous monitoring at the agency level. These include the following:

- *Spot-Checking*: The CISO should construct a capability that permits his team to spot-check compliance with various requirements of the information security program. For instance, there needs to be provision for occasional scans for wireless signals, laptop configurations, office walk-throughs, dumpster diving, physical access, social engineering, and user behavior as related to security awareness training

- *Preparatory Checking and Assistance Visits*: The information security function can assist system owners by performing security controls checks in advance of audits and inspections. The purpose of this exercise is to measure the system's compliance readiness in sufficient time to allow the system owner to take corrective action to increase preparedness before an audit begins. This effort is most effective if the information security function can closely approximate the approach that is expected to be used in the actual audit. A successful program of this nature can help to not only reduce audit findings but also to improve the agency's security posture.

- *Evaluate New Vulnerabilities*: Agencies should establish a process for obtaining up-to-date information on new vulnerabilities that includes the capability for evaluating them and their potential impact on agency systems. Information of this type can be obtained from US-CERT and a variety of vendor sites. This capability normally resides with the situational awareness team, and must be linked to the staffs (ISSOs) of infrastructure systems and major applications.

- *Enterprise Risk Assessment*: Agencies should perform an agency-wide assessment of risks at least every three years to ensure that they are able to maintain visibility of high-level risks that have an impact on agency resources and operations. This will provide them a means of continuously monitoring changes in risk exposure with respect to changing agency mission and objectives.

- *Security Impact Assessment*: Changes in the design, configuration, functions, or operation of authorized information systems must be addressed in a controlled, systematic method. The establishment of an effective security impact assessment process provides the information security function the information necessary to understand the nature, scope, and complexity of proposed changes to an information system prior to occurrence of the change, and to recommend requirements to be met as part of the system development project. This is an important part of a continuous monitoring process because it right-sizes the reauthorization process by focusing certification testing requirements only on those controls affected by the change.

- *Monitor Accuracy of System Security Documentation*: On an annual basis, system-level documentation should be reviewed to ensure that it is up to date, and reflects all changes since the previous update. The risk assessment must be reviewed to ensure that it addresses changes in system assets, threats, vulnerabilities, and controls. The system security plan should be reviewed to ensure the system is properly described, the categorization is valid, and the controls are described accurately. The system contingency plan should be reviewed to ensure that the results of testing have been addressed, procedures remain valid, resource requirements are current, and personal responsibilities are accurate.

- *Monitoring Property Losses*: The CISO should establish linkage to the physical property accountability function to ensure that the information security team is aware of losses of information technology equipment. This coordination can also lead to an awareness of physical security violations that have an impact on the security of sensitive information such as office insecurities and physical access violations.

- *Participation of Program Reviews*: When the agency has a program for reviewing the status of organizational programs, the information security program can benefit by including requirements for security as part of program and project reviews that are conducted periodically. Participation in such reviews gives the CISO an opportunity to present agency management a dashboard reflecting security compliance status and overall risk level of the program or project to the same degree that cost, schedule, and performance are addressed.

- *Periodic Performance Measurement*: Security requirements levied on agency executives and managers should be included as performance metrics for semiannual review. Additionally, security metrics for organizational elements should be prepared for quarterly and annual performance reviews. This could include metrics related to their completion of security tasks such as system contingency plan testing, annual controls testing, remediation of POA&M weaknesses, completion of user awareness and role-based training, and identification or formal appointment of personnel assigned significant security responsibilities.

- *Monitoring System Inventory*: The CISO should make provisions for review of the agency inventory of information technology systems annually to monitor for changes. Most agencies rely on quarterly or semiannual data calls to ensure that the inventory is current. The information security function should also position itself to review this updated information for impacts on the security of interconnected or hosted systems. This information can be compared against the results of a discovery scan to identify deltas.

- *Monitor Training Compliance*: To ensure that users are meeting required training requirements and are completing awareness and role-based training, user completion status should be monitored by the information security training and awareness staff throughout the year rather than just as a part of the annual FISMA audit. Associated with this is monitoring user behavior related to the training to ensure that users are adhering to required policies and are applying good security practices.

- *Monitor Corrective Action*: Violations of information security policy, procedures, and rules of behavior by users must be communicated to their supervisors for corrective action. The actions taken (or not taken) by business unit managers and supervisors must be monitored to determine if proper disciplinary action has been taken. This permits the CISO to measure the support of information security requirements by individual managers and business units, and provides an explanation for changes in user behavior (or the lack thereof) in response to security incidents

- *Threat Monitoring*: Threats to government agency information and systems are dynamic, requiring continual monitoring to ensure that protective controls employed by the agency remain viable. The information security function, primarily through the situational awareness capability, must monitor government information sources and industry sites for information on both threats to government agencies and global threats. This should include maintaining an awareness of known vulnerabilities that could potentially affect agency systems, and a process for assessing their impact, prioritizing the agency response in support of business units and system owners

Conclusion

After necessary security controls are put in place, organizations must employ monitoring mechanisms to ensure they remain viable and continue to provide necessary protection over time. The information security staff is charged with overseeing the agency's information security program to ensure that sensitive information is secured continually, not merely at a particular moment in time. To do this effectively, continuous monitoring capabilities must be effectively employed to maintain awareness of vulnerabilities in protective controls whenever they occur. The CISO plays the lead role in achieving this heightened

state of situational awareness through the development and maintenance of a continuous monitoring plan and strategy, which includes a
combination of technologies, processes, and skills to provide continuous and immediate visibility of the security posture of agency systems
and awareness of compliance with the established security policy.

11
LIFE-CYCLE ISSUES

One of the problems in implementing FISMA to date has been that an excessive amount of attention had to be concentrated initially on assessing legacy systems and bringing them into basic compliance. Of course, it is readily recognized that compliance with security requirements is far less expensive to build into systems while in development than it is for systems already in operation. Hence, the most effective way of ensuring compliance is to consider it during system development. It proved difficult to do this in the early days of FISMA, and significant amounts of funding were expended in what appeared to be wasteful efforts to assess legacy systems, the security for which would never be upgraded because of costs. It could be argued that certification and accreditation requirements should have been applied only to new systems and for upgrades of existing systems to avoid such costs.

In fact, to many people, FISMA and certification and accreditation or system authorization are all synonymous. Performance of C&A on a legacy system is less effective than on a system that is being acquired or is under development. This chapter will address how certification and accreditation can actually be leveraged as the primary means of addressing security requirements throughout the life cycle of an information system.

This chapter does not detail how security is integrated into each phase of the system development life cycle. Rather, it is presented to show how FISMA requirements can best be achieved by taking a life-cycle approach to their implementation. In fact, taking a life-cycle approach to the implementation of FISMA is the most practical approach to the security of government information technology systems. The requirements definition phase provides a primary opportunity for identifying system needs for protecting the information it will be processing. The acquisition/development phase should see necessary security controls integrated into the design of the system.

Testing of these security controls is most effectively performed as part of overall testing of the new system prior to its going into production. The operations phase provides ample opportunity to address the security posture of the system and its data, as well as the security impacts of evolving system requirements. Finally, the disposition phase should include provisions for safeguarding sensitive information as part of its decommissioning.

The CISO Role

The IT security function can influence his own fate by preaching in all seasons the need for early involvement of security. This helps him avoid being surprised by new system development efforts or acquisitions that are already well under way. In fact, people should get so tired of hearing his message on early security involvement in projects that they can recite it themselves. His guiding principle should be to be in a position to know about any information technology projects that are being planned, and to ensure he is aware of any "go lives."

Beyond stressing the importance of early security engagement, the CISO must find a way to stay in contact with program offices in order to be alert to upcoming projects and potential system changes. I will explore how he can do this more in Chapter 12. Because information technology investments thrive on funding, the CSIO should knock on all doors until he is accepted as a key player in the business case process. Accomplishing this will not only allow him to be aware of new projects, but will also offer an opportunity to ensure that funding requirements for security are appropriately addressed early in the conception of the project. He can also make a concerted effort to participate in budget planning sessions at his level to permit awareness of, and security involvement in, budget decisions.

In addition to the CIPC process, there are a number of other existing agency processes, with which he must ensure that his security team and his program processes connect. This includes testing, configuration management, change control, information technology strategy development, information technology business needs identification, and acquisition review. Information security has a significant role to play in each of these, and if it currently is not, then the CISO should prioritize integration. The IT security function should have a vote in the configuration control board and the change control process, and should actually be able to veto any change in which security concerns have not been addressed. Additionally, the information security function needs a seat at the table at the information technology strategy council to ensure that the needs of the information security program are considered in long-term planning for information technology. At the forum where business needs are presented for agencywide discussion, concurrence, and evaluation, the CISO can provide input on security impacts that may affect decisions about new initiatives, business needs, and technologies. It will take a significant effort to gain visibility of meetings and sessions that address issues which affect the information security program. Nevertheless, he will need to keep his ears open, and ensure he is on the list of addresses generally invited to all such meetings. The activities of the general counsel is a good model to follow in this regard.

The CISO should also be able to rely on a good relationship with the information technology services organization, which can help increase awareness of projects they are involved with that may have security implications. Of course, for this to be effective, the information technology services staff will need to understand how to identify the actions, activities, or initiatives that require involvement of the information security team, and there must be a relatively high level of trust between the two organizations. The CISO can meet with counterparts in the system development organization and enterprise architecture regularly. If they have planning sessions, encourage them to allow you to sit in first as a learning experience, but then as a regular contributor.

To be effective when attending meetings and boards such as these, the CISO or his representative must be up to date on new methodologies, processes, and technologies and their security impacts. The goal of IT security function participation in meetings and boards should be to effectively influence decision making.

Information Technology Governance

The requirements of the information security program must be addressed as part of an effective system development life cycle (SDLC) methodology. This allows those requirements to be considered along with all other business requirements that are being considered for new systems. When program requirements are integrated into the SDLC methodology and if the SDLC is up to date, useful to users, easy to use, consistent, and practical, then there is increased likelihood that information-security-related needs will be appropriately addressed at the appropriate stage of the system life cycle. This is, of course, the most important expectation the CISO can have for the SDLC process. When the information security function is able to assist in developing or updating the SDLC and PMM (project management process), then there is increased assurance that security requirements, tasks, activities, and artifacts will be comprehensively identified for performance or delivery at the optimum time. In addition, where possible, integrate security activities and deliverables into the agency's project management methodology if there is one separate from the SDLC. It is particularly important to include certification and accreditation activities in the PMM to permit their oversight by the project manager.

In most government agencies, the information security function relies on the CIO for support on taking an operational system off-line when necessary for security reasons or keeping a project from going live when unacceptable security risks exist. Support at this level needs to be promoted in the decision making of authorizing officials regarding the systems for which they are responsible. This support should also ensure that systems are not allowed to go into production without first undergoing security testing and without the concurrence of the information security function.

An effective life-cycle approach to security is supported by the creation of an enterprise architecture that has security fully integrated. Active enforcement of a well-crafted enterprise architecture ensures that the security policy and standards, along with approved solutions, are consistently addressed throughout the enterprise for all information technology projects. In fact, the enterprise architecture is one of the most effective means of ensuring FISMA compliance. Some agencies publish an information technology roadmap that identifies technologies that the agency forecasts for future implementation. The CISO must ensure that security tools and products are included in such forecasts, but more importantly, must ensure that his team is given the opportunity to review proposed technologies for their security impacts before being included in the final roadmap. Ideally, the information security function will employ a process that addresses security impacts, considerations, and requirements of new technologies prior to the appearance of any business need and will integrate them into the roadmap.

In order to address FISMA requirements with respect to the identification of information systems, one must pay strict attention to system definition and categorization. To ensure the validity of the system inventory, be careful about defining new systems. Ensure that they are actually new systems rather than just upgrades or modifications of existing systems. Failure to make this distinction can result in an inflated and inaccurate inventory. Another often-encountered problem is the existence of outdated, seldom-used systems that have not been properly deactivated or retired. You will also need to figure out how to address small office automation systems that process sensitive data in the system inventory. As fully as possible, they should be addressed as part of other systems rather than systems in their own right, in order to take advantage of the existence of control inheritance and to minimize the need for security documentation. The inventory should also be in alignment with the agency's portfolio of major information technology investments as used in the capital planning and investment (CPIC) process. Just as new information technology projects traverse the SDLC or project management methodology, ensure that information security is integrated into the review of Exhibit 300 and other business case review activities to ensure that security is adequately addressed.

One final word about information technology governance: security compliance is most easily achieved when the information technology environment is consolidated and information technology management has centralized authority over the way information technology is employed, maintained, and operated. Without such centralization, the CISO and the information security function must always work harder to ensure information security is included in all information technology projects throughout the agency. When information technology is centralized at the agency level, the implementation and enforcement of an enterprise information security program is greatly enhanced.

Requirements Definition Phase Issues

The CISO must continually reach out to business unit management and project managers to ensure that security is addressed along with the other business drivers affecting the requirements of a system and its design. The goal here is to work closely with system owners to identify business solutions that are secure from the beginning. The primary message to be communicated is that the system security categorization is done early, is done right, and is actually used to drive the decisions about how the system will protect the data it must process, as well as the activities that follow. Security personnel must communicate the need for protecting confidentiality, integrity, and availability of system data and can assist them in understanding this through the use of "what-if" scenarios, based on a clear picture of the business process. The use of the risk assessment methodology should also serve this purpose. Such an approach lends itself to better business unit and project team engagement because it goes beyond merely a statement of NIST SP 800-53 controls requirements and places controls needs in the context of the business itself.

In most every project, it will prove difficult to implement all the security controls normally required for a system irrespective of its categorization. This is because of process parameters, timing considerations, and resource limitations. Therefore, when defining the requirements for the system, the information security team can be helpful by explaining to the project team the process for submission of waivers and exceptions to information security policy requirements. They can also work with the business unit to assist them in identifying compensatory controls to address security impacts when business needs limit the implementation of prescribed controls. The team can also promote an effective approach to building security into system requirements by discouraging business owners from identifying particular solutions rather than specific requirements. They should be made to understand that there may be several solutions to achieving their requirements, and the selection of a specific solution as opposed to merely defining requirements could result in the selection of a less-than-ideal solution for their business need.

As part of this phase, the security team should focus on the review of acquisition documents to ensure that the requirements of information security policy have been satisfied as a basis for acquisition of a compliant design.

Development/Acquisition Phase Issues

A significant consideration in the development/acquisition phase is gaining assurance of the security of code. Remember the need to build in the requirement for use of secure coding practices into acquisition language in order to hold contract developers accountable for delivering secure code. You will also need to ensure that they use tools and processes that protect data during development and apply good design and coding practices. There is a large gap in the security of government data, as numerous and noteworthy incidents have been publicized in which developers using government information have failed to protect the confidentiality of that data, resulting in its compromise through unauthorized disclosure. They should be encouraged to use products that "desensitize" or anonymize any sensitive government data before its use in development and testing. Products such as this have the benefit of protecting sensitive data while closely approximating the characteristics of live data. Contract developers should be required in acquisition specifications to provide assurance that their programmers have been appropriately trained and are competent in secure coding techniques and practices. Inclusion of the security function into the acquisition review process will be necessary in order to ensure that standard security requirements are incorporated into acquisition specifications, and that requests for procurement and statements of work are appropriately reviewed prior to their approval.

In addition to addressing contract specifications for development-related security requirements, you should apply the principle of "trust but verify." You need to have additional assurance of secure code in delivered products by ensuring that code review tools and services are employed, and that the results are incorporated into the assessment of system controls. This can be accomplished as part of certification testing by means of a vulnerability assessment or security test and evaluation. There are a number of products that can be used to review code for common mistakes and vulnerabilities (for instance, cross-site scripting, remote code execution, SQL injection, and format string vulnerabilities). For more sensitive systems, the use of code review services provides an additional level of scrutiny. And, for your most sensitive systems, a combination of these two approaches along with a dedicated code review should be considered. When the quality of code is emphasized by including code review activities and milestones into the SDLC methodology, then the likelihood of secure code is greatly increased. Another approach that can be applied to facilitate the development of secure systems is the use of task order contract vehicles developed and managed by the information security team. This provides a practical path to ensuring that systems undergoing modernization meet security policy requirements and that necessary documentation is developed with requisite quality and timeliness. One of the more valuable inputs that the security team can provide to a project manager is timely information regarding the security of the system design. This is achieved by conducting an independent review of the design and proposed solutions. Often, the use of trained contractors performing independent validation and verification of work products is the most cost-effective way of ensuring that security specifications have been met in the design.

Testing of security controls should be integrated into the overall test plan for any new system coming online. This enhances efficiency of the SDLC development process and allows security testing to be performed in a manner that ensures adequate security testing is performed without unnecessary delays in the project schedule. This is facilitated by integration of the schedules and tasks of security testing into acceptance testing. In addition to modernization efforts, all new technologies must be assessed for security impacts from the perspective of adherence to the information security policy, and products being considered for deployment must undergo security testing before being allowed into production.

Operation and Maintenance Phase Issues

For operational systems, the same approach to testing must be applied for changes that affect security controls protecting the system and its data. A security impact assessment should be conducted in response to any significant change, which will lead to a determination of the scope and type of testing that will be required. Naturally, the process must be thoroughly documented and coordinated, and as a priority must include provisions for identifying the type of changes that constitute a significant change requiring such treatment. Additionally, the security function must also be able to monitor the system for potential vulnerabilities that could trigger the need for changes in security controls.

Providing Project Support

The effort that the information security function expends in supporting system development efforts will normally be far exceeded by the benefits of this involvement. The effectiveness of the effort can be enhanced if a single intake point for information technology projects has been established, and they are a part of it. As indicated earlier, becoming an active part of an overall information technology governance process also facilitates effective engagement in system development projects at the most opportune times.

The information security function is best served through membership in the integrated project team with active participation in all periodic meetings, activities, and planning. In this capacity, security team members must function as team players, and must be prepared to get their hands dirty working together with the other members of the team to solve problems. They must go beyond merely articulating why a solution will not provide requisite security. Security team members must work together with program managers to find solutions that are secure or alternatives to achieve security objectives. Security team members should put priority on helping to keep projects on schedule as much as possible. Full engagement should help them strike a balance between achieving risk-based security and meeting project milestones. This can be facilitated through the development of a security work plan that is integrated into the overall project management plan. This plan should include all certification and accreditation tasks to be performed, the steps required, and the work products to be delivered according to milestones.

Conclusion

Certification and accreditation can serve as the information security team's primary approach to addressing information security in system development and acquisition projects. Rather than mere use for assessment of compliance near the end of the implementation phase, the certification and accreditation process can lead to effective identification of risk-based security controls during requirements definition, and for validating the security of the system design during development.

Once an organization has made the commitment to address security early in the system development life cycle, then the information security function must be prepared to deliver full value to the process. This means that security personnel must have sufficient technical competence to evaluate technologies and to propose solutions and provide advice on specific projects under way. If they are not able to do this, then the greatest opportunity for addressing security in the most cost-effective manner will be lost.

12
OUTREACH

The Federal Information Security Management Act (FISMA) broadly disperses responsibility for information security well beyond the information technology security staff and the information technology operations function. This decentralized apportioning of responsibility represents a substantial departure from the traditional manner in which responsibility for implementation of enterprise information security was viewed. With FISMA, information technology security was no longer the exclusive domain of information technology security staff. Because of this, the engagement and involvement of all members of the organization became a necessity. The CISO, as the official with primary interest in the effective implementation of the agency's information technology security program, now had to reach out to all parties who have an identified role according to the FISMA legislation, to include the agency head, chief information officer, system owner, data owner, approving authority, and general user. In order for the CISO to ensure all these personnel perform their assigned FISMA role, he must ensure that they understand what their responsibilities are and must reach out to them effectively.

Additionally, FISMA's emphasis on risk management has changed the role of the information security function from being security "traffic cops" who make decisions on how security is to be achieved to one more focused on enabling business through the provision of sound security advice. Hence, security is no longer simply a binary formulation. In a significant shift, there is now a requirement that information security specialists understand the role of risk in establishing business needs for security and to enforce compliance with risk-based controls.

FISMA has therefore had an effect on the manner in which information security staff function and operate, with outreach across the organization greatly increasing in importance. The CISO must now look for opportunities for outreach, and must identify issues and activities that permit him to communicate with all those performing roles in making the enterprise information security program a success to ensure that risk to agency assets is effectively managed.

The purpose of this chapter is to share best practices on how the CISO can build relationships with individuals and elements of the organization to successfully share information and foster program support. The following graphic identifies organizational entities with which the CISO should establish strong relationships. (See Figure 12.1.)

This chapter will also address the changes in information security function approaches that permit a transition to risk management from absolute security.

Why the Need for Outreach?

The importance of outreach can best be understood from the perspective of the need to increase the visibility of the enterprise information security program in order to build support for it through the education of those on which the success of the program depends. Outreach efforts support a related need: to help those charged with security responsibilities understand the nature and importance of their role in order to perform it more effectively. To achieve these goals, outreach must be both vertical and horizontal across all elements of the organization, and from the highest echelons of organizational leadership down to the most common user. It must reach beyond internal entities and influence the performance of those who may be external to the organization and yet have a role to play in the security program. Outreach must implement both a top-down as well as a bottom-up approach. Outreach must be more than a completion of a communications project. It must be continuous, and it must be an integrated part of CISO activities and operations of the information security staff.

Building Relationships

As stated previously, the CISO must build relationships with individuals inside and outside the organization to obtain support for the enterprise information security program. To build effective, lasting bridges across the organization, it is better to use positive means

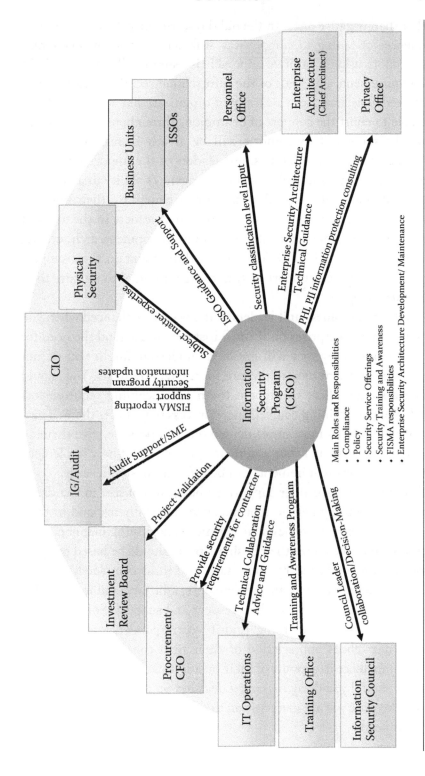

Figure 12.1

rather than negative ones. In the old days, stressing the negative consequences of failing to comply was sufficient, but today, encouraging support using a positive approach is essential. To communicate the requirements and goals of the information security program, you will need assistance from a variety of organizational elements. If you are able to enlist the support of champions throughout the organization, the success of your efforts will be greatly increased. This can be achieved by convincing business leaders of the importance of the effort by explaining its influence on the agency's ability to achieve its organizational goals, as well as the direct benefit on their business unit. Key targets for support should be senior leaders in the areas of information technology operations, system development, architecture, general counsel, and CFO. You can work to maintain their support by recognizing their support early and often in order to nurture their continued support.

Support of business unit leaders will always be enhanced when you avoid springing surprises on them. Most will understand the need for what you are doing, but will not be as understanding if you do not give them sufficient time to prepare for the requirements. You should make a special effort to prepare them for upcoming requirements (such as a new training course, a new process that affects them, a new set of controls that must implemented, etc.). If possible, give them an opportunity to discuss with you their opinions about how implementation of the new requirements can be effected most efficiently.

You can also gain their support by being responsive to the deadlines they are being held to. For instance, efficiently respond to their requests for security reviews in a timely and useful manner. Your response must recognize their business need, should be based on good coordination conducted by your staff, and must completely address the issue they are raising. Incomplete, late, arbitrary, and inapplicable staff work will not win you their respect and support. Sometimes an action such as hand-carrying priority correspondence can demonstrate your office's appreciation of their time constraints as well as your competence in support of their business need. Under no circumstances should you delay making a decision on a request for approval simply because you are in a position to do so. Prioritize responsiveness to their needs.

To demonstrate your commitment to customer support, you should widely publish contact numbers for key personnel in the information security program according to the issues, activities, and functions in which they are involved. This communicates your intention to make members of your team readily available to provide direct support when they have questions.

You should always be aware of initiatives that business units have under way and seek to contribute to them. Your team can reach out by offering to take part in all-hands meetings, open houses, off-site meetings, and the like to address security-related issues that may be of interest to members of the business unit staff.

The CISO should seek to establish positive relationships with all senior agency managers as a priority. However, there will be difficult relationships that the CISO will be tempted to consider hopeless and declare them as not worth the effort. Although senior leaders may not be inclined to offer support to you in what you are doing, you cannot afford to give up on any of them. Do not burn bridges with those who oppose your efforts or those who withdraw their support for some reason. Rather, increase your efforts to win back their support.

When dealing with business unit management, do not rely exclusively on e-mail even though it may be easy and fast. Take the time to make phone calls and to conduct face-to-face visits, preferably to their offices. This shows that you are willing to take the time to ensure that your message is clear and to do more than the minimum to communicate effectively.

You must always follow up on promises you make to business leaders. When they ask you a question, it is always important to get back to them as soon as possible with answers they can understand. Once again, you cannot afford to unnecessarily hold up their initiatives and actions because of unfilled promises or lack of a timely response.

Because security is usually thought of in negative terms by those outside the security community—at least when getting started—keep things positive as much as the situation allows. There will be times when you will have to address negative issues with them, so you should always to seek to present positive messages to create some semblance of balance, and to avoid a reaction of "Oh, here comes trouble" in their dealings with you.

Make it a point to meet with all newly assigned managers and executives to ensure they know who you are and give them a chance to get an introduction to the information security program from the horse's mouth. Early familiarization meetings provide you with an opportunity to ensure that they know and understand the role with which they have been charged.

One way the CISO can help build his relationship with customers is to create tools and aids that help them meet their security responsibilities. Create handbooks that guide them in how to engage security processes in simple terms. Provide them with access to databases and repositories of useful security information (the system inventory and the POA&M come to mind). Develop templates and samples that ease the burden of data gathering. Ensure that forms are easy to understand and complete in order to reduce the need for follow-up questions.

One of your main objectives in working with your customers is to give them stability. One of the least desirable qualities of a security organization is instability and inconsistency in providing security guidance. Seek always to provide a consistent message, useful information that is readily available when it is needed, and limit changes in guidance and instructions to the absolute minimum.

Another way to improve the effectiveness of working relationships with your supported customers is to seek feedback on how you are doing. This can be as simple as asking questions about your office's performance when engaging business leaders, or as formal as conducting a survey to obtain feedback from your customers on a wide range of support issues. Mature agencies will have established performance measurement programs that you can rely on for regular feedback. However, this should not be considered the most effective or the only means of obtaining input from your customers. Create an atmosphere where you are both reaching out to your customers for this information and in which they will not hesitate to provide you will useful performance information, both positive and negative.

The IT security function in most government agencies must deal with satellite offices and remote locations. Therefore, you must be prepared to travel to make frequent and regular contact with your customers who are located in other facilities, other cities, or perhaps other countries. Use these visits to understand how the requirements you have established are implemented away from headquarters, and to hear how remote offices and locations may be struggling to comply. The frequency of these trips will naturally depend on the size of the organization and the complexity of the security requirements with which each must deal. However, the initial visit to each site should occur as early as you can arrange it, and can then settle into a routine schedule over time.

Another means of making initial contact with key business leaders is to use training as a door opener. Under FISMA, most executives and senior leaders are charged with information security responsibilities. Consequently, each is required to undergo regular training to ensure they understand those responsibilities. While it would be easy enough to prepare a presentation to e-mail them to meet this requirement, it is always better to set up a desk-side meeting if possible. This is particularly true for newly assigned executives, who may appreciate the opportunity to put questions directly to you and to get to know you. Short (thirty minutes or less) briefings should be offered to newly assigned executives within the first 30 days of their assignment to ensure you are able to connect before they become deeply immersed in the routine of their positions and before they are called upon to perform their security responsibilities. This is particularly true in the case of authorizing officials and system owners. You must seek to get on the schedule of newly assigned agency heads and deputies even though it will be much more difficult to achieve due to the demands of their positions. Nevertheless, with good organization you can cover much ground with these senior officials in fifteen minutes. Consider providing them with targeted, succinct awareness to reinforce your message.

You can use annual awareness training as a means of highlighting security with business unit executives. For example, you can schedule meetings with them to discuss participation levels and at the same time seize the opportunity to discuss other program-related issues. Similarly, you can use policy changes or updates as an opportunity for meeting with business unit leaders to focus their attention on the change and to ensure they are aware of its potential impact.

Best Practices

There are numerous leading practices I have come to know and rely on in my experience with implementing the provisions of FISMA.

I offer the following for consideration with the hope they might be beneficial.

- When meeting with your customers, try to anticipate what issues may surface in order to be prepared to address them effectively, and to perhaps provide them an answer or solve a problem as early in the process as possible. It pays to do your homework and demonstrates your ability to be responsive to their needs. This can be accomplished by having an effective staff that maintains awareness of issues and stays abreast of initiatives under way in supported organizations.

- When problems arise, be prepared to take the first step to solve them. Waiting until a troubled customer comes to you is not the path to rapid resolution of problems. Deal with these situations as they arise, by taking the time to schedule a meeting or making a phone call directly to the customer to prevent miscommunication, and to prevent the issue from being blown out of proportion.

- The tasks of the CISO can be lessened by finding ways for your customers to more easily comply with security policies and program requirements. Not only can you provide helpful guidance, instructions, and tools as stated earlier, but within your capability, you can offer them resources to achieve your objectives. For instance, the CISO organization is well served by having a task order contract available to its customers through which information security services can be accessed easily and quickly. Or perhaps your office can centrally perform certain security services in order to lower costs and ensure that timelines are met. Putting yourself into a position to be able to offer such gifts will take planning and may take time due to the agency budgeting process. Nevertheless, it is clearly worth considering, not only for the sake of efficiency but also for building good customer relationships.

- When you have a problem with an organization, it is best to deliver bad news face to face. This requires not only boldness but also sensitivity. If you have identified significant problems with security of systems or major compliance issues, then take the time to prepare, schedule a meeting, and address the issue directly with the responsible executive.

- To gain their support, your customers must understand the reason for the requirements you establish for them and actions you take. This should be clear in your communications, both written and verbal.
- It never hurts to reward good customers. Single out those who are the biggest supporters of your program, reward them in some way for their support, and make a big deal of it. The idea is to draw attention not only to their individual achievement, but also to the security program itself.
- When you meet with executives for the first time, make it a point to give them your direct phone number so that they can contact you immediately and without filtering by aministrative staff. This also helps you establish trust with your business unit counterparts and customers. You can also improve the way your customers see your program by singling out early successes and declaring victory. This marks progress and builds a basis for continuous improvement of the program.
- Another potential approach is to consider issues requiring solution that can be addressed collectively. This approach permits using group involvement to find solutions and has the advantage of building collective support for the program. Think about how you can establish short-term, limited-scope work groups, planning teams, and task forces to support program goals and objectives. Of course, this will necessitate implementation or at least consideration of any recommendations such groups provide. Failure to respond appropriately can work against every good intention you may have initially had.
- Support your customers' needs for information about the program by making policies and guidance readily accessible and easy to understand and use. This can be achieved through the construction of a well-organized Web site that offers useful information that is well indexed and written in language that helps rather than hinders your customers.
- Another means of building support is to measure the performance of your customers in supporting the program. This must be done with sensitivity, recognizing that you will be

measuring failure as well as success. You will need to be skill-ful in identifying good metrics that your customers agree actually measure useful behavior and outcomes. You will need to administer the scoring process with fairness and transpar-ency, and must share positive results across the organiza-tion, while addressing substandard performance by omission in agencywide reporting, and through direct feedback with discussion of possible courses of action for improvement. The use of scorecards to objectively measure the performance of organizational elements or systems can be highly effective if well coordinated and administered. However, scoring of the performance of individual support of the program should be avoided as it can be interpreted to be on one hand vindictive or overtly flattering on the other.

CISO Awareness

Customer outreach begins with the CISO. To be effective, the CISO must try to understand the customer's situation and his business driv-ers in the context of his customers' needs and expectations from the information security program.

The CISO must be highly visible across the organization and, in particular, to senior management. He must do this by being seen, by participating in agency functions and forums, and through written communications. The CISO's name should be known by the entire workforce, and his face recognizable by the overwhelming majority.

He should invest the time to meet as many members of the staff as possible, and all managers and executives. Because of the time demands of the position, he will need to be persistent in his efforts to meet as many people as possible.

The CISO is expected to keep up with what is going on across the agency, even if it has little to do with security. This will enable him to relate to the issues his customers have to deal with and allow him to think about the pertinence of security as it relates to actual agency initiatives and activities. This awareness helps the CISO identify hot buttons and organizational or cultural landmines. Along the same lines, he must also be aware of hot buttons of personnel with whom he must interrelate. Perhaps they have had unpleasant experiences with security in the past. Often he will not know what sets them off until after the fact; but once it occurs, he should never forget the offending subject and the triggering action.

As he increases his knowledge of various agency-specific issues, he should find ways to highlight the attendant security considerations and implications. That is the CISO's job, and he may be the only official in a position to make key points at opportune times.

He can highlight security impacts by looking for security aspects of current events and relating them to actual situations in which his customers are involved. He can leverage widely known external events such as disasters, events, and incidents to enhance understanding of security principles and threats and further his outreach efforts.

He must make an effort to stay on top of what is happening across the organization through regular reading of news releases, agency announcements, minutes of meetings, blogs, and messages from key executives. The closer the message he is attempting to communicate can map to a current need, the greater its chance of being heard and remembered.

The CISO also has an obligation to keep senior management at the highest levels informed of the status of the program and to update them on the security impacts on key agency initiatives. The CISO should work to get on the calendar of the agency head on a periodic basis. In many cases, this will go beyond traditional patterns of communication, so he will have to build support for it one brick at a time. It may help to pitch it as a periodic program review.

The CISO will have to continually strive to educate himself on the nature of the agency's mission and how it is performed. It will not be necessary to be proficient in actually performing the technical work, but he will have to be able follow a conversation or speak intelligently about what is happening in the agency in terms of new initiatives, and to see their security impacts.

The CISO should also be aware of regular meetings, which he can attend to find out what is going on across the agency, to be in a position to offer assistance, and to increase his exposure. He should try to accept every invitation to participate, present, or attend. He can build on many existing forums for outreach and communication purposes, including the configuration management board, enterprise architecture council, privacy council, information technology business forum, and information technology strategic planning board. He should become part of these bodies and provide briefings and updates on the program whenever appropriate. On the other hand, if forums such as these do not exist, it may be worthwhile for the CISO to exert any influence he has to create them.

Finally, CISO awareness must also extend beyond the agency. To prepare for his outreach efforts, the CISO should reach out to other government agencies to seek best practices that could be beneficial in meeting agency customer needs. The CISO can contact his counterparts in other government agencies and share lessons learned and can seek out thought leaders to determine if there are other approaches available that might not have been considered. To further prepare for his role as agency advisor on all aspects of the information security program, he must stay in the loop on potential major government initiatives, legislation that is being considered, and new technologies, methodologies, and ideas that he may need to address. His efforts to stay in touch can be facilitated by volunteering to participate in cross-government working groups, by participation in panels, and by attending worthwhile conferences.

Information Sharing

The sharing of information about the information security program is one of the primary drivers for outreach. Timely dissemination of clearly understandable information about program objectives, status, security issues, and program initiatives should be an important consideration for the CISO. For example, he should consider that a solution or approach that proved successful for one program office could be applied just as successfully elsewhere, and perhaps even agencywide, thus warranting broader dissemination. This also serves the purpose of highlighting the support of an office as a positive example to other offices.

In the aftermath of incidents or audit findings, it may be beneficial to share information that would be helpful to offices that are required to cope with them. Lessons learned in other offices in response to security incidents can be maximized to demonstrate how the incident can be avoided elsewhere. Effective corrective actions should be shared to promote a more effective response to audit findings.

When sharing information about the information security program, it is necessary that the message be consistent. The information communicated by one member of the CISO's staff must be reliably consistent or the credibility of the office will be eroded, and the impact of the message will be lost. Information disseminated by the CISO's staff must be consistent not only with that which is verbally disseminated by other staff members, but also with the IT security policy, and with other written guidance that has been posted relating to the topic.

One idea for sharing information is a security road show. Associated with new information technology program initiatives, processes, or policies, consistency of message can be achieved by developing a communications plan and organizing a team to communicate information about it.

Some of the most fundamental, important information that should be shared is making sure business unit leaders know what the security organization does and how it can help them meet their mission objectives. You cannot assume that business unit managers understand your organization's reason for being, its mission, its organization, or even what the information security program is. Help them understand by reaching out to them and providing a short desk-side briefing to clarify any misconceptions they may have. Senior executives need to know about the information security organization, what it is responsible for, and perhaps just as important, what it is not responsible for. Dispelling myths that have arisen over time should be another objective of outreach to senior leaders. Additionally, outreach can help you ensure they know your role, your people, and your plans for improving the security of agency information systems and data.

A good means for information sharing is to schedule occasional meetings with business unit executives. This allows you to update them on program initiatives and activities and gives them the opportunity to bring up any issues and concerns that may have arisen.

For every initiative, you should consider the message that needs to go along with it. This can be as informal as merely thinking through how the action is going to be received, what response it may evoke, and how misunderstandings and misperceptions can be avoided. Two things that I have found helpful are to have a disinterested individual read the communication and provide you with feedback. He can let you know if the thinks it should be worded differently or the emphasis should be changed. Also, if there is a group that you can use to provide feedback on your initiative prior to committing to it, you may be well served to use it. Such a group can serve as a "murder board" and force you to defend your plans before they are implemented. For wide-ranging and long-term initiatives that will have a significant impact on the effectiveness of the program and activities of the organization, a communications plan is a must. It should address the nature of how the details of the initiative are going to be disseminated, who is responsible for communicating messages, the timing of communications, etc. Formally documenting your approach to rolling out a new project or initiative forces you to address issues that may have been overlooked previously, and provides a means for obtaining feedback from your staff, the CIO, and other vested stakeholders on how to best get out the word. Also remember to include communications tasks in all of your project plans.

Other ways to share information about the information security program include posting regular messages-of-the-day or daily notes that draw attention to information security program activities (such as upcoming training opportunities) or to a specific need (being alert for spear phishing attacks). More intentional efforts can result in information campaigns, open houses, security days, or information security conferences in which information security is the specific focus of attention. An information security newsletter is another effective means of drawing attention to the program and sharing information about it, to include security tips, lessons learned, and best practices. The same goes for the use of an information security Web page, which you should consider essential.

One of the best ways to share information is through the use of the ISSO structure, which represents the primary information security program stakeholders. Use of this network allows you to build consensus and to communicate program information rapidly and clearly to those who are most attuned to the need and can relay it most effectively to their organizations.

Preparing for Outreach

The CISO may be the face and voice of information security outreach efforts, but must be fully supported by his staff in order to be effective in this. All outreach activities need to be coordinated within the team so that all are aware of the initiative, understand it, and have the information necessary to support it, and to share information about it when required. Individuals who deal with members of the information security team are rapidly frustrated when staff give mixed signals and provide inconsistent information. This can be facilitated by organizing internally to enhance avenues for effective internal coordination in providing assistance and customer service externally.

Organizationally, you can designate POCs or leads for key customer organizations, depending on their importance to the information security program. Short of this, each team member should be required to identify a counterpart in every major supported organization to facilitate contact and information sharing. The CISO can maintain visibility of the effectiveness of staff support for outreach and customer service by requiring staff to report periodically on their customer contacts as part of regular office activity reporting.

At the individual level, it will be necessary to continually train staff in the importance of customer service. Serving the customer's needs should become an automatic reflex for the information security staff and must be a way of life. Each staff member must be taught to overcome their potential desire to tell customers "No, you can't." Rather than a compliance focused response like this, they should always begin by finding ways to help customers do their jobs, to keep their projects on schedule, and to meet their goals and objectives.

Staff must understand that with respect to customer service, every member of the team is an educator with a graduate degree in the information security program. The importance of customer service can be reinforced by its inclusion in individual performance plans as a separate critical performance element.

The CISO can foster customer service efforts by including it when defining success for his organization as he also gains the ability to define success for his customers. He must be able to do this not only to meet their immediate security-related needs (e.g., certification of the XYZ System), but also in terms of success, that is, their ability to meet their mission-related goals.

Finally, nothing is more beneficial to the success of customer outreach and service than excellent performance. Excellent delivery of all services from the information security function must be a priority, and overperforming in response to customers is not a vice.

Summary

The purpose of the CISO's outreach efforts is to ensure that all personnel who perform security functions actually know that security is part of their job, their business, and their projects. To be successful in this effort, outreach must be intentional, carefully considered, and thoroughly planned for in order to disseminate and receive the lifeblood of information the program requires. The information security staff must be focused on providing assistance to all who are supported or must support the enterprise information security program. Success in outreach depends on this focus on the customer by each member of the security team. This quest for outreach and information sharing must go beyond the CISO and his staff and must percolate to all who are required to perform information-security-related functions, to include the CIO, DAAs, system owners, ISSOs, and project managers.

PART III
SUMMARY

In the eight years since its passage, the Federal Information Security Management Act of 2002 (FISMA) has had a significant impact on information security management across the U.S. Government. Without FISMA, one can safely conclude that government information security management would appear far different than it does today. But one would have to also recognize that FISMA's impact has had both positive and negative aspects.

Negative Effects of FISMA

Although improvements resulting from FISMA are many and significant, that is not to say that the FISMA experience has been positive in every respect. In fact, the importance and relative success of FISMA have certainly been questioned to varying degrees at various points throughout its history.

The most important negative impact resulting from FISMA was a movement away from security risk management toward a focus on security compliance. At least in the early years after its passage, the response of government agencies to FISMA reflected this compliance focus and diminished the effectiveness of agency efforts to actually improve the security of government information and systems. This was unfortunate because, as noted in Chapter 1, the stated purpose of FISMA was to establish a comprehensive framework for securing information resources. However, rather than employing risk management principles included in the legislation, agencies responded by directing their efforts to address requirements identified in reporting guidance, which did not necessarily lead to establishment of holistic information security programs.

Strangely, the response of most government agencies to FISMA requirements was paradoxical. While their response focused on compliance, targeting activities necessary to meet OMB-prescribed reporting requirements, significant funds were expended to meet these minimal, compliance-based requirements. Many critics decried these expenditures as merely "checking the box," when in fact they could have been employed to good effect on managing real risks to their information resources. By losing sight of the actual purpose of FISMA and effective security risk management, agencies in many cases unnecessarily wasted critical resources in the process.

While there will always be a compliance aspect for any federal mandate, FISMA compliance efforts must always be balanced against the requirements of an overall enterprise information security risk management perspective. In fact, compliance should be considered one of several business drivers when considering risk to individual information systems, and when considering risk from an enterprise perspective.

Total costs for implementing FISMA since 2002 have not been calculated. Nevertheless, it is clear that it has been costly. As noted earlier, resources have not always been used effectively, and agency strategies for implementing FISMA have resulted in inefficient use of resources in many cases. However, one should not lose sight of the fact that not only compliance but also security requires the expenditure of resources. How effectively these resources are utilized is a function of good management principles, including careful planning. The FISMA legislation established accountability for effective security management, and provided a mechanism for identifying business needs for security and a means for quantifying necessary resources through its linkage to agency capital planning and investment control processes. FISMA proved to be a successful means of focusing management attention on information security and reaped the resource benefit this focus brought with it.

In hindsight, expectations for FISMA have proved unrealistic. No piece of legislation could possibly hope to meet the inflated expectations of critics of government information security efforts. Many consider it a failure because of his emphasis on compliance; others for failing to deliver "real security" in response to current threats. And still others for gobbling up government resources that could have been used more effectively for other purposes.

Improvements Resulting from FISMA

Arguably, a number of important improvements in government information security can be traced directly back to the enactment of FISMA. To varying degrees, agency information security programs have experienced improvements in the areas listed in the following table.

FISMA Improvements

Management support of information security
Institution of the agency-level CISO role
Decentralization of responsibilities for information security
Information security programs consistency
Broad acceptance of user training and awareness
Coordinated incident response
Identification of security controls baselines
Consistency of security controls testing
Contingency planning processes
Systems inventory processes
Quality and comprehensiveness of security documentation
Integration of security into the SDLC
Information security body of knowledge
Protection of personal privacy
CIO/OIG coordination
Government-level security coordination

These improvements are detailed in the following paragraphs:

- *Management Support of Information Security*: Prior to FISMA, dependable management support could only be found in the Department of Defense and other agencies with national security missions. Today, senior leaders are much more aware of the purpose of, need for, and their responsibilities concerning information security, thanks in large part to the manner in which FISMA has been implemented. Because of the emphasis on the need to comply with FISMA, there are few senior managers today who do not know what FISMA is. To them, the term "FISMA" has the connotation of meeting minimally acceptable security requirements in order to be compliant. Because of Congress' and OMB's emphasis on information security through FISMA, senior agency leaders have likewise learned the need to place emphasis on it at the agency level.

- *Institution of the Agency-Level CISO Role*: FISMA codified the requirement for a dedicated senior manager to oversee the enterprise information security program. Prior to FISMA, if there was an agency POC for information security, it was hidden in the bowels of the organization. FISMA for the first time established an independent information security function in support of the Chief Information Security Officer. This elevated the visibility and importance of the position and aligned with best practices employed in the private sector.

- *Decentralization of Information Security*: Thanks to FISMA, information security responsibilities now extend beyond those officials who previously "owned" information security. Primary responsibility for implementation of information security controls now resides with system owners, that is, business unit managers who exercise responsibility for the business process supported by the system. Additionally, enhanced responsibilities have now been instituted for the agency head and authorizing official to ensure that information security roles for these senior positions are defined.

- *Consistency of Government Information Security Programs*: Now that there is a legislative requirement that all executive branch agencies must adhere to, the level of consistency of agency-level information security management efforts has greatly improved. This is compounded by the fact that all agencies have migrated toward the common standards and guidance provided by NIST and toward implementation of Information Systems Security Line of Business (ISSLOB)-approved solutions. So, it is now possible to compare the requirements for and the effectiveness of information security programs in the great majority of agencies and departments.

- *User Training and Awareness*: Government agencies now more than ever emphasize training for those performing specialized information security tasks, and awareness for all system users. NIST's standardized curriculum is now generally followed, and ISSLOB course content is now widely employed in government agencies.

- *Incident Response Capabilities*: The ability of government agencies to identify, respond to, contain, investigate, and report security-related events and incidents has improved due to FISMA. Agencies now follow Department of Homeland Security guidance for categorizing and reporting security incidents, and routinely share incident-related information across agency boundaries, greatly improving coordination of incidents and events.

- *Identification of Security Controls Baselines*: FISMA mandated the implementation of security controls to protect the confidentiality, integrity, and availability of government information and information systems according to risk. OMB emphasized the importance of this requirement in its reporting guidance, and NIST has developed a comprehensive set of minimum security controls requirements in SP 800-53.

- *Security Controls Testing*: FISMA has brought on a common approach to the testing of security controls. Requirements for regular testing of controls contained in FISMA led OMB to emphasize annual testing of controls according to risk, and also led to the development of NIST SP 800-53A, which now provides detailed test procedures to guide testing personnel.

- *Contingency Planning*: Agencies have improved their level of contingency planning for their information systems as a result of the passage of FISMA. Once again, FISMA stated the requirement, OMB focused attention on the requirement through its reporting guidance, and NIST documented processes and approaches for implementing the requirement. Consequently, owners of the great majority of government systems develop contingency plans for their systems, and test those plans at least annually.

- *Systems Inventory*: FISMA has led to improvements in the capability of agencies to define, categorize, and track the accuracy of its inventory of information systems. Additionally, agencies have used the inventory as a means of managing their portfolios, implementing their enterprise architectures, and for cost-effectively modernizing systems to meet business requirements.

- *Security Documentation*: Requirements for security documentation resulting from FISMA have led to the development of standards for key security artifacts applicable to government information systems. Today, it is possible to review an up-to-date security plan, risk assessment, security test and evaluation, plan of action and milestones, and authorization letter for practically every major government information system.

- *Integration of Security into the SDLC*: FISMA mandated that agencies should integrate their security efforts into existing agency processes, including their approach to the system development life cycle. Consequently, security activities and artifacts are fully mapped to agency system development methodologies and IT project management plans in most government agencies. This has led to improved cost-effectiveness in the identification, integration, and implementation of risk-based security controls into the design of government information systems.

- *Information Security Body of Knowledge*: FISMA tasked the National Institute of Standards and Technology with development of information security standards and guidelines. Subsequently, NIST developed a much-used library of special publications to guide government agencies in the implementation of FISMA requirements. Additionally, NIST information security publications are widely accepted outside the U.S. Government, and are used widely in the private sector both domestically and internationally.

- *Protection of Privacy*: FISMA's establishment of the Information Security and Privacy Advisory Board ensured close linkage of security and privacy requirements. This was reinforced in OMB's inclusion of privacy in annual FISMA reporting. Consequently, needs for personal privacy have become an integrated part of security processes and practices. For example, privacy impact assessments are included in the information system authorization packages in most government agencies.

- *CIO/OIG Coordination:* The FISMA requirement for the agency OIG to conduct an annual evaluation of the agency information security program and practices to determine their effectiveness, coupled with the manner in which the annual FISMA report is structured, has meant that agency CIO staffs and OIG personnel have had to coordinate more closely on their FISMA-related activities. Additionally, agencies are required by FISMA to coordinate selected security incidents with OIG's investigations staff. In sum, this increased level of coordination has improved the ability of most agencies to integrate the efforts of their auditors into the overall approach to improving the effectiveness of their information security programs.

- *Government-Level Security Coordination:* Because of FISMA's assignment of roles and responsibilities along with OMB's centralizing role from the reporting perspective, there is far better coordination at the U.S. Government level than was ever been achieved previously. This situation was reinforced by the integrative role that the Department of Homeland Security has come to play and the manner in which NIST was able to standardize information security guidance across all sectors of the federal government.

FISMA and the Future

As we have seen, FISMA has led to myriad improvements in federal information security. Despite its shortcomings, FISMA as legislation has been a notable success. Nevertheless, eight years under the current statute have shown that several aspects warrant updating, if for no other reason than because government agencies have changed, as has the nature of the threat to government information systems and data.

- *Continuous Monitoring Focus:* There is a general consensus today that FISMA needs to be updated to reflect needs for real-time monitoring of risks to government information and systems. The idea here is that if continuous monitoring requirements are included in the legislation, there will be a greater likelihood that reporting requirements will reflect the need to report on metrics that actually improve the security of information resources. While OMB's reporting instructions for FY 2010 satisfy this view, the requirement is for the law itself to better address continuous monitoring needs.

- *Strengthening the Authority of the CISO*: The authority of the CISO according to FISMA as currently written derives from the Chief Information Officer and is restricted to "ensuring" compliance with FISMA. This means that the CISO must coordinate corrective action with agency managers when there is a failure to comply with the agency information security policy. Many have proposed that the CISO's authority for ensuring compliance be expanded to authorize actual enforcement of FISMA requirements. Ostensibly, this expanded authority would give the CISO the ability to cite violations of the information security policy and procedures. Similarly, other proposals pertain to the removal of the linkage between the CIO and the CISO found in the current statute. In some agencies, this could result in improved organizational effectiveness. However, this proposal also presents a risk of the CISO being considered by the CIO and his organization as an external auditor, thereby reducing his effectiveness in the process.

- *Accountability for Information Security*: Some legislators have proposed FISMA update legislation that would put teeth in FISMA requirements for management accountability. There have been proposals to include information security requirements in the job descriptions of all political appointees, senior executive service personnel, senior-level personnel, and managers, and enable the forfeiture of performance bonuses for failing to meet information security requirements based on the assessment of the Chief Information Security Officer. While this would clearly strengthen the authority of the CISO to ensure information security accountability at the personal level, it could be viewed by those falling under its purview as excessive and unnecessary.

No matter what changes to FISMA are proposed, or which modifications eventually find their way into a revision to the legislation, it is doubtful that any of them will substantially change its fabric. Although there is discussion about the need to update and strengthen FISMA, there is little serious conversation about the need to do away with FISMA entirely. The Federal Information Security Management Act has filled an important void for U.S. government agencies, and is now accepted as a critical business driver for agency information security programs and activities. The framework that FISMA provides, and the information security management principles and processes that it has spawned, ensure that it will continue to drive U.S. Government information security for at least the next decade.

Appendix A: The FISMA Legislation

TITLE III—INFORMATION SECURITY*

SEC. 301. INFORMATION SECURITY.

(a) SHORT TITLE.—This title may be cited as the "Federal Information Security Management Act of 2002".

(b) INFORMATION SECURITY.—

    (1) IN GENERAL.—Chapter 35 of title 44, United States Code, is amended by adding at the end the following new subchapter:

SUBCHAPTER III—INFORMATION SECURITY

§ 3541. Purposes The purposes of this subchapter are to—

(1) provide a comprehensive framework for ensuring the effectiveness of information security controls over information resources that support Federal operations and assets;

(2) recognize the highly networked nature of the current Federal computing environment and provide effective governmentwide management and oversight of the related information security risks, including coordination of information

---

* Extracted from http://csrc.nist.gov/drivers/documents/FISMA-final.pdf.

security efforts throughout the civilian, national security, and law enforcement communities;

(3) provide for development and maintenance of minimum controls required to protect Federal information and information systems;

(4) provide a mechanism for improved oversight of Federal agency information security programs;

(5) acknowledge that commercially developed information security products offer advanced, dynamic, robust, and effective information security solutions, reflecting market solutions for the protection of critical information infrastructures important to the national defense and economic security of the nation that are designed, built, and operated by the private sector; and

(6) recognize that the selection of specific technical hardware and software information security solutions should be left to individual agencies from among commercially developed products.

§ 3542. Definitions

(a) IN GENERAL.—Except as provided under subsection (b), the definitions under section 3502 shall apply to this subchapter.

(b) ADDITIONAL DEFINITIONS.—As used in this subchapter:

(1) The term 'information security' means protecting information and information systems from unauthorized access, use, disclosure, disruption, modification, or destruction in order to provide—

(A) integrity, which means guarding against improper information modification or destruction, and includes ensuring information nonrepudiation and authenticity;

(B) confidentiality, which means preserving authorized restrictions on access and disclosure, including means for protecting personal privacy and proprietary information; and

(C) availability, which means ensuring timely and reliable access to and use of information.

(2)(A) The term 'national security system' means any information system (including any telecommunications system) used or operated by an agency or by a contractor of an agency, or other organization on behalf of an agency—

    (i) the function, operation, or use of which—

        (I) involves intelligence activities;

        (II) involves cryptologic activities related to national security;

        (III) involves command and control of military forces;

        (IV) involves equipment that is an integral part of a weapon or weapons system; or

        (V) subject to subparagraph (B), is critical to the direct fulfillment of military or intelligence missions; or

    (ii) is protected at all times by procedures established for information that have been specifically authorized under criteria established by an Executive order or an Act of Congress to be kept classified in the interest of national defense or foreign policy.

(B) Subparagraph (A)(i)(V) does not include a system that is to be used for routine administrative and business applications (including payroll, finance, logistics, and personnel management applications).

(3) The term 'information technology' has the meaning given that term in section 11101 of title 40.

§ 3543. Authority and functions of the Director

(a) IN GENERAL.—The Director shall oversee agency information security policies and practices, including—

    (1) developing and overseeing the implementation of policies, principles, standards, and guidelines on information security, including through ensuring timely agency adoption of and compliance with standards promulgated under section 11331 of title 40;

    (2) requiring agencies, consistent with the standards promulgated under such section 11331 and the requirements of this subchapter, to identify and provide information

security protections commensurate with the risk and magnitude of the harm resulting from the unauthorized access, use, disclosure, disruption, modification, or destruction of—

(A) information collected or maintained by or on behalf of an agency; or

(B) information systems used or operated by an agency or by a contractor of an agency or other organization on behalf of an agency;

(3) coordinating the development of standards and guidelines under section 20 of the National Institute of Standards and Technology Act (15 U.S.C. 278g–3) with agencies and offices operating or exercising control of national security systems (including the National Security Agency) to assure, to the maximum extent feasible, that such standards and guidelines are complementary with standards and guidelines developed for national security systems;

(4) overseeing agency compliance with the requirements of this subchapter, including through any authorized action under section 11303 of title 40, to enforce accountability for compliance with such requirements;

(5) reviewing at least annually, and approving or disapproving, agency information security programs required under section 3544(b);

(6) coordinating information security policies and procedures with related information resources management policies and procedures;

(7) overseeing the operation of the Federal information security incident center required under section 3546; and

(8) reporting to Congress no later than March 1 of each year on agency compliance with the requirements of this subchapter, including—

(A) a summary of the findings of evaluations required by section 3545;

(B) an assessment of the development, promulgation, and adoption of, and compliance with, standards developed under section 20 of the National Institute of

Standards and Technology Act (15 U.S.C. 278g-3) and promulgated under section 11331 of title 40;

(C) significant deficiencies in agency information security practices;

(D) planned remedial action to address such deficiencies; and

(E) a summary of, and the views of the Director on, the report prepared by the National Institute of Standards and Technology under section 20(d)(10) of the National Institute of Standards and Technology Act (15 U.S.C. 278g–3).

(b) NATIONAL SECURITY SYSTEMS.—Except for the authorities described in paragraphs (4) and (8) of subsection (a), the authorities of the Director under this section shall not apply to national security systems.

(c) DEPARTMENT OF DEFENSE AND CENTRAL INTELLIGENCE AGENCY SYSTEMS.—(1) The authorities of the Director described in paragraphs (1) and (2) of subsection (a) shall be delegated to the Secretary of Defense in the case of systems described in paragraph (2) and to the Director of Central Intelligence in the case of systems described in paragraph (3).

(2) The systems described in this paragraph are systems that are operated by the Department of Defense, a contractor of the Department of Defense, or another entity on behalf of the Department of Defense that processes any information the unauthorized access, use, disclosure, disruption, modification, or destruction of which would have a debilitating impact on the mission of the Department of Defense.

(3) The systems described in this paragraph are systems that are operated by the Central Intelligence Agency, a contractor of the Central Intelligence Agency, or another entity on behalf of the Central Intelligence Agency that processes any information the unauthorized access, use, disclosure, disruption, modification, or destruction of which would have a debilitating impact on the mission of the Central Intelligence Agency.

§ 3544. Federal agency responsibilities

(a) IN GENERAL.—The head of each agency shall—

    (1) be responsible for—

        (A) providing information security protections commensurate with the risk and magnitude of the harm resulting from unauthorized access, use, disclosure, disruption, modification, or destruction of—

            (i) information collected or maintained by or on behalf of the agency; and

            (ii) information systems used or operated by an agency or by a contractor of an agency or other organization on behalf of an agency;

        (B) complying with the requirements of this subchapter and related policies, procedures, standards, and guidelines, including—

            (i) information security standards promulgated under section 11331 of title 40; and

            (ii) information security standards and guidelines for national security systems issued in accordance with law and as directed by the President; and

        (C) ensuring that information security management processes are integrated with agency strategic and operational planning processes;

    (2) ensure that senior agency officials provide information security for the information and information systems that support the operations and assets under their control, including through—

        (A) assessing the risk and magnitude of the harm that could result from the unauthorized access, use, disclosure, disruption, modification, or destruction of such information or information systems;

        (B) determining the levels of information security appropriate to protect such information and information systems in accordance with standards promulgated under section 11331 of title 40, for information security classifications and related requirements;

        (C) implementing policies and procedures to cost-effectively reduce risks to an acceptable level; and

(D) periodically testing and evaluating information security controls and techniques to ensure that they are effectively implemented;

(3) delegate to the agency Chief Information Officer established under section 3506 (or comparable official in an agency not covered by such section) the authority to ensure compliance with the requirements imposed on the agency under this subchapter, including—

(A) designating a senior agency information security officer who shall—

(i) carry out the Chief Information Officer's responsibilities under this section;

(ii) possess professional qualifications, including training and experience, required to administer the functions described under this section;

(iii) have information security duties as that official's primary duty; and

(iv) head an office with the mission and resources to assist in ensuring agency compliance with this section;

(B) developing and maintaining an agencywide information security program as required by subsection (b);

(C) developing and maintaining information security policies, procedures, and control techniques to address all applicable requirements, including those issued under section 3543 of this title, and section 11331 of title 40;

(D) training and overseeing personnel with significant responsibilities for information security with respect to such responsibilities; and

(E) assisting senior agency officials concerning their responsibilities under paragraph (2);

(4) ensure that the agency has trained personnel sufficient to assist the agency in complying with the requirements of this subchapter and related policies, procedures, standards, and guidelines; and

(5) ensure that the agency Chief Information Officer, in coordination with other senior agency officials, reports annually to the agency head on the effectiveness of the

agency information security program, including progress of remedial actions.

(b) AGENCY PROGRAM.—Each agency shall develop, document, and implement an agencywide information security program, approved by the Director under section 3543(a)(5), to provide information security for the information and information systems that support the operations and assets of the agency, including those provided or managed by another agency, contractor, or other source, that includes—

(1) periodic assessments of the risk and magnitude of the harm that could result from the unauthorized access, use, disclosure, disruption, modification, or destruction of information and information systems that support the operations and assets of the agency;

(2) policies and procedures that—

(A) are based on the risk assessments required by paragraph (1);

(B) cost-effectively reduce information security risks to an acceptable level;

(C) ensure that information security is addressed throughout the life cycle of each agency information system; and

(D) ensure compliance with—

(i) the requirements of this subchapter;

(ii) policies and procedures as may be prescribed by the Director, and information security standards promulgated under section 11331 of title 40;

(iii) minimally acceptable system configuration requirements, as determined by the agency; and

(iv) any other applicable requirements, including standards and guidelines for national security systems issued in accordance with law and as directed by the President;

(3) subordinate plans for providing adequate information security for networks, facilities, and systems or groups of information systems, as appropriate;

(4) security awareness training to inform personnel, including contractors and other users of information systems that support the operations and assets of the agency, of—

    (A) information security risks associated with their activities; and

    (B) their responsibilities in complying with agency policies and procedures designed to reduce these risks;

(5) periodic testing and evaluation of the effectiveness of information security policies, procedures, and practices, to be performed with a frequency depending on risk, but no less than annually, of which such testing—

    (A) shall include testing of management, operational, and technical controls of every information system identified in the inventory required under section 3505(c); and

    (B) may include testing relied on in [n] evaluation under section 3545;

(6) a process for planning, implementing, evaluating, and documenting remedial action to address any deficiencies in the information security policies, procedures, and practices of the agency;

(7) procedures for detecting, reporting, and responding to security incidents, consistent with standards and guidelines issued pursuant to section 3546(b), including—

    (A) mitigating risks associated with such incidents before substantial damage is done;

    (B) notifying and consulting with the Federal information security incident center referred to in section 3546; and

    (C) notifying and consulting with, as appropriate—

        (i) law enforcement agencies and relevant Offices of Inspector General;

        (ii) an office designated by the President for any incident involving a national security system; and

        (iii) any other agency or office, in accordance with law or as directed by the President; and

(8) plans and procedures to ensure continuity of operations for information systems that support the operations and assets of the agency.

(c) AGENCY REPORTING.—Each agency shall—

(1) report annually to the Director, the Committees on Government Reform and Science of the House of Representatives, the Committees on Governmental Affairs and Commerce, Science, and Transportation of the Senate, the appropriate authorization and appropriations committees of Congress, and the Comptroller General on the adequacy and effectiveness of information security policies, procedures, and practices, and compliance with the requirements of this subchapter, including compliance with each requirement of subsection (b);

(2) address the adequacy and effectiveness of information security policies, procedures, and practices in plans and reports relating to—

(A) annual agency budgets;

(B) information resources management under subchapter 1 of this chapter;

(C) information technology management under subtitle III of title 40;

(D) program performance under sections 1105 and 1115 through 1119 of title 31, and sections 2801 and 2805 of title 39;

(E) financial management under chapter 9 of title 31, and the Chief Financial Officers Act of 1990 (31 U.S.C. 501 note; Public Law 101–576) (and the amendments made by that Act);

(F) financial management systems under the Federal Financial Management Improvement Act (31 U.S.C. 3512 note); and

(G) internal accounting and administrative controls under section 3512 of title 31, (known as the 'Federal Managers Financial Integrity Act'); and

(3) report any significant deficiency in a policy, procedure, or practice identified under paragraph (1) or (2)—

(A) as a material weakness in reporting under section 3512 of title 31; and

(B) if relating to financial management systems, as an instance of a lack of substantial compliance under the Federal Financial Management Improvement Act (31 U.S.C. 3512 note).

(d) PERFORMANCE PLAN.—(1) In addition to the requirements of subsection (c), each agency, in consultation with the Director, shall include as part of the performance plan required under section 1115 of title 31 a description of—

(A) the time periods, and

(B) the resources, including budget, staffing, and training, that are necessary to implement the program required under subsection (b).

(2) The description under paragraph (1) shall be based on the risk assessments required under subsection (b)(2)(1).

(e) PUBLIC NOTICE AND COMMENT.—Each agency shall provide the public with timely notice and opportunities for comment on proposed information security policies and procedures to the extent that such policies and procedures affect communication with the public.

§ 3545. *Annual independent evaluation*

(a) IN GENERAL.—(1) Each year each agency shall have performed an independent evaluation of the information security program and practices of that agency to determine the effectiveness of such program and practices.

(2) Each evaluation under this section shall include—

(A) testing of the effectiveness of information security policies, procedures, and practices of a representative subset of the agency's information systems;

(B) an assessment (made on the basis of the results of the testing) of compliance with—

(i) the requirements of this subchapter; and

(ii) related information security policies, procedures, standards, and guidelines; and

(C) separate presentations, as appropriate, regarding information security relating to national security systems.

(b) INDEPENDENT AUDITOR.—Subject to subsection (c)—

    (1) for each agency with an Inspector General appointed under the Inspector General Act of 1978, the annual evaluation required by this section shall be performed by the Inspector General or by an independent external auditor, as determined by the Inspector General of the agency; and

    (2) for each agency to which paragraph (1) does not apply, the head of the agency shall engage an independent external auditor to perform the evaluation.

(c) NATIONAL SECURITY SYSTEMS.—For each agency operating or exercising control of a national security system, that portion of the evaluation required by this section directly relating to a national security system shall be performed—

    (1) only by an entity designated by the agency head; and

    (2) in such a manner as to ensure appropriate protection for information associated with any information security vulnerability in such system commensurate with the risk and in accordance with all applicable laws.

(d) EXISTING EVALUATIONS.—The evaluation required by this section may be based in whole or in part on an audit, evaluation, or report relating to programs or practices of the applicable agency.

(e) AGENCY REPORTING.—(1) Each year, not later than such date established by the Director, the head of each agency shall submit to the Director the results of the evaluation required under this section.

    (2) To the extent an evaluation required under this section directly relates to a national security system, the evaluation results submitted to the Director shall contain only a summary and assessment of that portion of the evaluation directly relating to a national security system.

(f) PROTECTION OF INFORMATION.—Agencies and evaluators shall take appropriate steps to ensure the protection of information which, if disclosed, may adversely affect information security. Such protections shall be commensurate with the risk and comply with all applicable laws and regulations.

(g) OMB REPORTS TO CONGRESS.—(1) The Director shall summarize the results of the evaluations conducted under this section in the report to Congress required under section 3543(a)(8).

(2) The Director's report to Congress under this subsection shall summarize information regarding information security relating to national security systems in such a manner as to ensure appropriate protection for information associated with any information security vulnerability in such system commensurate with the risk and in accordance with all applicable laws.

(3) Evaluations and any other descriptions of information systems under the authority and control of the Director of Central Intelligence or of National Foreign Intelligence Programs systems under the authority and control of the Secretary of Defense shall be made available to Congress only through the appropriate oversight committees of Congress, in accordance with applicable laws.

(h) COMPTROLLER GENERAL.—The Comptroller General shall periodically evaluate and report to Congress on—

(1) the adequacy and effectiveness of agency information security policies and practices; and

(2) implementation of the requirements of this subchapter.

§ 3546. Federal information security incident center

(a) IN GENERAL.—The Director shall ensure the operation of a central Federal information security incident center to—

(1) provide timely technical assistance to operators of agency information systems regarding security incidents, including guidance on detecting and handling information security incidents;

(2) compile and analyze information about incidents that threaten information security;

(3) inform operators of agency information systems about current and potential information security threats, and vulnerabilities; and

(4) consult with the National Institute of Standards and Technology, agencies or offices operating or exercising control of national security systems (including the National Security Agency), and such other agencies or

offices in accordance with law and as directed by the President regarding information security incidents and related matters.

(b) NATIONAL SECURITY SYSTEMS.—Each agency operating or exercising control of a national security system shall share information about information security incidents, threats, and vulnerabilities with the Federal information security incident center to the extent consistent with standards and guidelines for national security systems, issued in accordance with law and as directed by the President.

§ 3547. National security systems The head of each agency operating or exercising control of a national security system shall be responsible for ensuring that the agency—

(1) provides information security protections commensurate with the risk and magnitude of the harm resulting from the unauthorized access, use, disclosure, disruption, modification, or destruction of the information contained in such system;

(2) implements information security policies and practices as required by standards and guidelines for national security systems, issued in accordance with law and as directed by the President; and

(3) complies with the requirements of this subchapter.

§ 3548. Authorization of appropriations There are authorized to be appropriated to carry out the provisions of this subchapter such sums as may be necessary for each of fiscal years 2003 through 2007.

§ 3549. Effect on existing law Nothing in this subchapter, section 11331 of title 40, or section 20 of the National Standards and Technology Act (15 U.S.C. 278g–3) may be construed as affecting the authority of the President, the Office of Management and Budget or the Director thereof, the National Institute of Standards and Technology, or the head of any agency, with respect to the authorized use or disclosure of information, including with regard to the protection of personal privacy under section 552a of title 5, the disclosure of information under section 552 of title 5, the management and disposition of records under chapters 29, 31, or 33 of title 44, the management of

information resources under subchapter I of chapter 35 of this title, or the disclosure of information to the Congress or the Comptroller General of the United States. While this subchapter is in effect, subchapter II of this chapter shall not apply.

(2) CLERICAL AMENDMENT.—The table of sections at the beginning of such chapter 35 is amended by adding at the end the following:

SUBCHAPTER III—INFORMATION SECURITY

Sec.
3541. Purposes.
3542. Definitions.
3543. Authority and functions of the Director.
3544. Federal agency responsibilities.
3545. Annual independent evaluation.
3546. Federal information security incident center.
3547. National security systems.
3548. Authorization of appropriations.
3549. Effect on existing law.

(c) INFORMATION SECURITY RESPONSIBILITIES OF CERTAIN AGENCIES.—
  (1) NATIONAL SECURITY RESPONSIBILITIES.—
    (A) Nothing in this Act (including any amendment made by this Act) shall supersede any authority of the Secretary of Defense, the Director of Central Intelligence, or other agency head, as authorized by law and as directed by the President, with regard to the operation, control, or management of national security systems, as defined by section 3542(b)(2) of title 44, United States Code.
    (B) Section 2224 of title 10, United States Code, is amended—
      (i) in subsection (b), by striking "(b) OBJECTIVES AND MINIMUM REQUIREMENTS.—(1)" and inserting "(b) OBJECTIVES OF THE PROGRAM.—";
      (ii) in subsection (b), by striking paragraph (2); and

> > > (iii) in subsection (c), in the matter preceding paragraph (1), by inserting ", including through compliance with subchapter III of chapter 35 of title 44" after "infrastructure".

> (2) ATOMIC ENERGY ACT OF 1954.—Nothing in this Act shall supersede any requirement made by or under the Atomic Energy Act of 1954 (42 U.S.C. 2011 et seq.). Restricted data or formerly restricted data shall be handled, protected, classified, downgraded, and declassified in conformity with the Atomic Energy Act of 1954 (42 U.S.C. 2011 et seq.).

SEC. 302. MANAGEMENT OF INFORMATION TECHNOLOGY.

> (a) IN GENERAL.—Section 11331 of title 40, United States Code, is amended to read as follows:

§ 11331. Responsibilities for Federal information systems standards
> (a) STANDARDS AND GUIDELINES.—
> > (1) AUTHORITY TO PRESCRIBE.—Except as provided under paragraph (2), the Secretary of Commerce shall, on the basis of standards and guidelines developed by the National Institute of Standards and Technology pursuant to paragraphs (2) and (3) of section 20(a) of the National Institute of Standards and Technology Act (15 U.S.C. 278g–3(a)), prescribe standards and guidelines pertaining to Federal information systems.
> > (2) NATIONAL SECURITY SYSTEMS.—Standards and guidelines for national security systems (as defined under this section) shall be developed, prescribed, enforced, and overseen as otherwise authorized by law and as directed by the President.
> (b) MANDATORY REQUIREMENTS.—
> > (1) AUTHORITY TO MAKE MANDATORY.—Except as provided under paragraph (2), the Secretary shall make standards prescribed under subsection (a)(1) compulsory and binding to the extent determined necessary by the Secretary to improve the efficiency of operation or security of Federal information systems.

(2) REQUIRED MANDATORY STANDARDS.—(A) Standards prescribed under subsection (a)(1) shall include information security standards that—

   (i) provide minimum information security requirements as determined under section 20(b) of the National Institute of Standards and Technology Act (15 U.S.C. 278g–3(b)); and

   (ii) are otherwise necessary to improve the security of Federal information and information systems.

   (B) Information security standards described in sub-paragraph (A) shall be compulsory and binding.

(c) AUTHORITY TO DISAPPROVE OR MODIFY.—The President may disapprove or modify the standards and guidelines referred to in subsection (a)(1) if the President determines such action to be in the public interest. The President's authority to disapprove or modify such standards and guidelines may not be delegated. Notice of such disapproval or modification shall be published promptly in the Federal Register. Upon receiving notice of such disapproval or modification, the Secretary of Commerce shall immediately rescind or modify such standards or guidelines as directed by the President.

(d) EXERCISE OF AUTHORITY.—To ensure fiscal and policy consistency, the Secretary shall exercise the authority conferred by this section subject to direction by the President and in coordination with the Director of the Office of Management and Budget.

(e) APPLICATION OF MORE STRINGENT STANDARDS.—The head of an executive agency may employ standards for the cost-effective information security for information systems within or under the supervision of that agency that are more stringent than the standards the Secretary prescribes under this section if the more stringent standards—

(1) contain at least the applicable standards made compulsory and binding by the Secretary; and

(2) are otherwise consistent with policies and guidelines issued under section 3543 of title 44.

(f) DECISIONS ON PROMULGATION OF STANDARDS. —The decision by the Secretary regarding the promulgation of any standard under this section shall occur not later than 6 months after the submission of the proposed standard to the Secretary by the National Institute of Standards and Technology, as provided under section 20 of the National Institute of Standards and Technology Act (15 U.S.C. 278g–3).

(g) DEFINITIONS.—In this section:

    (1) FEDERAL INFORMATION SYSTEM.—The term 'Federal information system' means an information system used or operated by an executive agency, by a contractor of an executive agency, or by another organization on behalf of an executive agency.

    (2) INFORMATION SECURITY.—The term 'information security' has the meaning given that term in section 542(b)(1) of title 44.

    (3) NATIONAL SECURITY SYSTEM.—The term 'national security system' has the meaning given that term in section 3542(b)(2) of title 44.

(b) CLERICAL AMENDMENT.—The item relating to section 11331 in the table of sections at the beginning of chapter 113 of such title is amended to read as follows:

    11331. Responsibilities for Federal information systems standards.

SEC. 303. NATIONAL INSTITUTE OF STANDARDS AND TECHNOLOGY.

Section 20 of the National Institute of Standards and Technology Act (15 U.S.C. 278g–3), is amended by striking the text and inserting the following:

(a) IN GENERAL.—The Institute shall—

    (1) have the mission of developing standards, guidelines, and associated methods and techniques for information systems;

    (2) develop standards and guidelines, including minimum requirements, for information systems used or operated by an agency or by a contractor of an agency or other

organization on behalf of an agency, other than national security systems (as defined in section 3542(b)(2) of title 44, United States Code); and

(3) develop standards and guidelines, including minimum requirements, for providing adequate information security for all agency operations and assets, but such standards and guidelines shall not apply to national security systems.

(b) MINIMUM REQUIREMENTS FOR STANDARDS AND GUIDELINES.—

The standards and guidelines required by subsection (a) shall include, at a minimum—

(1)(A) standards to be used by all agencies to categorize all information and information systems collected or maintained by or on behalf of each agency based on the objectives of providing appropriate levels of information security according to a range of risk levels;

(B) guidelines recommending the types of information and information systems to be included in each such category; and

(C) minimum information security requirements for information and information systems in each such category;

(2) a definition of and guidelines concerning detection and handling of information security incidents; and

(3) guidelines developed in conjunction with the Department of Defense, including the National Security Agency, for identifying an information system as a national security system consistent with applicable requirements for national security systems, issued in accordance with law and as directed by the President.

(c) DEVELOPMENT OF STANDARDS AND GUIDELINES.—In developing standards and guidelines required by subsections (a) and (b), the Institute shall—

(1) consult with other agencies and offices and the private sector (including the Director of the Office of Management and Budget, the Departments of Defense and Energy, the National Security Agency, the General Accounting Office, and the Secretary of Homeland Security) to assure—

(A) use of appropriate information security policies, procedures, and techniques, in order to improve information security and avoid unnecessary and costly duplication of effort; and

(B) that such standards and guidelines are complementary with standards and guidelines employed for the protection of national security systems and information contained in such systems;

(2) provide the public with an opportunity to comment on proposed standards and guidelines;

(3) submit to the Secretary of Commerce for promulgation under section 11331 of title 40, United States Code—

(A) standards, as required under subsection (b)(1)(A), no later than 12 months after the date of the enactment of this section; and

(B) minimum information security requirements for each category, as required under subsection (b)(1)(C), no later than 36 months after the date of the enactment of this section;

(4) issue guidelines as required under subsection (b)(1)(B), no later than 18 months after the date of the enactment of this section;

(5) to the maximum extent practicable, ensure that such standards and guidelines do not require the use or procurement of specific products, including any specific hardware or software;

(6) to the maximum extent practicable, ensure that such standards and guidelines provide for sufficient flexibility to permit alternative solutions to provide equivalent levels of protection for identified information security risks; and

(7) to the maximum extent practicable, use flexible, performance-based standards and guidelines that permit the use of off-the-shelf commercially developed information security products.

(d) INFORMATION   SECURITY   FUNCTIONS.—The Institute shall—

(1) submit standards developed pursuant to subsection (a), along with recommendations as to the extent to which

these should be made compulsory and binding, to the Secretary of Commerce for promulgation under section 11331 of title 40, United States Code;

(2) provide technical assistance to agencies, upon request, regarding—

   (A) compliance with the standards and guidelines developed under subsection (a);

   (B) detecting and handling information security incidents; and

   (C) information security policies, procedures, and practices;

(3) conduct research, as needed, to determine the nature and extent of information security vulnerabilities and techniques for providing cost-effective information security;

(4) develop and periodically revise performance indicators and measures for agency information security policies and practices;

(5) evaluate private sector information security policies and practices and commercially available information technologies to assess potential application by agencies to strengthen information security;

(6) assist the private sector, upon request, in using and applying the results of activities under this section;

(7) evaluate security policies and practices developed for national security systems to assess potential application by agencies to strengthen information security;

(8) periodically assess the effectiveness of standards and guidelines developed under this section and undertake revisions as appropriate;

(9) solicit and consider the recommendations of the Information Security and Privacy Advisory Board, established by section 21, regarding standards and guidelines developed under subsection (a) and submit such recommendations to the Secretary of Commerce with such standards submitted to the Secretary; and

(10) prepare an annual public report on activities undertaken in the previous year, and planned for the coming year, to carry out responsibilities under this section.

(e) DEFINITIONS.—As used in this section—
  (1) the term 'agency' has the same meaning as provided in section 3502(1) of title 44, United States Code;
  (2) the term 'information security' has the same meaning as provided in section 3542(b)(1) of such title;
  (3) the term 'information system' has the same meaning as provided in section 3502(8) of such title;
  (4) the term 'information technology' has the same meaning as provided in section 11101 of title 40, United States Code; and
  (5) the term 'national security system' has the same meaning as provided in section 3542(b)(2) of title 44, United States Code.

(f) AUTHORIZATION OF APPROPRIATIONS.—There are authorized to be appropriated to the Secretary of Commerce $20,000,000 for each of fiscal years 2003, 2004, 2005, 2006, and 2007 to enable the National Institute of Standards and Technology to carry out the provisions of this section.

SEC. 304. INFORMATION SECURITY AND PRIVACY ADVISORY BOARD.

Section 21 of the National Institute of Standards and Technology Act (15 U.S.C. 278g–4), is amended—
  (1) in subsection (a), by striking "Computer System Security and Privacy Advisory Board" and inserting "Information Security and Privacy Advisory Board";
  (2) in subsection (a)(1), by striking "computer or telecommunications" and inserting "information technology";
  (3) in subsection (a)(2)—
    (A) by striking "computer or telecommunications technology" and inserting "information technology"; and
    (B) by striking "computer or telecommunications equipment" and inserting "information technology";
  (4) in subsection (a)(3)—
    (A) by striking "computer systems" and inserting "information system"; and

(B) by striking "computer systems security" and inserting "information security";

(5) in subsection (b)(1) by striking "computer systems security" and inserting "information security";

(6) in subsection (b) by striking paragraph (2) and inserting the following:

"(2) to advise the Institute, the Secretary of Commerce, and the Director of the Office of Management and Budget on information security and privacy issues pertaining to Federal Government information systems, including through review of proposed standards and guidelines developed under section 20; and

(7) in subsection (b)(3) by inserting "annually" after "report";

(8) by inserting after subsection (e) the following new subsection:

"(f) The Board shall hold meetings at such locations and at such time and place as determined by a majority of the Board.";

(9) by redesignating subsections (f) and (g) as subsections (g) and (h), respectively; and

(10) by striking subsection (h), as redesignated by paragraph (9), and inserting the following:

"(h) As used in this section, the terms 'information system' and 'information technology' have the meanings given in section 20.".

SEC. 305. TECHNICAL AND CONFORMING AMENDMENTS.

(a) COMPUTER SECURITY ACT.—Section 11332 of title 40, United States Code, and the item relating to that section in the table of sections for chapter 113 of such title, are repealed.

(b) FLOYD D. SPENCE NATIONAL DEFENSE AUTHOR-IZATION ACT FOR FISCAL YEAR 2001.—The Floyd D. Spence National Defense Authorization Act for Fiscal Year 2001 (Public Law 106–398) is amended by striking section 1062 (44 U.S.C. 3531 note).

(c) PAPERWORK REDUCTION ACT.—(1) Section 3504(g) of title 44, United States Code, is amended—

(A) by adding "and" at the end of paragraph (1);

(B) in paragraph (2)—

    (i) by striking "sections 11331 and 11332(b) and (c) of title 40" and inserting "section 11331 of title 40 and subchapter II of this chapter"; and

    (ii) by striking "; and" and inserting a period; and

(C) by striking paragraph (3).

(2) Section 3505 of such title is amended by adding at the end—

  (c) INVENTORY OF MAJOR INFORMATION SYSTEMS.
—(1) The head of each agency shall develop and maintain an inventory of major information systems (including major national security systems) operated by or under the control of such agency.

    (2) The identification of information systems in an inventory under this subsection shall include an identification of the interfaces between each such system and all other systems or networks, including those not operated by or under the control of the agency.

    (3) Such inventory shall be—

      (A) updated at least annually;

      (B) made available to the Comptroller General; and

      (C) used to support information resources management, including—

        (i) preparation and maintenance of the inventory of information resources under section 3506(b)(4);

        (ii) information technology planning, budgeting, acquisition, and management under section 3506(h), subtitle III of title 40, and related laws and guidance;

        (iii) monitoring, testing, and evaluation of information security controls under subchapter II;

        (iv) preparation of the index of major information systems required under section 552(g) of title 5, United States Code; and

        (v) preparation of information system inventories required for records management under chapters 21, 29, 31, and 33.

(4) The Director shall issue guidance for and oversee the implementation of the requirements of this subsection.

(3) Section 3506(g) of such title is amended—

(A) by adding "and" at the end of paragraph (1);

(B) in paragraph (2)—

(i) by striking "section 11332 of title 40" and inserting "subchapter II of this chapter"; and

(ii) by striking "; and" and inserting a period; and

(C) by striking paragraph (3).

TITLE IV—AUTHORIZATION OF APPROPRIATIONS AND EFFECTIVE DATES

SEC. 401. AUTHORIZATION OF APPROPRIATIONS.

Except for those purposes for which an authorization of appropriations is specifically provided in title I or II, including the amendments made by such titles, there are authorized to be appropriated such sums as are necessary to carry out titles I and II for each of fiscal years 2003 through 2007.

SEC. 402. EFFECTIVE DATES.

(a) TITLES I AND II.—

(1) IN GENERAL.—Except as provided under paragraph (2), titles I and II and the amendments made by such titles shall take effect 120 days after the date of enactment of this Act.

(2) IMMEDIATE ENACTMENT.—Sections 207, 214, and 215 shall take effect on the date of enactment of this Act.

Appendix B: OMB FISMA Reporting Guidelines*

EXECUTIVE OFFICE OF THE PRESIDENT
OFFICE OF MANAGEMENT AND BUDGET
WASHINGTON, D.C. 20503

M-10-15   April 21, 2010

MEMORANDUM FOR HEADS OF EXECUTIVE
DEPARTMENTS AND AGENCIES

FROM: Jeffrey Zients
              Deputy Director for Management
              Vivek Kundra
              Federal Chief Information Officer
              Howard A. Schmidt
              Cybersecurity Coordinator

SUBJECT: FY 2010 Reporting Instructions for the Federal Information Security Management Act and Agency Privacy Management

This memorandum provides instructions for meeting your agency's FY 2010 reporting requirements under the Federal Information Security Management Act of 2002 (FISMA) (Title III, Pub. L. No. 107-347).

---

* Extracted from http://www.whitehouse.gov/sites/default/files/omb/assets/memoranda-2010/m10-15.pdf.

It also includes reporting instructions on your agency's privacy management program.

Agencies need to be able to continuously monitor security-related information from across the enterprise in a manageable and actionable way. Chief Information Officers (CIOs), Chief Information Security Officers (CISOs), and other agency management all need to have different levels of this information presented to them in ways that enable timely decision making. To do this, agencies need to automate security-related activities, to the extent possible, and acquire tools that correlate and analyze security-related information. Agencies need to develop automated risk models and apply them to the vulnerabilities and threats identified by security management tools.

The Department of Homeland Security (DHS) will provide additional operational support to Federal agencies in securing Federal systems. DHS will monitor and report agency progress to ensure the effective implementation of this guidance.

For FY 2010, FISMA reporting for agencies through CyberScope, due November 15, 2010, will follow a three-tiered approach:

1. Data feeds directly from security management tools
2. Government-wide benchmarking on security posture
3. Agency-specific interviews

This three-tiered approach is a result of the task force established in September 2009 to develop new, outcome-focused metrics for information security performance for Federal agencies. This task force concentrated on developing metrics that would advance the security posture of agencies and departments.

Understanding that metrics are a policy statement about what Federal entities should concentrate resources on, the task force developed metrics that will push agencies to examine their risks and make substantial improvements in their security. Participants in the task force included: the Federal CIO Council; the Council of Inspectors General on Integrity and Efficiency; the National Institute of Standards and Technology; the Department of Homeland Security; the Information Security and Privacy Advisory Board; and the President's Cybersecurity Coordinator. In addition, the Government Accountability Office (GAO) served as an observer to this taskforce.

CyberScope is the platform for the FY 2010 FISMA submission process. Agencies should note that a Personnel Identity Verification card, compliant with Homeland Security Presidential Directive 12, is required for access to CyberScope. No FISMA submissions will be accepted outside of CyberScope. For information related to Cyber-Scope, please visit: https://max.omb.gov/community/x/EgQrFQ.

CIOs, Inspectors General, and the Senior Agency Officials for Privacy will all report through CyberScope. Microagencies will also report using the automated collection tool. CyberScope training dates for all agencies will be published on the Max Portal page. The due date for FISMA reporting through CyberScope is November 15, 2010.

1. Data feeds directly from security management tools

Agencies should not build separate systems for reporting. Any reporting should be a by-product of agencies' continuous monitoring programs and security management tools. Therefore, the task force has developed a set of data elements that can be easily fed from agency security monitoring systems. Agencies are already required to report each quarter. Beginning with the 3rd quarter of FY2010, agencies will be required to report on this new information. Agencies will continue to report on this information through the FY2010 annual reporting cycle. Beginning January 1, 2011, agencies will be required to report on this new information monthly.

The new data feeds will include summary information, not detailed information, in the following areas for CIOs:

- Inventory
- Systems and Services
- Hardware
- Software
- External Connections
- Security Training
- Identity Management and Access

If agencies are unable to provide direct feeds from their security management tools, they will be required to provide a data feed through an Excel template as an XML upload to CyberScope. In the coming months, an XML schema for uploading the required data and a roadmap for the development of this reporting structure will be released.

Please note that microagencies (agencies with fewer than 100 full time equivalent employees) are asked to report a subset of this data. When such agencies log into CyberScope, they will be presented with the subset.

2. Government-wide benchmarking on security posture

A set of questions on the security posture of the agencies will also be asked in CyberScope. All agencies, except microagencies, will be required to respond to these questions in addition to the data feeds described above.

As in previous years, for the annual report, the agency head should submit an electronic copy of an official signed letter that provides a comprehensive overview of the adequacy and effectiveness of information security policies, procedures, and practices, and compliance with the requirements of FISMA for the agency. CyberScope allows for the submissions of these letters. Agency reports must reflect the agency head's determination of the adequacy and effectiveness of information security and privacy policies, procedures, and practices.

3. Agency-specific interviews

As a follow-up to the questions described above, a team of government security specialists will interview all agencies individually on their respective security postures.

These interviews will be focused on specific threats that each agency faces as a function of its unique mission. The information collected in these interviews will also inform the FY 2010 Report on FISMA to the Congress.

This process is designed to shift our efforts away from a culture of paperwork reports. The focus must be on implementing solutions that actually improve security.

Inspectors General Reporting

The Inspectors General (IGs) assisted the task force in a parallel effort to update and strengthen the metrics collected by the IGs. The effort focused on the agencies' management performance, in line with the requirements of FISMA. The IGs will assess agency performance in the following programs:

- Certification and Accreditation
- Configuration Management
- Security Incident Management
- Security Training
- Remediation/Plans of Actions and Milestones
- Remote Access
- Identity Management
- Continuous Monitoring
- Contractor Oversight
- Contingency Planning

Senior Agency Officials for Privacy Reporting

Agencies should also submit the following information related to OMB Memorandum M-07-16, of May 22, 2007, "Safeguarding Against and Responding to the Breach of Personally Identifiable Information."* This information should be provided in separate documents submitted through CyberScope and should include the following items for your agency:

- Breach notification policy if it has changed significantly since last year's report;
- Progress update on eliminating unnecessary use of Social Security Numbers; and
- Progress update on review and reduction of holdings of personally identifiable information.

Agency staff may contact Matt Coose, matt.coose@dhs.gov, or Suzanne Lightman, slightman@omb.eop.gov, with questions.

Attachment:

- FY 2010 Frequently Asked Questions on Reporting for FISMA

---

* http://www.whitehouse.gov/omb/memoranda/fy2007/m07-16.pdf.

FY 2010 Frequently Asked Questions on Reporting for the
Federal Information Security Management Act and
Agency Privacy Management*

Sending Reports to Congress and GAO

1. When should my agency send our annual report to Congress and the Government Accountability Office (GAO)?

After review by and notification from OMB, agencies shall forward their transmittal letter with a report generated by CyberScope to the appropriate Congressional Committees. Transmittal of agency reports to Congress shall be made by, or be consistent with guidance from, the agency's Congressional or Legislative Affairs office to the following: Committees on Oversight and Government Reform and Science and Technology of the House, the Committees on Government Affairs and Commerce, Science, and Transportation of the Senate, and the Congressional authorization and appropriations committees for each individual agency. In prior years, the Committees have provided to OMB specific points of contact for receiving the reports. As in the past, if such are provided to OMB, we will notify the agencies. In

---

* Extracted from http://www.whitehouse.gov/sites/default/files/omb/assets/
memoranda_2010/m10-15.pdf.

addition, agencies must forward a copy of their printed reports to the Government Accountability Office (GAO).

Submission Instructions and Templates

2. Which set of questions should my agency fill out in CyberScope?

All agencies, except for microagencies, should complete the Chief Information (CIO), Inspector General (IG) and Senior Agency Official for Privacy (SAOP) questions in CyberScope for submission to OMB no later than November 15, 2010.

Microagencies (i.e., agencies employing 100 or fewer FTEs) should answer the abbreviated questions for their annual report. Micro-agencies will be automatically presented with the correct questions within CyberScope.

Please note that only submissions through CyberScope will be accepted by OMB.

3. When should program officials, SAOPs, CIOs, and IGs share the results of their reviews?

While the goal of FISMA is stronger agency- and Government-wide security, information regarding an agency's information security pro-gram should be shared as it becomes available. This helps promote timely correction of weaknesses in the agency's information systems and resolution of issues. Waiting until the completion of a report or the year's end does not promote stronger information system security.

As in previous years, the agency head should submit a signed letter that provides a comprehensive overview of the adequacy and effec-tiveness of information security policies, procedures, and practices, and compliance with the requirements of FISMA for the agency. CyberScope will require that agencies upload a PDF of this letter with the agency head's signature prior to accepting the agency's FY 2010 report submission.

4. Should agencies set an internal FISMA reporting cut-off date?

Yes. OMB suggests agencies set an internal cut-off date for data col-lection and report preparation. A cut-off date should permit adequate time for meaningful internal review and comment and resolution of any disputes before finalizing the agency's report to OMB. With respect to an IG's review of the CIO's or SAOP's work product, such review does not in itself fulfill FISMA's requirement for IGs to independently evaluate an agency's program including testing the effectiveness of a representative subset of the agency's information systems.

5. Why are there questions in CyberScope that do not correspond to a NIST SP 800-53 security control?

Not all FISMA questions concern NIST SP 800-53 compliance. OMB, in our management role under FISMA, is looking at the current maturity level of cyber security in the agencies, not just the compliance. The intention is for the questions to evolve over the years as cyber security matures.

6. Is the use of CyberScope mandatory?

Yes, OMB will only accept submissions through CyberScope. Full instructions for the use of the tool will be available by May 2010 along with a test version. Webinar training on the use of CyberScope will also be available by May.

Additional information, including a project schedule and detailed CyberScope FAQs, will be made available on the Max portal at: https://max.omb.gov/community/x/EgQrFQ

Security Reporting

7. Must agencies report at both an agency wide level and by individual component?

Yes. Agencies must provide an overall agency view of their security and privacy program but most of the topic areas also require specific responses for each of the major components (e.g., bureaus or operating divisions). Thus, the agencies' and OMB's reports can distinguish good performing components from poor performers and more accurately reflect the overall agency performance.

Please note that CyberScope will require reporting by component in several areas as well as at the agency level.

8. Should all of my agency's information systems be included as part of our FISMA report?

Yes. Section 3544(a)(1)(A) states: "The head of each agency shall be responsible for providing information security protections commensurate with the risk and magnitude of the harm resulting from unauthorized access, use, disclosure, disruption, modification, or destruction of (i) information collected or maintained by or on behalf of the agency; and (ii) information systems used or operated by an agency or by a contractor of an agency or other organization on behalf of an agency." Your agency's annual FISMA report therefore summarizes the performance of your agency's program to secure all of your agency's information and information systems, in any form or format, whether automated or manual. NIST Special Publication 800-37 Revision 1 (issued February 2010) provides guidance on establishing information system boundaries which can help you identify your systems.

9. Must the Department of Defense and the Director of National Intelligence (DNI) follow OMB policy and NIST guidance?

Provided that DOD and DNI internal security standards and policies are as stringent as OMB's policies and NIST's standards, they must only follow OMB's reporting policies. However, please note that NIST publication SP-800-53 Revision 3 (issued in August 2009) was developed jointly by NIST, the Department of Defense (DOD) and the intelligence community through the Joint Task Force Transformation Initiative Interagency Working Group. Therefore, DOD and the intelligence community must follow this publication.

10. What reporting is required for national security systems?

FISMA requires annual reviews and reporting of all systems, including national security systems. Agencies can choose to provide responses to the questions in the template either in aggregate or separate from their non-national security systems.

Agencies shall describe how they are implementing the requirements of FISMA for national security systems. When management and internal control oversight of an agency's national security programs and systems are handled differently than non-national security programs, a description of and explanation for the differences is required. DOD and the DNI shall report on compliance with their policies and guidance. Note that SP 800-53 Revision 3 was developed jointly by NIST, the Department of Defense (DOD) and the intelligence community through the Joint Task Force Transformation Initiative Interagency Working Group.

The CIO for the DNI reports on systems processing or storing sensitive compartmentalized information (SCI) across the intelligence community and those other systems for which the DNI is the principal accrediting authority. Agencies shall follow the intelligence community reporting guidance for these systems. SCI systems shall only be reported via the intelligence community report. However, this separate reporting does not alter an agency head's responsibility for overseeing the security of all operations and assets of the agency or component. Therefore, copies of separate reporting must also be provided to the agency head for their use.

To assist oversight by appropriate national security authorities, it is important to specify where practicable which portion of the agency report pertains to national security systems.

NIST Standards and Guidelines

11. Is use of National Institute of Standards and Technology (NIST) publications required?

Yes. For non-national security programs and information systems, agencies must follow NIST standards and guidelines. For legacy information systems, agencies are expected to be in compliance with NIST standards and guidelines within one year of the publication date unless otherwise directed by OMB. The one year compliance date for revisions to NIST publications applies only to the new and/or updated material in the publications. For information systems under development or for legacy systems undergoing significant changes, agencies are expected to be in compliance with the NIST publications immediately upon deployment of the information system.

12. Are NIST guidelines flexible?

Yes. While agencies are required to follow NIST standards and guidelines in accordance with OMB policy, there is flexibility within NIST's guidelines (specifically in the 800-series) in how agencies apply them. However, Federal Information Processing Standards (FIPS) are mandatory. Unless specified by additional implementing policy by OMB, NIST guidelines generally allow agencies latitude in their application. Consequently, the application of NIST guidelines by agencies can result in different security solutions that are equally acceptable and compliant with the guideline.

General

13. Are the security requirements outlined in the Act limited to information in electronic form?

No. Section 3541 of FISMA provides the Act's security requirements apply to "information and information systems" without distinguishing by form or format; therefore, the security requirements outlined in FISMA apply to Federal information in all forms and formats (including electronic, paper, audio, etc.).

14. Does OMB give equal weight to the assessments by the agency and the IG? What if the two parties disagree?

OMB gives equal weight to both assessments. In asking different questions of each party, OMB seeks complementary and not conflicting reporting. While OMB guidelines require a single report from each agency, OMB expects the report to represent the consolidated views of the agency and not separate views of various reviewers.

15. FISMA, OMB policy, and NIST standards require agency security programs to be risk-based. Who is responsible for deciding the acceptable level of risk (e.g., the CIO, program officials and system owners, or the IG)? Are the IGs' independent evaluations also to be risk-based? What if they disagree?

The agency head ultimately is responsible for deciding the acceptable level of risk for their agency. System owners, program officials, and CIOs provide input for this decision. Such decisions must reflect policies from OMB and standards and guidance from NIST (particularly FIPS 199 and FIPS 200). An information system's Authorizing Official takes responsibility for accepting any residual risk, thus they are held accountable for managing the security for that system.

IG evaluations are intended to independently assess if the agency is applying a risk-based approach to their information security programs and the information systems that support the conduct of agency missions and business functions. When reviewing the assessment in support of an individual security authorization, for example, the IG would generally assess whether: 1) the assessment was performed in the manner prescribed in NIST guidance and agency policy; 2) controls are being implemented as stated in any planning documentation;

and 3) continuous monitoring is adequate given the system impact level of the system and information.

16. Could you provide examples of high impact systems?
In some respects, the answer to this question is unique to each agency depending on their mission requirements. At the same time, some examples are relatively obvious and common to all agencies. As a rebuttable presumption, all cyber critical infrastructure and key resources identified in an agency's Homeland Security Policy Directive – 7 (HSPD-7) plans are high impact, as are all systems identified as necessary to support agency continuity of operations. Systems necessary for continuity of operations purposes include, for example, telecommunications systems identified in agency reviews under OMB's June 30, 2005, memorandum M-05-16, "Regulation on Maintaining Telecommunications Service During Crisis or Emergency in Federally-owned Buildings," implementing Section 414 the Transportation, Treasury, Independent Agencies, and General Government Appropriations Act, 2005 (Division H of Public Law 108-447).

Additionally, information systems used by agencies to provide services to other agencies such as under E-Government initiatives and lines of business, could also be high impact, but are at least moderate impact. The decision as to information system impact level in this circumstance must be agreed to by the provider and all of its customers.

17. My IG says the agency's inventory of major information systems is less than 96% complete. How do I reconcile the differing lists?
OMB expects agency IGs to provide to the agency CIO and OMB the list of systems they've identified as not being part of the agency's inventory.

18. When OMB asks if an agency has a process, are you also asking if the process is implemented and is effective?
Yes. OMB wants to know whether processes are working effectively to safeguard information and information systems. An ineffective process cannot be relied upon to achieve its information security and privacy objectives. To gauge the effectiveness of a particular IT security program process, we rely on responses to questions asked of the agency IG.

19. We often find security weaknesses requiring additional and significant resources to correct such discoveries seldom coincide with the budget process. Can we delay correction until the next budget cycle?

No. Agencies must plan for security needs as they develop new and operate existing systems and as security weaknesses are identified.

OMB's policies regarding information security funding were articulated in OMB Memorandum M-00-07 dated February 28, 2000. They remain in effect, were repeated in OMB Memorandum M-06-19, and are included in OMB's budget preparation guidance, i.e., Circular A-11. In brief, agencies must do two specific things. First, they must integrate security into and fund it over the lifecycle of each system as it is developed. This requirement was codified in section 3544(b)(2)(C) of FISMA. Second, the operations of legacy (steady-state) systems must meet security requirements before funds are spent on new systems (development, modernization or enhancement).

As an example of this policy in practice, if an agency has a legacy system without a current security authorization (certified and accredited), or for which a contingency plan has not been tested, these actions must be completed before spending funds on a new system. A simple way to accomplish this is to redirect the relatively modest costs of security authorization or contingency plan testing from the funds intended for development, modernization or enhancement.

OMB recognizes other unanticipated security needs may arise from time-to-time. In such cases, agencies should prioritize available resources to correct the most significant weaknesses. Correcting such weaknesses would still be required prior to spending funds on development on an interim basis, and NIST's Special Publication 800-53 Revision 3 "Recommended Security Controls for Federal Information Systems" provides guidance for using these compensating controls.

20. You are no longer asking agencies to report significant deficiencies in the annual FISMA report. Don't we have to report them?

Not in your annual FISMA report to OMB. However, agencies must maintain all documentation supporting a finding of a significant deficiency and make it available in a timely manner upon request by OMB or other oversight authorities.

FISMA requires agencies to report a significant deficiency as: 1) a material weakness under FMFIA and 2) an instance of a lack of substantial compliance under FFMIA, if related to financial management systems. (See OMB Circular A-123 for further information on reporting significant deficiencies.) As you know, all security weaknesses must be included in and tracked on your plan of action and milestones.

A significant deficiency is defined as a weakness in an agency's overall information systems security program or management control structure, or within one or more information systems that significantly restricts the capability of the agency to carry out its mission or compromises the security of its information, information systems, personnel, or other resources, operations, or assets. In this context, the risk is great enough that the agency head and outside agencies must be notified and immediate or near-immediate corrective action must be taken.

21. Should my agency's regulatory and information collection activities apply FISMA and privacy requirements?

Yes and Federal regulatory and information collection activities depend upon quality information protected from unauthorized access, use, disclosure, disruption, modification, or destruction.

Federal regulatory and information collection activities often require Federal agencies, and entities (e.g., contractors, private companies, non-profit organizations) which operate on behalf of Federal agencies, to collect, create, process, or maintain Federal government information. When developing regulations, agencies must ensure information security and privacy law and policy are applied where appropriate. Your agency's information collection activities (subject to the Paperwork Reduction Act and OMB's rule providing implementing guidance found at 5 CFR 1320), including those activities conducted or sponsored by other entities on behalf of your agency, must also ensure procedures for adequately securing and safeguarding Federal information are consistent with existing law and policy.

If your agency promulgates regulations requiring entities which operate on behalf of your agency to collect, create, process, or maintain Federal information, then procedures established by the regulation for adequately securing and safeguarding this information must be consistent with existing law and policy (e.g., FISMA, the Privacy

Act, the E-Gov Act, OMB security and privacy policy, and NIST standards and guidelines), regardless of whether the information is being held at the Agency or with the entity collecting, processing, or maintaining the information on behalf of the agency.

22. Are agencies allowed to utilize data services in the private sector, including "software as a service" and "software subscription" type solutions?
Yes. Agencies are permitted to utilize these types of agreements and arrangements, provided appropriate security controls are implemented, tested, and reviewed as part of your agency's information security program. We encourage agencies to seek out and utilize private sector, market-driven solutions resulting in cost savings and performance improvements - provided agency information is protected to the degree required by FISMA, FISMA implementing standards, and associated guidance. As with other contractor services and relationships, agencies should include these software solutions and subscriptions as they complete their annual security reviews.

23. How do agencies ensure FISMA compliance for connections to non-agency systems? Do Statement of Auditing Standards No. 70 (SAS 70) audits meet the requirements of FISMA and implementing policies and guidance?
NIST Special Publication 800-47 "Security Guide for Interconnecting Information Technology Systems" (August 2002) provides a management approach for interconnecting IT systems, with an emphasis on security. The document recommends development of an Interconnection Security Agreement (ISA) and a Memorandum of Understanding (MOU). The ISA specifies the technical and security requirements of the interconnection, and the MOU defines the responsibilities of the participating organizations. The security guide recommends regular communications between the organizations throughout the life cycle of the interconnection. One or both organizations shall review the security controls for the interconnection at least annually or whenever a significant change occurs to ensure the controls are operating properly and are providing appropriate levels of protection.

Security reviews may be conducted by designated audit authorities of one or both organizations, or by an independent third party. Both organizations shall agree on the rigor and frequency of reviews as well as a reporting process.

SAS 70 audits may or may not meet the requirements of FISMA. The private sector relies on Statement on Auditing Standards (SAS) No. 70, to ensure among other purposes compliance with Section 404 of the Sarbanes-Oxley Act of 2002, requiring management assessment of internal controls. While SAS 70 reports may be sufficient to determine contractor compliance with OMB Circular A-123 and financial statement audit requirements, it is not a pre-determined set of control objectives or control activities, and therefore is not in itself sufficient to meet FISMA requirements. In addition, it is not always clear the extent to which specific systems supporting the Government activity or contract are actually reviewed as part of a particular audit. In determining whether SAS 70 reports provide sufficient evidence of contractor system FISMA compliance, it is the agency's responsibility to ensure:

- The scope of the SAS 70 audit was sufficient, and fully addressed the specific contractor system requiring FISMA review.
- The audit encompassed all controls and requirements of law, OMB policy and NIST guidelines.

To reduce burden on agencies and service providers and increase efficiency, agencies and IGs should share with their counterparts at other agencies any assessment described above.

Security Authorization (C&A)

24. Why place such an emphasis on the security authorization of agency information systems?

The security authorization process when applied to agency information systems, provides a systematic approach for assessing security controls to determine their overall effectiveness; that is, the extent to which operational, technical, and managerial security controls are implemented correctly, operating as intended, and producing the desired outcome with respect to meeting the security requirements for the system. Understanding the overall effectiveness of the security controls implemented in the information system is essential in determining the risk to the organization's operations and assets, to individuals, to other organizations, and to the nation resulting from the use of the system.

Agencies are reminded the security authorization process is more than just planning. The continuous monitoring phase (discussed in NIST Special Publications 800-37 Revision 1 and 800-53 Revision 3) must include an appropriate set of management, operational, and technical controls including controls over physical access to systems and information. Agency officials and IGs should be advised of the results of this monitoring as appropriate. OMB asks CIOs to present a quantitative assessment and the IGs a qualitative assessment of the security authorization process.

25. Is a security authorization required for all information systems? OMB Circular A-130 requires a security authorization to process only for general support systems and major applications.

Yes, security authorizations are required for all Federal information systems. Section 3544(b)(3) of FISMA refers to "subordinate plans for providing adequate information security for networks, facilities, and systems or groups of information systems" and does not distinguish between major or other applications. Smaller "systems" and "applications" may be included as part of the assessment of a larger system-as allowable in NIST guidance and provided an appropriate risk assessment is completed and security controls are implemented.

26. Does OMB recognize interim authority to operate for security authorizations?

No. The security authorization process has been required for many years, and it is important to measure the implementation of this process to improve consistency and quality Government-wide. Introducing additional inconsistency to the Government's security program would be counter to FISMA's goals.

Testing

27. Must all agency information systems be tested and evaluated annually?

Yes, all information systems used or operated by an agency or by a contractor of an agency or other organization on behalf of an agency must be tested at least annually. FISMA (section 3544(b)(5)) requires each agency to perform for all systems "periodic testing and evaluation of the effectiveness of information security policies, procedures, and practices, to be performed with a frequency depending on risk, but no less than annually." This review shall include the testing of management, operational, and technical controls.

28. How can agencies meet the annual testing and evaluation (review) requirement?

To satisfy the annual FISMA assessment requirement, organizations can draw upon the security control assessment results from any of the following sources, including but not limited to:

- security assessments conducted as part of an information system security authorization or re-authorization process;
- continuous monitoring activities; or
- testing and evaluation of the information system as part of the ongoing system development life cycle process (provided that the testing and evaluation results are current and relevant to the determination of security control effectiveness).

Existing security assessment results can be reused to the extent that they are still valid and are supplemented with additional assessments as needed. Reuse of assessment information is critical in achieving a broad-based, cost-effective, and fully integrated security program capable of producing the needed evidence to determine the actual security status of the information system.

FISMA does not require an annual assessment of all security controls employed in an organizational information system. In accordance with OMB policy, organizations must determine the necessary depth and breadth of an annual review and assess a subset of the security controls based on several factors, including: (i) the FIPS 199 security categorization of the information system; (ii) the specific security controls selected and employed by the organization to protect the information system; (iii) the relative comprehensiveness of the most recent past review, (iv) the adequacy and successful implementation of the plan of action and milestone (POA&M) for weaknesses in the system, (v) advice from IGs or US-CERT on threats and vulnerabilities at your agency, and (vi) the level of assurance (or confidence) that the organization must have in determining the effectiveness of the security controls in the information system, among others.

It is expected agencies will assess all of the security controls in the information system during the three-year authorization cycle, and agencies can use the current year's assessment results obtained during security assessments to meet the annual FISMA assessment requirement.

29. What NIST guidelines must agencies use for their annual testing and evaluations?

Agencies are required to use FIPS 200/NIST Special Publication 800-53 for the specification of security controls and NIST Special Publications 800-37 and 800-53A for the assessment of security control effectiveness. DOD and DNI may use their internal policies, directives and guidance provided that they are as stringent as the NIST security standards.

30. Why should agencies conduct continuous monitoring of their security controls?

Continuous monitoring of security controls is a cost-effective and important part of managing enterprise risk and maintaining an accurate understanding of the security risks confronting your agency's information systems. Continuous monitoring of security controls is required as part of the security authorization process to ensure controls remain effective over time (e.g., after the initial security authorization or reauthorization of an information system) in the face of changing threats, missions, environments of operation, and technologies.

Agencies should develop an enterprise-wide strategy for selecting subsets of their security controls to be monitored on an ongoing basis to ensure all controls are assessed during the three-year authorization cycle. A robust and effective continuous monitoring program will ensure important procedures included in an agency's security authorization package (e.g., as described in system security plans, security assessment reports, and POAMs) are updated as appropriate and contain the necessary information for authorizing officials to make credible risk-based decisions regarding the security state of the information system on an ongoing basis. This will help make the security authorization process more dynamic and responsive to today's federal missions and rapidly changing conditions. NIST Special Publications 800-37, 800-53, and 800-53A provide guidance on continuous monitoring programs.

31. Do agencies need to test and evaluate (review) security controls on low impact information systems?
Yes. While the depth and breadth of security controls testing and evaluation (review) will vary based on information system risk and system impact level, agencies are required to do annual testing and evaluation (review) of ALL systems. NIST Special Publications 800-37 and 800-53A provide guidance on assessment of security controls in low-impact information systems.

Configuration Management

32. What are minimally acceptable system configuration requirements?
FISMA (section 3544(b)(2)(D)(iii)) requires each agency to develop minimally acceptable system configuration requirements and ensure compliance with them. Common security configurations provide a baseline level of security, reduce risk from security threats and vulnerabilities, and save time and resources. This allows agencies to improve system performance, decrease operating costs, and ensure public confidence in the confidentiality, integrity, and availability of Government information.

Agencies are to cite the frequency by which they implement system configuration requirements. Security configuration checklists are now available for computer software widely used within the Federal Government, and they can be found on the NIST Computer Security Division web site (see: http://checklists.nist.gov) as well as the NSA System and Network Attack Center web site. Agencies must document and provide NIST with any deviations from the common security configurations (send documentation to checklists@nist.gov) and be prepared to justify why they are not using them. IGs should review such use.

In FY 2007, OMB issued policy for agencies to adopt security configurations for Windows XP and VISTA, as well as policy for ensuring new acquisitions include common security configurations. For more information, see OMB Memorandum M-07-11 "Implementation of Commonly Accepted Security Configurations for Windows Operating Systems," at: http://www.whitehouse.gov/omb/memoranda/fy2007/m07-11.pdf, and OMB Memorandum M-07-18 "Ensuring New Acquisitions Include Common Security Configurations," at: http://www.whitehouse.gov/omb/memoranda/fy2007/m07-18.pdf, respectively. The acquisition language in OMB M-07-18 was published in the Federal Register, FAR 2007-004. For all contracts, the following language should be included, to encompass Federal Desktop Core Configurations:

> "(d) In acquiring information technology, agencies shall include the appropriate information technology security policies and requirements, including use of common security configurations available from the National Institute of Standards and Technology's website at http://checklists.nist.gov. Agency contracting officers should consult with the requiring official to ensure the appropriate standards are incorporated."

33. Why must agencies explain their performance metrics in terms of FIPS 199 categories?

FISMA directed NIST to develop a standard to categorize all information and information systems based upon the need to provide appropriate levels of information security according to a range of risk levels. "Federal Information Processing Standard 199: Standards for Security Categorization of Federal Information and Information Systems" (issued February 2004) defines three levels of potential impact on organizations or individuals should there be a breach of security (i.e., a loss of confidentiality, integrity, or availability). These impact levels are: low, moderate and high. Agencies must categorize their information and information systems using one of these three categories in order to comply with the minimum security requirements described in FIPS 200 and to determine which security controls in NIST Special Publication 800-53 are required. While NIST guidance does not apply to national security systems nor DOD nor DNI, OMB expects all agencies to implement a reasonably similar process.

Plan of Action and Milestones (POA&M)

34. What is required of agency POA&Ms?

As outlined in previous guidance (OMB M-04-25, "FY 2004 Reporting Instructions for the Federal Information Security Management Act") Agency POA&Ms must:

1. Be tied to the agency's budget submission through the unique project identifier of a system. This links the security costs for a system with the security performance of a system.
2. Include all security weaknesses found during any other review done by, for, or on behalf of the agency, including GAO audits, financial system audits, and critical infrastructure vulnerability assessments. These plans should be the authoritative agency-wide management tool, inclusive of all evaluations.
3. Be shared with the agency IG to ensure independent verification and validation of identified weaknesses and completed corrective actions.
4. Be submitted to OMB upon request.

While agencies are no longer required to follow the exact format prescribed in the POA&M examples in M-04-25, they must still include all of the associated data elements in their POA&Ms. To facilitate compliance with POA&M reporting requirements, agencies may choose to utilize the FISMA reporting services of a Shared Service Center as part of the Information Security Line of Business. Please note that these FISMA reporting services are **not** mandatory.

35. Can a POA&M process be effective even when correcting identified weaknesses is untimely?

Yes. The purpose of a POA&M is to identify and track security weaknesses in one location. A POA&M permits agency officials and oversight authorities to identify when documented corrective actions are both timely and untimely. In either circumstance, the POA&M has served its intended purpose. Agency managers can use the POA&M process to focus resources to resolve delays.

Contractor Monitoring and Controls

36. Must Government contractors abide by FISMA requirements?

Yes. Also, each agency must ensure their contractors are abiding by FISMA requirements. Section 3544(a)(1)(A)(ii) describes Federal agency security responsibilities as including "information systems used or operated by an agency or by a contractor of an agency or other organization on behalf of an agency." Section 3544(b) requires each agency to provide information security for the information and "information systems that support the operations and assets of the agency, including those provided or managed by another agency, contractor, or other source." This includes services which are either fully or partially provided, including agency hosted, outsourced, and software-as-a-service (SaaS) solutions.

Because FISMA applies to both information and information systems used by the agency, contractors, and other organizations and sources, it has somewhat broader applicability than prior security law. That is, agency information security programs apply to all organizations (sources) which possess or use Federal information – or which operate, use, or have access to Federal information systems (whether automated or manual) – on behalf of a Federal agency. Such other organizations may include contractors, grantees, State and local Governments, industry partners, providers of software subscription services, etc. FISMA, therefore, underscores longstanding OMB policy concerning sharing Government information and interconnecting systems.

Therefore, Federal security requirements continue to apply and the agency is responsible for ensuring appropriate security controls (see OMB Circular A-130, Appendix III). Agencies must develop policies for information security oversight of contractors and other users with privileged access to Federal data. Agencies must also review the security of other users with privileged access to Federal data and systems.

Finally, because FISMA applies to Federal information and information systems, in certain limited circumstances its requirements also apply to a specific class of information technology to which Clinger-Cohen did not, i.e., "equipment that is acquired by a Federal contractor incidental to a Federal contract." Therefore, when Federal information is used within incidentally acquired equipment, the agency continues to be responsible and accountable for ensuring FISMA requirements are met.

37. Could you provide examples of "incidental" contractor equipment which is not subject to FISMA?

In considering the answer to this question, it is essential to remember FISMA requires agencies to provide security protections "...commensurate with the risk and magnitude of harm resulting from unauthorized access, use, disclosure, disruption, modification, or destruction of information collected or maintained by or on behalf of the agency; and information systems used or operated by an agency or other organization on behalf of an agency." This includes services which are either fully or partially provided by another source, including agency hosted, outsourced, and SaaS solutions.

A corporate human resource or financial management system acquired solely to assist managing corporate resources assigned to a Government contract could be incidental, provided the system does not use agency information or interconnect with an agency system.

38. Could you provide examples of agency security responsibilities concerning contractors and other sources?

FISMA requires agencies to provide security protections "...commensurate with the risk and magnitude of harm resulting from unauthorized access, use, disclosure, disruption, modification, or destruction of information collected or maintained by or on behalf of the agency; and information systems used or operated by an agency or other organization on behalf of an agency." This includes full or partial operations.

While we cannot anticipate all possible combinations and permutations, there are five primary categories of contractors as they relate to securing systems and information: 1) service providers, 2) contractor support, 3) Government Owned, Contractor Operated facilities (GOCO), 4) laboratories and research centers, and 5) management and operating contracts.

> 1) Service providers — this encompasses typical outsourcing of system or network operations, telecommunications services, or other managed services (including those provided by another agency and subscribing to software services).
> Agencies are fully responsible and accountable for ensuring all FISMA and related policy requirements are implemented and reviewed and such must be included in the

terms of the contract. Agencies must ensure identical, not "equivalent," security procedures. For example, annual reviews, risk assessments, security plans, control testing, contingency planning, and security authorization (C&A) must, at a minimum, explicitly meet guidance from NIST. Additionally, IGs shall include some contractor systems in their "representative subset of agency systems," and not doing so presents an incomplete independent evaluation.

Agencies and IGs should to the maximum extent practicable, consult with other agencies using the same service provider, share security review results, and avoid the unnecessary burden on the service provider and the agencies resulting from duplicative reviews and re-reviews. Additionally, provided they meet FISMA and policy requirements, agencies and IGs should accept all or part of the results of industry-specific security reviews performed by an independent auditor on the commercial service provider.

In the case of agency service providers, they must work with their customer agencies to develop suitable arrangements for meeting all of FISMA's requirements, including any special requirements for one or more particular customer agencies. Any arrangements should also provide for an annual evaluation by the IG of one agency. Thereafter, the results of that IG evaluation would be shared with all customer agencies and their respective IGs.

2) Contractor support — this encompasses on- or off-site contractor technical or other support staff.

Agencies are fully responsible and accountable for ensuring all FISMA and related policy requirements are implemented and reviewed and such must be included in the terms of the contract. Agencies must ensure identical, not "equivalent," security procedures. Specifically, the agency is responsible for ensuring the contractor personnel receive appropriate training (i.e., user awareness training and training on agency policy and procedures).

3) Government Owned, Contractor Operated (GOCO) — For the purposes of FISMA, GOCO facilities are agency

components and their security requirements are identical to those of the managing Federal agency in all respects. Security requirements must be included in the terms of the contract.

4) Laboratories and research facilities — For the purposes of FISMA, laboratories and research facilities are agency components and their security requirements are identical to those of the managing Federal agency in all respects. Security requirements must be included in the terms of the contract or other similar agreement.

5) Management and Operating Contracts — For the purposes of FISMA, management and operating contracts include contracts for the operation, maintenance, or support of a Government-owned or -controlled research, development, special production, or testing establishment.

39. Should agencies include FISMA requirements in grants and contracts?

Yes, as with the Government Information Security Reform Act of 2000, agency contracts including but not limited to those for IT services must reflect FISMA requirements.

The Federal Acquisition Regulation, Subpart 7.1—Acquisition Plans, requires heads of agencies to ensure agency planners on information technology acquisitions comply with the information technology security requirements in the Federal Information Security Management Act (44 U.S.C. 3544), OMB's implementing policies including Appendix III of OMB Circular A-130, and guidance and standards from NIST.

When applicable, agencies must also include FISMA's security requirements in the terms and conditions of grants.

40. How deeply into contractor, state, or grantee systems must a FISMA review reach? To the application, to the interface between the application and their network, or into the corporate network/infrastructure?

This question has a two-part answer. First, FISMA's requirements follow agency information into any system which uses it or processes it on behalf of the agency. That is, when the ultimate responsibility and accountability for control of the information continues to reside with the agency, FISMA applies. Second, with respect to system interconnections, as a general rule, OMB assumes agency responsibility and accountability extends to the interface between Government systems (or contractor systems performing functions on behalf of the agency) and corporate systems and networks. For example, a corporate network, human resource, or financial management system would not be covered by FISMA requirements, provided the agency has confirmed appropriate security of the interface between them and any system using Government information or those operating on behalf of the agency. See also the discussions concerning interconnection agreements and security authorization boundaries.

41. Are all information systems operated by a contractor on behalf of an agency subject to the same type of security authorization process?
Yes, they must be addressed in the same way. As with agency-operated systems, the level of effort required for security authorization depends on the impact level of the information contained on each system. Security authorization of a system with an impact level of low will be less rigorous and costly than a system with a higher impact level. More information on system security categorization is available in FIPS Pub 199 and NIST Special Publication 800-60 "Guide for Mapping Types of Information and Information Systems to Security Categories."

FISMA is unambiguous regarding the extent to which security authorizations and annual IT security assessments apply. To the extent that contractor, state, or grantee systems process, store, or house Federal Government information (for which the agency continues to be responsible for maintaining control), their security controls must be assessed against the same NIST criteria and standards as if they were a Government-owned or -operated system. The security authorization boundary for these systems must be carefully mapped to ensure that Federal information: (a) is adequately protected, (b) is segregated from the contractor, state or grantee corporate infrastructure, and (c) there is an interconnection security agreement in place to address connections from the contractor, state or grantee system containing the agency information to systems external to the security authorization boundary.

42. Who is responsible for the POA&M process for contractor systems owned by the contractor?

The agency is responsible for ensuring the contractor corrects weaknesses discovered through self-assessments and independent assessments. Any weaknesses are to be reflected in the agency's POA&M.

Training

43. Do employees who never access electronic information systems need annual security and privacy awareness training?

Yes, FISMA and OMB policy (Memorandum M-07-17, Attachment I.A.2.d.) require all employees to receive annual security and privacy awareness training, and they must be included as part of your agency's training totals. When administering your security and privacy awareness training programs, it is important to remember: (i) all employees collect, process, access and/or maintain government information, in some form or format, to successfully perform their duties and support the agency's mission; and (ii) information is processed in various forms and formats, including paper and electronic, and information systems are a discrete set of information resources organized for the collection, processing, maintenance, transmission, and dissemination of information, in accordance with defined procedures, whether automated or manual.

44. OMB asks agencies whether they have provided information security training and awareness to all employees, including contractors. Is it the agency's responsibility to ensure contractors have security training if they are hired to perform IT security functions? Wouldn't they already be trained by their companies to perform this work?

The agency should include in its contract the requirements for level of skill and experience. However, contractors must be trained on agency-specific security policies and procedures, including rules of behavior. Agencies may explain the type of awareness training they provide to contractors as part of the response to section B.6.c.

45. What resources are available to assist agencies in providing annual information security and privacy training to their employees?

The Information System Security Line of Business (ISSLOB) has been working with agencies to develop a standardized curriculum, and, to select information security Shared Service Centers (SSC). The ISSLOB SSC's provide an efficient and cost-effective solution for agencies to procure general information security training for employees and contractors. For more information on this program, contact the ISSLOB program management office at the Department of Homeland Security.

Privacy Reporting

46. Which agency official should complete the privacy questions in this FISMA report?
These questions shall be completed or supervised by the Senior Agency Official for Privacy (SAOP). Since privacy management may fall into areas of responsibility likely held by several program officials, e.g., the CIO, the Privacy Act Officer, etc., the SAOP shall consult with these officials when responding to these questions, and note (Section D, part IV) those who contributed and/or reviewed the responses to the questions.

47. What does it mean for a system of records notice (SORN) to be "current"?
A SORN is "current" if that document satisfies the applicable requirements under the Privacy Act and there have been no subsequent substantive changes to the system which would necessitate republication of the notice in the Federal Register.

48. Must agencies publish a SORN for all systems?
No. As required by the Privacy Act (5 U.S.C. 552a), agencies must publish a SORN for systems with records about individuals maintained in a system of records covered by the Privacy Act.

49. Are agencies required to conduct a privacy impact assessment (PIA) for information technology systems that contain or administer information in identifiable form strictly about Federal employees (including contractors)?
The legal and policy requirements addressing Federal agency computer security apply equally to Federal IT systems containing identifiable

information about members of the public and to systems containing identifiable information solely about agency employees (or contractors). That is, as a practical matter, all systems containing information in identifiable form fall subject to the same technical, administrative and operational security controls. Although neither Section 208 of the E-Government Act, nor OMB's implementing guidance mandate agencies conduct PIAs on electronic systems containing information about Federal employees (including contractors), OMB encourages agencies to scrutinize their internal business processes and the handling of identifiable information about employees to the same extent they scrutinize processes and information handling procedures involving information collected from or about members of the public (OMB Memorandum M-03-22, Section II.B.3.a.).

50. If an agency chooses to conduct a PIA on systems which only contain information about Federal employees (including contractors), should these be included in the total number of systems reported?

No, agencies should count only those systems which require a PIA under the E-Government Act. OMB recognizes some agencies choose to conduct a PIA on systems containing information about Federal employees (including contractors), or conduct a "threshold analysis" to determine whether a formal PIA is required for the system. While OMB applauds this level of dedication to privacy awareness and encourages agencies to continue pursuing these efforts, including these additional assessments inhibits meaningful evaluation of agency compliance with Section 208 of the E-Government Act of 2002.

Electronic Authentication

51. What is Electronic Authentication (e-authentication)?

In December 2003, OMB issued Memorandum M-04-04, "E-Authentication Guidance for Federal Agencies", which requires agencies to review new and existing electronic transactions to ensure the authentication processes provide the appropriate level of assurance. It establishes and describes four levels of identity assurance for electronic transactions requiring authentication. Specifically, agencies are to determine assurance levels using the following steps:

1. Conduct an e-authentication risk assessment of the e-government system.
2. Map identified risks to the appropriate assurance level.
3. Select technology based on e-authentication technical guidance.
4. Validate that the implemented system has achieved the required assurance level.
5. Periodically reassess the system to determine technology refresh requirements.

An e-authentication application is an application that meets the following criteria:

1. Is web-based;
2. Requires authentication; and
3. Extends beyond the borders of your enterprise (e.g. multi-agency, government-wide, or public facing)

For additional e-authentication requirements, please refer to NIST Special Publication 800-63, "Electronic Authentication Guidance" at http://csrc.nist.gov/publications.

Homeland Security Presidential Directive 12 (HSPD-12)

52. When reporting how many Personal Identity Verification (PIV) credentials are being used for authentication to systems, does my agency include only those implementations where the PIV authentication (PIVAUTH) certificate is being used for authentication?
Yes, for access to logical systems, an application is PIV-enabled when at authentication the presented Public Key Infrastructure (PKI) certificate is validated under Federal Common Policy as a valid PIV Authentication Certificate and that the corresponding "PIV Auth Key" on the card correctly responds to the cryptographic challenge in the authentication protocol to gain access. This includes implementing a credential revocation checking capability, which may be accomplished by 'caching' revocation information from the credential issuer, provided the cache is refreshed at least once every 18 hours. For additional information, refer to NIST FIPS 201 at www.nist.gov and Federal PKI Policy at www.idmanagement.gov.

53. What guidance does my agency follow when implementing the use of the PIV credentials for physical access control?

NIST Special Publication (SP) 800-116, *"A Recommendation for the Use of PIV Credentials in Physical Access Control Systems,"* provides guidance concerning the use of the PIV credential for physical access. Agencies should not include in the count of PIV-enabled physical access control any situations where the PIV credential is being used to support legacy systems, including but not limited to situations where physical access control systems use PIV credential modifications (such as additional legacy antennas, MAG Stripe, 3D Barcode, 2D Barcode, etc.) Nor should agencies count manual physical access control (i.e. using the PIV credential as a "flash-pass"). In all situations, at a minimum, the digital credential (content-signer) used to sign the PIV containers must be validated before accepting a card holder unique identifier (CHUID) or biometric assertion.

54. For the purposes of HSPD-12 implementation, what is meant by "federal facilities" or "systems?"

You may refer to Page 3 of OMB Memorandum 05-24, *"Implementation of Homeland Security Presidential Directive (HSPD) 12 – Policy for a Common Identification Standard for Federal Employees and Contractors,"* for a definition of federally controlled facilities and information systems. Each agency is expected to have identified all of its facilities and is to report on whether all the physical access control systems and card readers controlling access to these facilities have been upgraded to be HSPD-12 compliant in accordance with NIST and GSA guidance. When reporting the number of FISMA systems enabled to use PIV credentials, it is expected that all applications included as part of the FISMA system use the PIV credential as the means to gain access. Additionally, physical access control systems which include servers, databases, workstations and appliances in either shared or isolated networks are to be included in the count of reported systems.

For additional questions regarding HSPD-12, please contact Carol Bales at cbales@omb.eop.gov, 202-395-9915 or visit www.idmanagement.gov.

Automated Risk Model

55. What is meant by an "automated risk model"?
It is envisioned that agencies will not only collate their data from their current disparate systems; they will be able to have greater visibility and focus on their most significant vulnerabilities at any time. In order to do this, agencies need to develop a risk model that is then incorporated into the tool in order to highlight the information they need. Agencies can use such utilize the National Vulnerability Database (including vulnerability risk assessments from the Common Vulnerability Scoring System) or similar vulnerability information to develop their risk model.

Definitions

Adequate Security (defined in OMB Circular A-130, Appendix III, (A)(2)(a)): Security is commensurate with the risk and magnitude of the harm resulting from the loss, misuse, or unauthorized access to or modification of information. This includes assuring that systems and applications used by the agency operate effectively and provide appropriate confidentiality, integrity, and availability, through the use of cost-effective management, personnel, operational, and technical controls.

Capital Planning and Investment Control Process (as defined in OMB Circular A-130, (6)(c)): A management process for ongoing identification, selection, control, and evaluation of investments in information resources. The process links budget formulation and execution, and is focused on agency missions and achieving specific program outcomes.

General Support System or System (defined in OMB Circular A-130, Appendix III, (A)(2)(c)): An interconnected set of information resources under the same direct management control which shares common functionality. A system normally includes hardware, software, information, data, applications, communications, and people. A system can be, for example, a local area network (LAN) including smart terminals that supports a branch office, an agency-wide backbone, a communications network, a departmental data processing center including its operating system and utilities, a tactical radio network, or a shared information processing service organization (IPSO).

Information Security (defined by FISMA, section 3542(b)(1) (A-C)): Protecting information and information systems from unauthorized access, use, disclosure, disruption, modification, or destruction in order to provide: (A) integrity, which means guarding against improper information modification or destruction, and includes ensuring information non-repudiation and authenticity; (B) confidentiality, which means preserving authorized restrictions on access and disclosure, including means for protecting personal privacy and proprietary information; and (C) availability, which means ensuring timely and reliable access to and use of information.

Information System (defined in OMB Circular A-130, (6)(q)): The term "information system" means a discrete set of information resources organized for the collection, processing, maintenance, transmission, and dissemination of information, in accordance with defined procedures, whether automated or manual.

Information Technology (defined by the Clinger-Cohen Act of 1996, sections 5002, 5141 and 5142): Any equipment or interconnected system or subsystem of equipment that is used in the automatic acquisition, storage, manipulation, management, movement, control, display, switching, interchange, transmission, or reception of data or information. For purposes of this definition, equipment is used by an agency whether the agency uses the equipment directly or it is used by a contractor under a contract with the agency which (1) requires the use of such equipment or (2) requires the use, to a significant extent, of such equipment in the performance of a service or the furnishing of a product. Information technology includes computers, ancillary equipment, software, firmware and similar procedures, services (including support services), and related resources. It does not include any equipment that is acquired by a Federal contractor incidental to a Federal contract.

Major Acquisition/Investment (defined in OMB Circular A-11, section 300): Major acquisition/investment means a system or project requiring special management attention because of its importance to the mission or function of the agency, a component of the agency or another organization; is for financial management and obligates more than $500,000 annually; has significant program or policy implications; has high executive visibility; has high development, operating or maintenance costs or is defined as major by the agency's capital planning and investment control process.

Major Application (defined in OMB Circular A-130, (A)(2)(d)): A major application is an application that requires special attention to security due to the risk and magnitude of the harm resulting from the loss, misuse, or unauthorized access to or modification of the information in the application. Note: All Federal applications require some level of protection. Certain applications, because of the information in them, however, require special management oversight and should be treated as major. Adequate security for other applications should be provided by the security of the systems in which they operate.

Major Information System (defined in OMB Circular A-130): A major information system is an information system that requires special management attention because of its importance to an agency mission; its high development, operating, or maintenance costs; or its significant role in the administration of agency programs, finances, property, or other resources.

National Security System (defined in FISMA, section 3542 (b)(2) (A-B))

(A) The term "national security system" means any information system (including any telecommunications system) used or operated by an agency or by a contractor of an agency, or other organization on behalf of an agency—

    (i) the function, operation, or use of which—

        (I) involves intelligence activities;

        (II) involves cryptologic activities related to national security;

(III) involves command and control of military forces;

(IV) involves equipment that is an integral part of a weapon or weapons system; or

(V) subject to subparagraph (B), is critical to the direct fulfillment of military or intelligence missions; or

(ii) is protected at all times by procedures established for information that have been specifically authorized under criteria established by an Executive order or an Act of Congress to be kept classified in the interest of national defense or foreign policy.

(B) Subparagraph (A)(i)(V) does not include a system that is to be used for routine administrative and business applications (including payroll, finance, logistics, and personnel management applications).

Plan of Action and Milestone (defined in OMB Memorandum M-02-01): A plan of action and milestones (POA&M), also referred to as a corrective action plan, is a tool that identifies tasks that need to be accomplished. It details resources required to accomplish the elements of the plan, any milestones in meeting the task, and scheduled completion dates for the milestones. The purpose of the POA&M is to assist agencies in identifying, assessing, prioritizing, and monitoring the progress of corrective efforts for security weaknesses found in programs and systems.

Privacy Impact Assessment (PIA) (See OMB Memorandum M-03-22): A process for examining the risks and ramifications of using information technology to collect, maintain and disseminate information in identifiable form from or about members of the public, and for identifying and evaluating protections and alternative processes to mitigate the impact to privacy of collecting such information.

Security Controls (defined in FIPS 199): Security controls are defined as the management, operational, and technical controls (i.e., safeguards or countermeasures) prescribed for an information system to protect the confidentiality, integrity, and availability of the system and its information.

Security Program (defined by FISMA, Section 3544(b)(1-8)): Each agency shall develop, document, and implement an agency wide information security program, approved by the Director under section 3543(a)(5), to provide information security for the information and information systems that support the operations and assets of the agency, including those provided or managed by another agency, contractor, or other source.

Significant Deficiency: A significant deficiency is a weakness in an agency's overall information systems security program or management control structure, or within one or more information systems, that significantly restricts the capability of the agency to carry out its mission or compromises the security of its information, information systems, personnel, or other resources, operations, or assets. In this context, the risk is great enough that the agency head and outside agencies must be notified and immediate or near-immediate corrective action must be taken.

As required in FISMA (section 3544(c)(3)), agencies are to report any significant deficiency in policy, procedure, or practice as a material weakness in reporting under FMFIA and if relating to financial management systems, as an instance of a lack of substantial compliance under FFMIA.

System Assessment: A comprehensive assessment of the management and operational and technical security controls in an information system, made in support of security accreditation, to determine the extent to which the controls are implemented correctly, operating as intended, and producing the desired outcome with respect to meeting the security requirements of the system.

System of Records Notice (SORN): A SORN is a statement providing to the public notice of the existence and character of a group of any records under the control of any agency from which information is retrieved by the name of the individual or by some identifying number, symbol, or other identifying particular assigned to the individual. The Privacy Act of 1974 requires this notice to be published in the Federal Register upon establishment or substantive revision of the system, and establishes what information about the system must be included.

Appendix C: OMB FISMA FY10 Reporting Questionnaires

Part 1—Chief Information Officer*

Section 1: System Inventory

1. Provide the number of Agency-owned and contractor systems by component with the following information:
   a. FIPS 199 risk category
   b. Certification and accreditation status
   c. Whether annual testing occurred
   d. Whether a tested contingency plan exists
   e. The number of systems assessed at E-Authentication levels 3 or 4

Section 2: Hardware Inventory

2. Provide the number of all desktops connected to the Agency's network.
3. Provide the number of all laptops connected to the Agency's network.
4. Provide the number of all servers connected to the Agency's network.

---

* Extracted from http://www.federalnewsradio.com/docs/fismametrics_cio2010.pdf.

5. Does the Agency have a capability to identify hardware assets by:
   a. IP Address?
   b. Hardware names(s)?
   c. Purpose of each system?
   d. The hardware owner?
6. Provide the number of all firewalls connected to the Agency's network according to the Agency's asset inventory.
7. Provide the number of all routers connected to the Agency's network according to the Agency's asset inventory.
8. Provide the number of all switches connected to the Agency's network according to the Agency's asset inventory.
9. Provide the number of all other devices connected to the Agency's network according to the Agency's asset inventory.
10. Does the Agency have the technical ability to identify the introduction of unauthorized hardware to its networks?
    a. What percentage of the Agency's networks does this cover? *Please provide a range within 10%.*
    b. Does the Agency block the introduction of unauthorized hardware to its networks?
    c. Is there a process to respond if unauthorized hardware is detected? Has this process been tested?

Section 3: Software Inventory

11. Provide an inventory of software authorized to run on the Agency's networks. (Operating System Software, Windows 2007, Vista)
12. Provide an inventory of software authorized to run on the Agency's networks. (Non-FDCC, All other software - Adobe, Databases)
13. How frequently updated is the Agency's inventory of all software run on the Agency's networks, recording at least the operating system, version number, patch level, and the applications installed on it?
13a. Does the Agency technically scan and discover/inventory all software not authorized to run on its networks?

1. If yes, is this capability manual, partially automated or fully automated?
2. What percentage of the Agency's networks does this cover? *Please provide a range within 10%.*
3. Is there a process to respond if unauthorized software is detected?
4. Does the Agency have the capability to (block, notify, or quarantine) the introduction of unauthorized software to its networks? *Choose all that apply.*
5. Has the Agency tested this capability?

Section 4: Connections Inventory

14. What percentage of internet traffic goes through a TIC compliant gateway? *Please provide a range within 10%.*
15. Can the Agency provide a real-time inventory of all of its external connections as defined in the TIC architecture? For this question, real-time is defined as *"within 24 hours."*
    a. How frequently updated is the Agency's inventory of all of its external connections as defined in the TIC architecture?
    b. Does the Agency have the capability to monitor for external connections that are not TIC compliant?
    c. What is the frequency of monitoring for external connections that are not TIC compliant?
16. Is the Agency a TICAP or Seeking Service?
    a. Has the Agency undergone the Department of Homeland Security (DHS) TCV assessment of the 51 Critical Capabilities?
    b. What was the Agency's score? *Please provide a range within 10%.*
    c. How many outstanding items has the Agency corrected to date?
    d. Does the Agency have a remediation plan with dates?

Section 5: Configuration Management

Operating System
    a. Average number of systems found not in compliance.
    b. Total number of patches needed.

    c. Total number of critical patches needed.

    d. Average time to apply high security criticality patch to 95% of machines.

    e. Number of patches applied in last 30 days.

    f. Average success rate of patches applied.

    g. Number of issues identified.

    h. Number of issues remediated.

Operating System

    a. Is a standard baseline security configuration defined?

    b. What is the basis of the standard baseline security configuration?

       1. NIST Checklist Used

       2. DOD Gold Standard

22. For each of the authorized operating system software chosen in the previous question:

    a. What is the percentage of installations that can be technically scanned for compliance with a standard baseline? *Please provide a range within 10%.*

       1. For that percentage, what is the frequency of scanning of all installations that can be scanned? *Please provide the response measured as the average number of days.*

   22b. If an installation is not compliant, does the Agency have a procedure for response and mitigation?

Section 6: Integration of Security into SDLC

19. What number of new Agency-owned systems (by FIPS 199 level) went live during the reporting period?

    a. What number of new systems used NIST SP 800-53 controls where applicable as system design requirements?

    b. What number of new systems used NIST SP 800-53A to test controls in the process of system acceptance testing?

20. What number of Agency-owned systems (by FIPS 199 level) are currently in development?

    a. What number of systems in development used NIST SP 800-53 controls where applicable as system design requirements?

    b. What number of systems in development used NIST SP 800-53A to test controls in the process of system acceptance testing?

21. Is the Agency in the process of acquiring contractor-owned systems? If yes, what systems?
    a. What number of contractor-operated systems have contracts with applicable FAR clauses?
    b. How many of those include applicable NIST SP 800-53 security requirements in the contract or equivalent language?

Section 7: Security Incident Management

22. Does the Agency have an Incident Response Capability (whether in-house or as part of managed security services contract)?
    a. Does the Agency have a Security Operations Center operating as the incident response center?
23. Does the Agency participate in DHS/US-CERT threat briefings? (e.g., JACKE)
    a. Why not and what are the Agency's plans to participate?
    b. Does the Agency face particular barriers to participation?
24. Does the Agency have access to US-CERT publications? (e.g. SARS)
25. In the last year, did the Agency perform network penetration testing on any of the Agency's networks?
    a. If yes, was the Agency's NOC/SOC capability exercised during the test?
    b. What tools, techniques, and technologies does the Agency use for incident detection?
       1. How many systems (or networks of systems) are protected using the tools, techniques and technologies listed above?
26. In the last year, how many times has a security incident resulted in a system being unavailable?
    a. What was the average time the system was unavailable?

Section 8: Training

27. Can the Agency determine, at any point in time, the annual security awareness training status of all employees and contractors?
28. Can the Agency determine, at any point in time, the specialized security training of all employees with significant security responsibilities?

   a. Number with log-in privileges.

   b. Number with log-in privileges given annual security awareness training

   c. Number with significant security responsibilities

   d. Number with significant security responsibilities provided specialized security training (employees only).

   e. Cost of providing security awareness training.

   f. Cost of providing specialized security training.

29. Does the Agency security awareness training:

   a. Address phishing?

   b. Cover the subject of remote access?

   c. Cover the subject of Web 2.0 technologies?

   d. Cover the subject of Peer-to-Peer technologies?

30. Number with significant security responsibilities who have security-related certifications?

   a. Please identify the type and number of security-related certifications.

Section 9: Identity & Access Management

31. Does the Agency have an Agency-wide policy requiring the use of Personal Identity Verification (PIV) credentials for physical and logical access control in accordance with HSPD-12? If no, then when does the Agency expect to issue such a policy?

   a. If no, then when does the Agency expect to issue such a policy?

32. Provide the following regarding PIV implementation status:

   a. Number of employees eligible for PIV cards.

   b. Number of employees with PIV cards.

   c. Number of employees with PIV readers and middleware.

   d. Number of contractors eligible for PIV cards.

   e. Number of contractors with PIV cards.

   f. Number of contractors with PIV readers and middleware.

33. How many systems in the reported system inventory, other than remote access solutions, use another type of two-factor authentication method other than a PIV credential?

34. Does the Agency use PIV credential for authentication to the network?
35. How many systems in the Agency's reported system inventory from Question 1 use PIV credentials for use authentication?
36. How many systems in the reported system inventory, other than remote access solutions, use another type of two-factor authentication method other than a PIV credential?
    a. How many of those facilities use readers that are HSPD-12 compliant?
37. Please provide the URL to the agency's progress update for HSPD-12 implementation. Note: This does not have to be a working URL.
38. Of the systems in the Agency's reported inventory assessed at E-authentication levels 3 or 4, what percentage of those require two-factor or multi-factor authentication for non-Federal users (e.g. citizens, business partners)? *Please provide a range within 10%.*

Section 10: Remote Access Management

39. Does the Agency permit remote access in the Agency for authorized users?
40. Does the Agency's remote access policy require two-factor authentication for remote access (including VPN, dial-up, and other forms)?
41. Has the Agency deployed, piloted or researched a zero-footprint solution? (e.g. Citrix, Thumb drive, etc.)
42. What is the Agency's total number of remote access points?
43. What percentage of remote access solutions (i.e. the cryptographic portions, if any) use FIPS 140-2 validated cryptographic modules? *Please provide a range within 10%.*
44. What number of users has remote access to the Agency networks?
    a. What number of those use PIV credentials?
    b. What number of those use another form of two-factor authentication for remote access?
45. What percentage of the Agency's connections prohibit split tunneling (as defined by NIST)?

46. Can the Agency detect, in real-time, remote access connections to its networks?
    a. When the Agency detects a remote connection, can the Agency determine if it is authorized? If a connection is not authorized, can the Agency block it?

47. For Government Furnished Equipment (GFE), does the Agency correct deviations, clean viruses and malware? If yes, what number?

48. Is Agency information permitted to be stored on the local device?

49. Does the Agency use a "time-out" function for remote access and mobile devices requiring user re-authentication after at least 30 minutes of activity?

50. Does the Agency permit non-GFE to connect remotely to your networks?
    a. For non-GFE, does the Agency limit access/functionality (e.g. email only, web browsing, restricted network drive access, etc.)?

51. What is the percentage of portable computers (laptops) that have all user data encrypted with FIPS 140-2 validated encryption? *Please provide a range within 10%.*

52. What is the percentage of non-laptop, portable electronic devices (e.g. smart phones, portable hard drives, etc.) that have all user data encrypted with FIPS 140-2 validated encryption? *Please provide a range within 10%.*

Section 11: Data Leakage Protection

53. Does the Agency have a data sensitivity based labeling scheme?
    a. Does the Agency have the technical capability to apply the labeling scheme to the actual data?
    b. Does the Agency have a Data Leakage Protection (DLP) to leverage the labeled data?
    c. Does the Agency have technical controls to disable compromised mobile devices (i.e. lost or stolen devices)?
    d. Does the Agency have the technical capability to see data leaving the perimeter and to determine if the data traffic is legitimate?

Section 12: Real-Time Security Status Management

54. Does the Agency have an automated capability to provide real-time enterprise-wide cybersecurity situational awareness?
    a. Is the tool SCAP compliant?
55. Does the automated capability integrate the following:
    a. Intrusion Detection/Prevention Sensor Data?
    b. Anti-Virus/Anti-Malware/Anti-Spyware?
    c. System Log Data?
56. Web: Does the Agency white-list or black-list URLs?
57. Does the Agency employ E-mail authentication (i.e. digital signature) either at the gateway or per user?

Part 2—Inspector General*

Section 1: System Inventory

1. Provide the number of Agency-owned and contractor systems by component with the following information:
   a. FIPS 199 risk category
   b. Certification and accreditation status
   c. Whether annual testing occurred
   d. Whether a tested contingency plan exists
   e. The number of systems assessed at E-Authentication levels 3 or 4

Section 2: Status of Certification and Accreditation Program

1. Check one:
   a. The Agency has established and is maintaining a certification and accreditation program that is generally consistent with NIST's and OMB's FISMA requirements. Although improvement opportunities may have been identified by the OIG, the program includes the following attributes:
      1. Documented policies and procedures describing the roles and responsibilities of participants in the certification and accreditation process.

---

* Extracted from http://www.federalnewsradio.com/docs/fismametrics_IG2010.pdf.

2. Establishment of accreditation boundaries for agency information systems.
3. Categorizes information systems.
4. Applies applicable minimum baseline security controls.
5. Assesses risks and tailors security control baseline for each system.
6. Assessment of the management, operational, and technical security controls in the information system.
7. Risks to Agency operations, assets, or individuals analyzed and documented in the system security plan, risk assessment, or an equivalent document.
8. The accreditation official is provided:
    i. the security assessment report from the certification agent providing the results of the independent assessment of the security controls and recommendations for corrective actions;
    ii. the plan of action and milestones from the information system owner indicating actions taken or planned to correct deficiencies in the controls and to reduce or eliminate vulnerabilities in the information system; and
    iii. the updated system security plan with the latest copy of the risk assessment.
  b. The Agency has established and is maintaining a certification and accreditation program. However, the Agency needs to make significant improvements as noted below.
  c. The Agency has not established a certification and accreditation program.

2. If b. checked above, check areas that need significant improvement:
  a. Certification and accreditation policy is not fully developed.
  b. Certification and accreditation procedures are not fully developed or consistently implemented.
  c. Information systems are not properly categorized (FIPS 199/SP 800-60).
  d. Accreditation boundaries for agency information systems are not adequately defined.

  e. Minimum baseline security controls are not adequately applied to information systems (FIPS 200/SP 800-53).

  f. Risk assessments are not adequately conducted (SP 800-30).

  g. Security control baselines are not adequately tailored to individual information systems (SP 800-30).

  h. Security plans do not adequately identify security requirements (SP 800-18).

  i. Inadequate process to assess security control effectiveness (SP800-53A).

  j. Inadequate process to determine risk to agency operations, agency assets, or individuals, or to authorize information systems to operate (SP 800-37).

  k. Inadequate process to continuously track changes to information systems that may necessitate reassessment of control effectiveness (SP 800-37).

  l. Other

3. Comments:

Section 3: Status of Security Configuration Management

4. Check one:

  a. The Agency has established and is maintaining a security configuration management program that is generally consistent with NIST's and OMB's FISMA requirements. Although improvement opportunities may have been identified by the OIG, the program includes the following attributes:

   1. Documented policies and procedures for configuration management.

   2. Standard baseline configurations.

   3. Scanning for compliance and vulnerabilities with baseline configurations.

   4. FDCC baseline settings fully implemented and/or any deviations from FDCC baseline settings fully documented.

   5. Documented proposed or actual changes to the configuration settings.

      6. Process for the timely and secure installation of software patches.

  b. The Agency has established and is maintaining a security configuration management program. However, the Agency needs to make significant improvements as noted below.

  c. The Agency has not established a security configuration management program.

5. If b. checked above, check areas that need significant improvement:

  a. Configuration management policy is not fully developed.

  b. Configuration management procedures are not fully developed or consistently implemented.

  c. Software inventory is not complete (NIST 800-53: CM-8).

  d. Standard baseline configurations are not identified for all software components (NIST 800-53: CM-8).

  e. Hardware inventory is not complete (NIST 800-53: CM-8).

  f. Standard baseline configurations are not identified for all hardware components (NIST 800-53: CM-2).

  g. Standard baseline configurations are not fully implemented (NIST 800-53: CM-2).

  h. FDCC is not fully implemented (OMB) and/or all deviations are not fully documented.

  i. Software scanning capabilities are not fully implemented (NIST 800-53: RA-5, SI-2).

  j. Configuration-related vulnerabilities have not been remediated in a timely manner (NIST 800-53: CM-4, CM-6, RA-5, SI-2).

  k. Patch management process is not fully developed (NIST 800-53: CM-3, SI-2).

  l. Other

6. Comments:

7. Software Name

  a. Software Version

Section 4: Status of Incident Response & Reporting Program

8. Check one:
    a. The Agency has established and is maintaining an incident response and reporting program that is generally consistent with NIST's and OMB's FISMA requirements. Although improvement opportunities may have been identified by the OIG, the program includes the following attributes:
        1. Documented policies and procedures for responding and reporting to incidents.
        2. Comprehensive analysis, validation and documentation of incidents.
        3. When applicable, reports to US-CERT within established timeframes.
        4. When applicable, reports to law enforcement within established timeframes.
        5. Responds to and resolves incidents in a timely manner to minimize further damage.
    b. The Agency has established and is maintaining an incident response and reporting program. However, the Agency needs to make significant improvements as noted below.
    c. The Agency has not established an incident response and reporting program.
9. If b. checked above, check areas that need significant improvement:
    a. Incident response and reporting policy is not fully developed.
    b. Incident response and reporting procedures are not fully developed or consistently implemented.
    c. Incidents were not identified in a timely manner (NIST 800-53, 800-61, and OMB M-07-16, M-06-19).
    d. Incidents were not reported to US-CERT as required (NIST 800-53, 800-61, and OMB M-07-16, M-06-19).
    e. Incidents were not reported to law enforcement as required.
    f. Incidents were not resolved in a timely manner (NIST 800-53, 800-61, and OMB M-07-16, M-06-19).

    g. Incidents were not resolved to minimize further damage (NIST 800-53, 800-61, and OMB M-07-16, M-06-19).

    h. There is insufficient incident monitoring and detection coverage (NIST 800-53, 800-61, and OMB M-07-16, M-06-19).

    i. Other

10. Comments:

Section 5: Status of Security Training Program

11. Check one:

    a. The Agency has established and is maintaining a security training program that is generally consistent with NIST's and OMB's FISMA requirements. Although improvement opportunities may have been identified by the OIG, the program includes the following attributes:

       1. Documented policies and procedures for security awareness training.

       2. Documented policies and procedures for specialized training for users with significant information security responsibilities.

       3. Appropriate training content based on the organization and roles.

       4. Identification and tracking of all employees with login privileges that need security awareness training.

       5. Identification and tracking of employees without login privileges that require security awareness training.

       6. Identification and tracking of all employees with significant information security responsibilities that require specialized training.

    b. The Agency has established and is maintaining a security training program. However, the Agency needs to make significant improvements as noted below.

    c. The Agency has not established a security training program.

12. If b. checked above, check areas that need significant improvement:

    a. Security awareness training policy is not fully developed.

    b. Security awareness training procedures are not fully developed or consistently implemented.

    c. Specialized security training policy is not fully developed.

    d. Specialized security training procedures are not fully developed or sufficiently detailed (SP 800-50, SP 800-53).

    e. Training material for security awareness training does not contain appropriate content for the Agency (SP 800-50, SP 800-53).

    f. Identification and tracking of employees with login privileges that require security awareness training is not adequate (SP 800-50, SP 800-53).

    g. Identification and tracking of employees without login privileges that require security awareness training is not adequate (SP 800-50, SP 800-53).

    h. Identification and tracking of employees with significant information security responsibilities is not adequate (SP 800-50, SP 800-53).

    i. Training content for individuals with significant information security responsibilities is not adequate (SP 800-53, SP 800-16).

    j. Less than 90% of employees with login privileges attended security awareness training in the past year.

    k. Less than 90% of employees, contractors, and other users with significant security responsibilities attended specialized security awareness training in the past year.

    l. Other

13. Comments:

Section 6: Status of Plans of Actions & Milestones (POA&M) Program

14. Check one:

    a. The Agency has established and is maintaining a POA&M program that is generally consistent with NIST's and OMB's FISMA requirements and tracks and monitors known information security weaknesses. Although improvement opportunities may have been identified by the OIG, the program includes the following attributes:

1. Documented policies and procedures for managing all known IT security weaknesses.
2. Tracks, prioritizes and remediates weaknesses.
3. Ensures remediation plans are effective for correcting weaknesses.
4. Establishes and adheres to reasonable remediation dates.
5. Ensures adequate resources are provided for correcting weaknesses.
6. Program officials and contractors report progress on remediation to CIO on a regular basis, at least quarterly, and the CIO centrally tracks, maintains, and independently reviews/validates the POAM activities at least quarterly.

b. The Agency has established and is maintaining a POA&M program that tracks and remediates known information security weaknesses. However, the Agency needs to make significant improvements as noted below.

c. The Agency has not established a POA&M program.

15. If b. checked above, check areas that need significant improvement:

a. POA&M Policy is not fully developed.
b. POA&M procedures are not fully developed or consistently implemented.
c. POA&Ms do not include all known security weaknesses (OMB M-04-25).
d. Remediation actions do not sufficiently address weaknesses (NIST SP 800-53, Rev. 3, Sect. 3.4 Monitoring Security Controls).
e. Initial date of security weaknesses are not tracked (OMB M-04-25).
f. Security weaknesses are not appropriately prioritized (OMB M-04-25).
g. Estimated remediation dates are not reasonable (OMB M-04-25).

h. Initial target remediation dates are frequently missed (OMB M-04-25).

i. POA&Ms are not updated in a timely manner (NIST SP 800-53, Rev. 3, Control CA-5, and OMB M-04-25).

j. Costs associated with remediating weaknesses are not identified (NIST SP 800-53, Rev. 3, Control PM-3 & OMB M-04-25).

k. Agency CIO does not track and review POA&Ms (NIST SP 800-53, Rev. 3, Control CA-5, and OMB M-04-25).

l. Other

16. Comments:

Section 7: Status of Remote Access Program

17. Check one:

a. The Agency has established and is maintaining a remote access program that is generally consistent with NIST's and OMB's FISMA requirements. Although improvement opportunities may have been identified by the OIG, the program includes the following attributes:

1. Documented policies and procedures for authorizing, monitoring, and controlling all methods of remote access.

2. Protects against unauthorized connections or subversion of authorized connections.

3. Users are uniquely identified and authenticated for all access.

4. If applicable, multi-factor authentication is required for remote access.

5. Authentication mechanisms meet NIST Special Publication 800-63 guidance on remote electronic authentication, including strength mechanisms.

6. Requires encrypting sensitive files transmitted across public networks or stored on mobile devices and removable media such as CDs and flash drives.

7. Remote access sessions are timed-out after a maximum of 30 minutes of inactivity after which re-authentication is required.

    b. The Agency has established and is maintaining a remote access program. However, the Agency needs to make significant improvements as noted below.

    c. The Agency has not established a program for providing secure remote access.

18. If b. checked above, check areas that need significant improvement:

    a. Remote access policy is not fully developed.

    b. Remote access procedures are not fully developed or consistently implemented.

    c. Telecommuting policy is not fully developed (NIST 800-46, Section 5.1).

    d. Telecommuting procedures are not fully developed or sufficiently detailed (NIST 800-46, Section 5.4).

    e. Agency cannot identify all users who require remote access (NIST 800-46, Section 4.2, Section 5.1).

    f. Multi-factor authentication is not properly deployed (NIST 800-46, Section 2.2, Section 3.3).

    g. Agency has not identified all remote devices (NIST 800-46, Section 2.1).

    h. Agency has not determined all remote devices and/or end user computers have been properly secured (NIST 800-46, Section 3.1 and 4.2).

    i. Agency does not adequately monitor remote devices when connected to the agency's networks remotely (NIST 800-46, Section 3.2).

    j. Lost or stolen devices are not disabled and appropriately reported (NIST 800-46, Section 4.3, US-CERT Incident Reporting Guidelines).

    k. Remote access rules of behavior are not adequate (NIST 800-53, PL-4).

    l. Remote access user agreements are not adequate (NIST 800-46, Section 5.1, NIST 800-53, PS-6).

    m. Other

19. Comments:

Section 8: Status of Account and Identity Management Program

20. Check one:

   a. The Agency has established and is maintaining an account and identity management program that is generally consistent with NIST's and OMB's FISMA requirements and identifies users and network devices. Although improvement opportunities may have been identified by the OIG, the program includes the following attributes:

      1. Documented policies and procedures for account and identity management.
      2. Identifies all users, including federal employees, contractors, and others who access Agency systems.
      3. Identifies when special access requirements (e.g., multi-factor authentication) are necessary.
      4. If multi-factor authentication is in use, it is linked to the Agency's PIV program.
      5. Ensures that the users are granted access based on needs and separation of duties principles.
      6. Identifies devices that are attached to the network and distinguishes these devices from users.
      7. Ensures that accounts are terminated or deactivated once access is no longer required.

   b. The Agency has established and is maintaining an account and identify management program that identifies users and network devices. However, the Agency needs to make significant improvements as noted below.

   c. The Agency has not established an account and identify management program.

21. If b. checked above, check areas that need significant improvement:

   a. Account management policy is not fully developed.
   b. Account management procedures are not fully developed or consistently implemented.
   c. Active Directory is not properly implemented (NIST 800-53, AC-2).
   d. Other Non-Microsoft account management software is not properly implemented (NIST 800-53, AC-2).

    e. Agency cannot identify all User and Non-User Accounts (NIST 800-53, AC-2).

    f. Accounts are not properly issued to new users (NIST 800-53, AC-2).

    g. Accounts are not properly terminated when users no longer require access (NIST 800-53, AC-2).

    h. Agency does not use multi-factor authentication where required (NIST 800-53, IA-2).

    i. Agency has not adequately planned for implementation of PIV for logical access (HSPD 12, FIPS 201, OMB M-05-24, OMB M-07-06, OMB M-08-01).

    g. Excessive administrative privileges have been granted Privileges granted are excessive or result in capability to perform conflicting functions. (NIST 800-53, AC-2, AC-6).

    h. Agency does not use dual accounts for administrators (NIST 800-53, AC-5, AC-6).

    i. Network devices are not properly authenticated (NIST 800-53, IA-3).

    j. Other

22. Comments:

Section 9: Status of Continuous Monitoring Program

23. Check one:

    a. The Agency has established an entity-wide continuous monitoring program that assesses the security state of information systems that is generally consistent with NIST's and OMB's FISMA requirements. Although improvement opportunities may have been identified by the OIG, the program includes the following attributes:

        1. Documented policies and procedures for continuous monitoring.

        2. Documented strategy and plans for continuous monitoring, such as vulnerability scanning, log monitoring, notification of unauthorized devices, sensitive new accounts, etc.

        3. Ongoing assessments of selected security controls (system-specific, hybrid, and common) that have been

performed based on the approved continuous monitoring plans.

4. Provides system authorizing officials and other key system officials with security status reports covering updates to security plans and security assessment reports, as well as POA&M additions.

b. The Agency has established an entity-wide continuous monitoring program that assesses the security state of information systems. However, the Agency needs to make significant improvements as noted below.

c. The Agency has not established a continuous monitoring program.

24. If b. checked above, check areas that need significant improvement:

a. Continuous monitoring policy is not fully developed.

b. Continuous monitoring procedures are not fully developed or consistently implemented.

c. Strategy or plan has not been fully developed for entity-wide continuous monitoring (NIST 800-37).

d. Ongoing assessments of selected security controls (system-specific, hybrid, and common) have not been performed (NIST 800-53, NIST 800-53A).

e. The following were not provided to the system authorizing official or other key system officials: security status reports covering continuous monitoring results, updates to security plans, security assessment reports, and POA&Ms (NIST 800-53, NIST 800-53A).

f. Other

25. Comments:

Section 10: Status of Contingency Planning Program

26. Check one:

a. The Agency established and is maintaining an entity-wide business continuity/disaster recovery program that is generally consistent with NIST's and OMB's FISMA requirements. Although improvement opportunities may have been identified by the OIG, the program includes the following attributes:

1. Documented business continuity and disaster recovery policy providing the authority and guidance necessary to reduce the impact of a disruptive event or disaster.
2. The agency has performed an overall Business Impact Assessment.
3. Development and documentation of division, component, and IT infrastructure recovery strategies, plans and procedures.
4. Testing of system specific contingency plans.
5. The documented business continuity and disaster recovery plans are ready for implementation.
6. Development of training, testing, and exercises (TT&E) approaches.
7. Performance of regular ongoing testing or exercising of continuity/disaster recovery plans to determine effectiveness, and to maintain current plans.

b. The Agency has established and is maintaining an entity-wide business continuity/disaster recovery program. However, the Agency needs to make significant improvements as noted below.

c. The Agency has not established a business continuity/disaster recovery program.

27. If b. checked above, check areas that need significant improvement:

a. Contingency planning policy is not fully developed.
b. Contingency planning procedures are not fully developed or consistently implemented.
c. An overall business impact assessment has not been performed (NIST SP 800-34).
d. Development of organization, component, or infrastructure recovery strategies and plans has not been accomplished (NIST SP 800-34).
e. A business continuity/disaster recovery plan has not been developed (FCD1, NIST SP 800-34).
f. A business continuity/disaster recovery plan has been developed, but not fully implemented (FCD1, NIST SP 800-34).

    g. System contingency plans missing or incomplete (FCD1, NIST SP 800-34, NIST SP 800-53).

    h. Critical systems contingency plans are not tested (FCD1, NIST SP 800-34, NIST SP 800-53).

    i. Training, testing, and exercises approaches have not been developed (FCD1, NIST SP 800-34,NIST 800-53).

    j. Training, testing, and exercises approaches have been developed, but are not fully implemented (FCD1, NIST SP 800-34, NIST SP 800-53).

    k. Disaster recovery exercises were not successful revealed significant weaknesses in the contingency planning. (NIST SP 800-34).

    l. After-action plans did not address issues identified during disaster recovery exercises (FCD1, NIST SP 800-34).

    m. Critical systems do not have alternate processing sites (FCD1, NIST SP 800-34, NIST SP 800-53).

    n. Alternate processing sites are subject to same risks as primary sites (FCD1, NIST SP 800-34, NIST SP 800-53).

    o. Backups of information are not performed in a timely manner (FCD1, NIST SP 800-34, NIST SP 800-53).

    p. Backups are not appropriately tested (FCD1, NIST SP 800-34, NIST SP 800-53).

    q. Backups are not properly secured and protected (FCD1, NIST SP 800-34, NIST SP 800-53).

    r. Other

28. Comments:

Section 11: Status of Agency Program to Oversee Contractor Systems

29. Check one:

    a. The Agency has established and maintains a program to oversee systems operated on its behalf by contractors or other entities. Although improvement opportunities may have been identified by the OIG, the program includes the following attributes:

        1. Documented policies and procedures for information security oversight of systems operated on the Agency's behalf by contractors or other entities

2. A complete inventory of systems operated on the Agency's behalf by contractors or other entities.

3. The inventory identifies interfaces between these systems and Agency-operated systems.

4. The agency requires agreements (MOUs, Interconnect Service Agreements, contracts, etc.) for interfaces between these systems and those that is owns and operates.

5. The inventory, including interfaces, is updated at least annually.

6. Systems that are owned or operated by contractors or entities are subject to and generally meet NIST and OMB's FISMA requirements.

7. The Agency obtains sufficient assurance that security controls of systems operated by contractors or others on its behalf are effectively implemented and comply with federal and agency guidelines.

b. The Agency has established and maintains a program to oversee systems operated on its behalf by contractors or other entities. However, the Agency needs to make significant improvements as noted below.

c. The Agency does not have a program to oversee systems operated on its behalf by contractors or other entities.

30. If b. checked above, check areas that need significant improvement:

a. Policies to oversee systems operated on the Agency's behalf by contractors or other entities are not fully developed.

b. Procedures to oversee systems operated on the Agency's behalf by contractors or other entities are not fully developed or consistently implemented.

c. The inventory of systems owned or operated by contractors or other entities is not sufficiently complete.

d. The inventory does not identify interfaces between contractor/entity-operated systems to Agency owned and operated systems.

e. The inventory of contractor/entity-operated systems, including interfaces, is not updated at least annually.

  f. Systems owned or operated by contractors and entities are not subject to NIST and OMB's FISMA requirements (e.g., certification and accreditation requirements).

  g. Systems owned or operated by contractor's and entities do not meet NIST and OMB's FISMA requirements (e.g., certifications and accreditation requirements).

  h. Interface agreements (e.g., MOUs) are not properly documented, authorized, or maintained.

  i. Other

31. Comments:

Part 3—Senior Agency Official for Privacy[*]

Question 1: Information Security Systems

  a. Number of Federal systems that contain personal information in an identifiable form

  b. Number of systems in column a. for which a Privacy Impact Assessment (PIA) is required under the E-Government Act

  c. Number of systems in column b. covered by a current PIA

  d. Number of systems in column d. for which a current SORN has been published in the Federal Register

Question 2: Links to PIAs and SORNs

  a. Provide the URL of the centrally located page on the agency web site that provides working links to agency PIAs or N/A if not applicable.

  b. Provide the URL of the centrally located page on the agency web site that provides working links to the published SORNs or N/A if not applicable.

Question 3: Senior Agency Official for Privacy (SAOP) Responsibilities

  a. Can your agency demonstrate with documentation that the SAOP participates in all agency information privacy compliance activities?

  b. Can your agency demonstrate with documentation that the SAOP participates in evaluating the privacy implications of

---

[*] Extracted from http://www.federalnewsradio.com/docs/fismametrics_saop2010.pdf.

legislative, regulatory, and other policy proposals, as well as testimony and comments under OMB Circular A-19?

c. Can your agency demonstrate with documentation that the SAOP participates in assessing the impact of the agency's use of technology on privacy and the protection of personal information?

Question 4: Information Privacy Training and Awareness

a. Does your agency have a policy in place to ensure that all personnel (employees, contractors, etc.) with access to Federal data are generally familiar with information privacy laws, regulations, and policies, and understand the ramifications of inappropriate access and disclosure?

b. Does your agency have a program for job-specific and comprehensive information privacy training for all personnel (employees, contractors, etc.) that handle personal information, that are directly involved in the administration of personal information or information technology systems, or that have significant information security responsibilities?

5. Does the agency have a written policy or process for each of the following?

a. PIA Practices
   1. Determining whether a PIA is needed
   2. Conducting a PIA
   3. Evaluating changes in technology or business practices that are identified during the PIA process
   4. Ensuring systems owners, privacy officials, and IT experts participate in conducting the PIA
   5. Making PIAs available to the public as required by law and OMB policy
   6. Monitoring the agency's systems and practices to determine when and how PIAs should be updated
   7. Assessing the quality and thoroughness of each PIA and performing reviews to ensure that appropriate standards for PIAs are maintained

b. Web Privacy Practices
1. Determining circumstances where the agency's web-based activities warrant additional consideration of privacy implications
2. Making appropriate updates and ensuring continued compliance with stated web privacy policies
3. Requiring machine-readability of public-facing agency web sites (i.e., use of P3P)

Question 6: Reviews Mandated by the Privacy Act of 1974, the E-Government Act of 2002, and the Federal Agency Data Mining Reporting Act of 2007

a. Section Contracts
b. Records Practices
c. Routine Uses
d. Matching Programs
e. Training
f. Violations: Civil Action
g. Violations: Remedial Action
h. System of Records Notices
i. (e)(3) Statements
j. Privacy Impact Assessments and Updates
k. Data Mining Impact Assessment

Question 7: Written Privacy Complaints

Indicate the number of written complaints for each type of privacy issue received by the SAOP or others at the agency

a. Process and Procedural — consent, collection, and appropriate notice
b. Redress — non-Privacy Act inquiries seeking resolution of difficulties or concerns about privacy matters
c. Operational — inquiries regarding Privacy Act matters not including Privacy Act requests for access and/or correction
d. Referrals — complaints referred to another agency with jurisdiction

Question 8: Policy Compliance Review

    a. Does the agency have current documentation demonstrating review of the agency's compliance with information privacy laws, regulations, and policies?

    b. Can the agency provide documentation of planned, in progress, or completed corrective actions necessary to remedy deficiencies identified in compliance reviews?

    c. Does the Agency use technologies that enable continuous auditing of compliance with stated privacy policies and practices?

    d. Does the Agency coordinate with the agency's Inspector General on privacy program oversight?

Question 9: Information About Advice and Guidance Provided by the SAOP

Please select "Yes" or "No" to indicate if the SAOP has provided formal written advice or guidance in each of the listed categories, and briefly describe the advice or guidance if applicable.

    a. Agency policies, orders, directives, or guidance governing the agency's handling of personally identifiable information

    b. Written agreements (either interagency or with non-Federal entities) pertaining to information sharing, computer matching, and similar issues

    c. The agency's practices for conducting, preparing, and releasing SORNs and PIAs

    d. Reviews or feedback outside of the SORN and PIA process (e.g., formal written advice in the context of budgetary or programmatic activities or planning)

    e. Privacy training (either stand-alone or included with training on related issues)

Question 10: Agency Use of Web Management and Customization Technologies (e.g., "cookies," "tracking technologies")

    a. Does the agency use web management and customization technologies on any web site or application?

    b. Does the agency annually review the use of web management and customization technologies to ensure compliance with all laws, regulations, and OMB guidance?

c. Can the agency demonstrate, with documentation, the continued justification for, and approval to use, web management and customization technologies?

d. Can the agency provide the notice language or citation for the web privacy policy that informs visitors about the use of web management and customization technologies?

Appendix D: Consensus Audit Guidelines

The following is an extract from *Twenty Critical Controls for Effective Cyber Defense: Consensus Audit Guidelines*, Version 2.3, November 13, 2009. The CAG project led by John Gilligan was initiated early in 2008 as a response to the extreme data losses experienced by leading companies in the US defense industrial base (DIB).

Critical Control 1: Inventory of Authorized and Unauthorized Devices

Organizations must first establish information owners and asset owners, deciding and documenting which organizations and individuals are responsible for each component of information and device. Some organizations maintain asset inventories using specific large-scale enterprise commercial products dedicated to the task or they use free solutions to track and then sweep the network periodically for new assets connected to the network. In particular, when effective organizations acquire new systems, they record the owner and features of each new asset, including its network interface MAC address, a unique identifier hard-coded into most network interface cards and devices. This mapping of asset attributes and owner-to-MAC address can be stored in a free or commercial database management system.

Then, with the asset inventory assembled, many organizations use tools to pull information from network assets such as switches and routers regarding the machines connected to the network. Using securely authenticated and encrypted network management protocols, tools can retrieve MAC addresses and other information from network devices that can be reconciled with the organization's asset inventory of servers, workstations, laptops, and other devices.

Going further, effective organizations configure free or commercial network scanning tools to perform network sweeps on a regular basis, such as every 12 hours, sending a variety of different packet types to identify devices connected to the network. Before such scanning can take place, organizations should verify that they have adequate bandwidth for such periodic scans by consulting load history and capacities for their networks. In conducting inventory scans, scanning tools could send traditional ping packets (ICMP Echo Request), looking for ping responses to identify a system at a given IP address. Because some systems block inbound ping packets, in addition to traditional pings, scanners can also identify devices on the network using TCP SYN or ACK packets. Once they have identified IP addresses of devices on the network, some scanners provide robust fingerprinting features to determine the operating system type of the discovered machine.

In addition to active scanning tools that sweep the network, other asset identification tools passively listen on network interfaces looking for devices to announce their presence by sending traffic. Such passive tools can be connected to switch span ports at critical places in the network to view all data flowing through such switches, maximizing the chance of identifying systems communicating through those switches.

Wireless devices (and wired laptops) may periodically join a network and then disappear making the inventory of currently available systems churn significantly. Likewise, virtual machines can be difficult to track in asset inventories when they are shut down or paused, because they are merely files in some host machine's file system. Additionally, remote machines accessing the network using VPN technology may appear on the network for a time, and then be disconnected from it. Each machine, whether physical or virtual, directly connected to the network or attached via VPN, currently running or shut down, should be included in an organization's asset inventory.

Critical Control 2: Inventory of Authorized and Unauthorized Software

Commercial software and asset inventory tools are widely available and in use in many enterprises today. The best of these tools provide an inventory check of hundreds of common applications used in enterprises, pulling information about the patch level of each installed program to ensure that it is the latest version and leveraging standardized application names, such as those found in the Common Platform Enumeration (CPE) specification.

Features that implement whitelists and blacklists of programs allowed to run or blocked from executing are included in many modern end-point security suites. Moreover, commercial solutions are increasingly bundling together anti-virus, anti-spyware, personal firewall, and host-based Intrusion Detection Systems and Intrusion Prevention Systems (IDS and IPS), along with software white listing and black listing. In particular, most endpoint security solutions can look at the name, file system location, and/or cryptographic hash of a given executable to determine whether the application should be allowed to run on the protected machine. The most effective of these tools offer custom whitelists and blacklists based on executable path, hash, or regular expression matching. Some even include a graylist function that allows administrators to define rules for execution of specific programs only by certain users and at certain times of day, and blacklists based on specific signatures.

Critical Control 3: Secure Configurations for Hardware
and Software on Laptops, Workstations, and Servers

Organizations can implement this control by developing a series of images and secure storage servers for hosting these standard images. Then, commercial and/or free configuration management tools can be employed to measure the settings of managed machines' operating system and applications to look for deviations from the standard image configurations used by the organization. Some configuration management tools require that an agent be installed on each managed system, while others remotely login to each managed machine using administrator credentials. Either approach or combinations of the two approaches can provide the information needed for this control.

Critical Control 4: Secure Configurations for Network Devices
such as Firewalls, Routers, and Switches

Some organizations use commercial tools that evaluate the rule set
of network filtering devices to determine whether they are consistent
or in conflict, providing an automated sanity check of network filters
and search for errors in rule sets or ACLs that may allow unintended
services through the device. Such tools should be run each time significant changes are made to firewall rule sets, router ACLs, or other
filtering technologies.

Critical Control 5: Boundary Defense

One element of this control can be implemented using free or commercial IDSs and sniffers to look for attacks from external sources
directed at DMZ and internal systems, as well as attacks originating
from internal systems against the DMZ or Internet. Security personnel should regularly test these sensors by launching vulnerability-
scanning tools against them to verify that the scanner traffic triggers
an appropriate alert. The captured packets of the IDS sensors should
be reviewed using an automated script each day to ensure that log vol-
umes are within expected parameters and that the logs are formatted
properly and have not been corrupted.

Additionally, packet sniffers should be deployed on DMZs to look
for HTTP traffic that bypasses HTTP proxies. By sampling traffic
regularly, such as over a 3-hour period once per week, information
security personnel search for HTTP traffic that is neither sourced
by nor destined for a DMZ proxy, implying that the requirement for
proxy use is being bypassed.

To identify back-channel connections that bypass approved DMZs,
network security personnel can establish an Internet-accessible system to use as a receiver for testing outbound access. This system is
configured with a free or commercial packet sniffer. Then, security
personnel connect a sending test system to various points on the
organization's internal network, sending easily identifiable traffic to
the sniffing receiver on the Internet. These packets can be generated
using free or commercial tools with a payload that contains a custom
file used for the test. When the packets arrive at the receiver system,

the source address of the packets should be verified against accept-able DMZ addresses allowed for the organization. If source addresses are discovered that are not included in legitimate, registered DMZs, more detail can be gathered by using a traceroute tool to determine the path packets take from the sender to the receiver system.

Critical Control 6: Maintenance, Monitoring, and Analysis of Audit Logs

Most free and commercial operating systems, network services, and firewall technologies offer logging capabilities. Such logging should be activated, with logs sent to centralized logging servers. Firewalls, proxies, and remote access systems (VPN, dial-up, etc.) should all be configured for verbose logging, storing all the information available for logging should a follow-up investigation be required. Furthermore, operating systems, especially those of servers, should be configured to create access control logs when a user attempts to access resources without the appropriate privileges. To evaluate whether such log-ging is in place, an organization should periodically scan through its logs and compare them with the asset inventory assembled as part of Critical Control 1, to ensure that each managed item actively con-nected to the network is periodically generating logs.

Analytical programs for reviewing logs can be useful, but the capa-bilities employed to analyze audit logs is quite wide-ranging, includ-ing just a cursory examination by a human. Actual correlation tools can make audit logs far more useful for subsequent manual inspec-tion by people. Such tools can be quite helpful in identifying subtle attacks. However, these tools are neither a panacea nor a replacement for skilled information security personnel and system administrators. Even with automated log analysis tools, human expertise and intu-ition are often required to identify and understand attacks.

Critical Control 7: Application Software Security

Source code testing tools, web application security scanning tools, and object code testing tools have proven useful in securing appli-cation software, along with manual application security penetration testing by testers who have extensive programming knowledge as well as application penetration testing expertise. The Common Weakness Enumeration (CWE) initiative is utilized by many such tools to identify the weaknesses that they find. Organizations can also use CWE to determine which types of weaknesses they are most interested in addressing and removing. A broad community effort to identify the "Top 25 Most Dangerous Programming Errors" is also available as a minimum set of important issues to investigate and address during the application development process. When evaluating the effectiveness of testing for these weaknesses, the Common Attack Pattern Enumeration and Classification (CAPEC) can be used to organize and record the breadth of the testing for the CWEs as well as a way for testers to think like attackers in their development of test cases.

Critical Control 8: Controlled Use of Administrative Privileges

Built-in operating system features can extract lists of accounts with superuser privileges, both locally on individual systems and on overall domain controllers. To verify that users with high-privileged accounts do not use such accounts for day-to-day web surfing and e-mail reading, security personnel could periodically gather a list of running processes in an attempt to determine whether any browsers or e-mail readers are running with high privileges. Such information gathering can be scripted, with short shell scripts searching for a dozen or more different browsers, e-mail readers, and document editing programs running with high privileges on machines. Some legitimate system administration activity may require the execution of such programs over the short term, but long-term or frequent use of such programs with administrative privileges could indicate that an administrator is not adhering to this control.

Additionally, to prevent administrators from accessing the web using their administrator accounts, administrative accounts can be configured to use a web proxy of 127.0.0.1 in some operating systems that allow user-level configuration of web proxy settings. Furthermore, in some environments, administrator accounts do not require the ability to receive e-mail. These accounts can be created without an e-mail box on the system.

To enforce the requirement for password length of 12 or more characters, built-in operating system features for minimum password length can be configured, which prevent users from choosing short passwords. To enforce password complexity (requiring passwords to be a string of pseudo-random characters), built-in operating system settings or third-party password complexity enforcement tools can be applied.

Critical Control 9: Controlled Access Based on Need to Know

This control is often implemented using the built-in separation of administrator accounts from non-administrator accounts included in most operating systems. While these features are available in most systems, it is important that organizations diligently implement and follow procedures for when administrator-level accounts should be used versus non-administrator accounts.

Critical Control 10: Continuous Vulnerability Assessment and Remediation

A large number of vulnerability scanning tools are available to evaluate the security configuration of systems. Some enterprises have also found commercial services using remotely managed scanning appliances to be effective as well. To help standardize the definitions of discovered vulnerabilities in multiple departments of an agency or even across agencies, it is preferable to use vulnerability scanning tools that measure security flaws and map them to vulnerabilities and issues categorized using one or more of the following industry-recognized vulnerability, configuration, and platform classification schemes and languages: CVE, CCE, OVAL, CPE, CVSS, and/or XCCDF.

Advanced vulnerability scanning tools can be configured with user credentials to login to scanned systems and perform more comprehensive scans than can be achieved without login credentials. For example, organizations can run scanners every week or every month without credentials for an initial inventory of potential vulnerabilities. Then, on a less frequent basis, such as monthly or quarterly, the organization can run the same scanning tool with user credentials or a different scanning tool that supports scanning with user credentials to find additional vulnerabilities. The frequency of scanning activities, however, should increase as the diversity of an organization's systems increases to account for the varying patch cycles of each vendor.

In addition to the scanning tools that check for vulnerabilities and misconfigurations across the network, various free and commercial tools can evaluate security settings and configurations of local machines on which they are installed. Such tools can provide fine-grained insight into unauthorized changes in configuration or the introduction of security weaknesses inadvertently by administrators.

Effective organizations link their vulnerability scanners with problem-ticketing systems that automatically monitor and report progress on fixing problems and that make visible unmitigated critical vulnerabilities to higher levels of management to ensure the problems are solved.

The most effective vulnerability scanning tools compare the results of the current scan with previous scans to determine how the vulnerabilities in the environment have changed over time. Security personnel use these features to conduct vulnerability trending from month-to-month.

As vulnerabilities related to unpatched systems are discovered by scanning tools, security personnel should determine and document the amount of time that elapsed between the public release of a patch for the system and the occurrence of the vulnerability scan. If this time window exceeds the organization's benchmarks for deployment of the given patch's criticality level, security personnel should note the delay and determine if a deviation was formally documented for the system and its patch. If not, the security team should work with management to improve the patching process.

Additionally, some automated patching tools may not detect or install certain patches, due to error on the vendor's or administrator's part. Because of this, all patch checks should reconcile system patches with a list of patches each vendor has announced on its website.

Critical Control 11: Account Monitoring and Control

Although most operating systems include capabilities for logging information about account usage, these features are sometimes disabled by default. Even when such features are present and active, they often do not provide fine-grained detail about access to the system by default. Security personnel can configure systems to record more detailed information about account access, and utilize home-grown scripts or third-party log analysis tools to analyze this information and profile user access of various systems.

Critical Control 12: Malware Defenses

Relying on policy and user action to keep anti-malware tools up to date has been widely discredited, as many users have not proven able to keep such tools up to date consistently. To ensure anti-virus signatures are up to date, effective organizations use automation. They use the built-in administrative features of enterprise end-point security suites to verify that anti-virus, anti-spyware, and host-based IDS features are active on every managed system. They run automated assessments daily and review the results to find and mitigate systems that have deactivated such protections, as well as systems that do not have the latest malware definitions. For added security in depth, and for those systems that may fall outside the enterprise anti-malware coverage, some organizations use network access control technology that tests machines for compliance with security policy before allowing them to connect to the network.

Some enterprises deploy free or commercial honeypot and tarpit tools to identify attackers in their environment. Security personnel should continuously monitor honeypots and tarpits to determine whether traffic is directed to them and account logins are attempted. When they identify such events, these personnel should gather the source address from which this traffic originates and other details associated with the attack for a follow-on investigation.

Critical Control 13: Limitation and Control of Network Ports, Protocols, and Services

Port scanning tools are used to determine which services are listening on the network for a range of target systems. In addition to determining which ports are open, effective port scanners can be configured to identify the version of the protocol and service listening on each discovered open port. This list of services and their versions are compared against an inventory of services required by the organization for each server and workstation, in an asset management system, such as those described in Critical Control 1. Recently added features in these port scanners are being used to determine the changes in services offered by scanned machines on the network since the previous scan, helping security personnel identify differences over time.

Critical Control 14: Wireless Device Control

Effective organizations run commercial wireless scanning, detection, and discovery tools as well as commercial wireless intrusion detection systems. Additionally, the security team could periodically capture wireless traffic from within the borders of a facility and use free and commercial analysis tools to determine whether the wireless traffic was transmitted using weaker protocols or encryption than the organization mandates. When devices relying on weak wireless security settings are identified, they should be found within the organization's asset inventory and either reconfigured more securely or denied access to the agency network.

Additionally, the security testing team could employ remote management tools on the wired network to pull information about the wireless capabilities and devices connected to managed systems.

Critical Control 15: Data Loss Prevention

Commercial DLP solutions are available to look for exfiltration attempts and detect other suspicious activities associated with a protected network holding sensitive information. Organizations deploying such tools should carefully inspect their logs and follow-up on any discovered attempts, even those that are successfully blocked, to transmit sensitive information out of the organization without authorization.

Additional Controls

The following sections identify additional controls that are important but cannot be fully automatically or continuously monitored to the same degree as the controls covered earlier in this document.

Critical Control 16: Secure Network Engineering

To help ensure a consistent, defensible network, the architecture of each network should be based on a template that describes the overall layout of the network and the services it provides. Organizations should prepare network diagrams for each of their networks that show network components such as routers, firewalls, and switches, along with significant servers and groups of client machines.

Critical Control 17: Penetration Tests and Red Team Exercises

Each organization should define a clear scope and rules of engagement for penetration testing and red team analyses. The scope of such projects should include, at least, systems with the highest value information and production processing functionality of the organization. Other, lowered value systems may also be tested to see if they can be used as pivot points to compromise higher-valued targets. The rules of engagement for penetration tests and red team analyses should describe, at a minimum, times of day for testing, duration of tests, and overall test approach.

Critical Control 18: Incident Response Capability

After defining detailed incident response procedures, the incident response team should engage in periodic scenario-based training, working through a series of attack scenarios fine-tuned to the threats and vulnerabilities the organization faces. These scenarios help ensure that team members understand their role on the incident response team and also help prepare them to handle incidents.

Critical Control 19: Data Recovery Capability

Once per quarter, a testing team should evaluate a random sample of system backups by attempting to restore them on a test bed environment. The restored systems should be verified to ensure that the operating system, application, and data from the backup are all intact and functional.

Critical Control 20: Security Skills Assessment
and Appropriate Training to Fill Gaps

The key to upgrading skills is measurement – not with certification examinations, but with assessments that show both the employee and the employer where knowledge is sufficient and where the gaps are. Once the gaps have been identified, those employees who have the requisite skills and knowledge can be called upon to mentor the employees who need skills improvement or the organization

Summary

This document has been developed through the collaboration of a diverse set of security experts. While there is no such thing as absolute protection, proper implementation of the security controls identified in this document will ensure that an organization is protecting against the most significant attacks. As attacks change, additional controls or tools become available, or the state of common security practice advances, this document will be updated to reflect what is viewed by the collaborating authors as the most important security controls to defend against cyber attacks.

Appendix E: Bibliography

Computer Security Act of 1987 (Public Law 100-235), January 8, 1988.

E-Government Act of 2002 (Public Law 107-347), December 17, 2002.

Federal Information Security Management Act of 2002 (Public Law 107-347), (also referred to as Title III of the E-Government Act of 2002), December 17, 2002.

Federal Information Processing Standard (FIPS) Publication 199, Standards for Security Categorization of Federal Information and Information Systems, February 2004.

FIPS Publication 200, Security Controls for Federal Information Systems, March 2006.

General Accounting Office GAO/AIMD-12.19.6, Federal Information System Controls Audit Manual (FISCAM), February 2009.

Government Information Security Reform Act (Public Law 106-398), October 30, 2000.

International Organization for Standardization (ISO)/International Electrotechnical Commission (IEC) ISO/IEC 27002:2005, Information Technology—Security Techniques—Code of Practice for Information Security Management, July 2007. Office of Management and Budget, Circular A-123, Management's Responsibility for Internal Control, December 2004.

National Institute of Standards and Technology (NIST) Special Publication 800-12, An Introduction to Computer Security: The NIST Handbook, October 1995.

NIST Special Publication 800-16, Information Technology Security Training Requirements: A Role- and Performance-Based Model, April 1998.

NIST Special Publication 800-18 Revision 1, Guide for Developing Security Plans for Federal Information Systems, February 2006.

NIST Special Publication 800-26, Security Self-Assessment Guide for Information Technology Systems, August 2001.

NIST Special Publication 800-30, Risk Management Guide for Information Technology Systems, July 2002.

NIST Special Publication 800-34 Revision 1, Contingency Planning Guide for Information Technology Systems, May 2010.

NIST Special Publication 800-37 Revision 1, Guide for Applying the Risk Management Framework to Federal Information Systems: A Security Life Cycle Approach, February 2010.

NIST Special Publication 800-39 Draft, Managing Risk from Information Systems: An Organizational Perspective, April 3, 2008.

NIST Special Publication 800-40 Version 2, Creating a Patch and Vulnerability Management Program, November 2005.

NIST Special Publication 800-47, Security Guide for Interconnecting Information Technology Systems, August 2002.

NIST Special Publication 800-50, Building an Information Technology Security Awareness and Training Program, October 2003.

NIST Special Publication 800-53 Revision 3, Recommended Security Controls for Federal Information Systems and Organizations, August 2009.

NIST Special Publication 800-53A, Guide for Assessing the Security Controls in Federal Information Systems and Organizations, Building Effective Security Assessment Plans, May 5, 2010.

NIST Special Publication 800-60 Revision 1, Guide for Mapping Types of Information and Information Systems to Security Categories, August 2008.

NIST Special Publication 800-64 Revision 2, Security Considerations in the System Development Life Cycle, October 2008.

NIST Special Publication 800-70 Revision 1, National Checklist Program for IT Products—Guidelines for Checklist Users and Developers, September 2009.

NIST Special Publication 800-100, Information Security Handbook: A Guide for Managers, October 2006.

Office of Management and Budget, Circular A-130, Appendix III, Transmittal Memorandum #4, Management of Federal Information Resources, November 2000.

Index